Taste of Home

EVERYDAY
slow
cooker
& ONE DISH RECIPES

Now It's Easier Than Ever to Serve Comforting Dishes...Any Day of the Week!

Taste of Home, the world's No. 1 cooking magazine, extends you a heartfelt welcome to Everyday Slow Cooker & One Dish Recipes. With the busy schedules and activity-packed days of folks and families everywhere, recipes that require less time, preparation and cleanup have never been more popular than they are now.

If you fall into the camp of the hectic and harried, this book may be the answer to your prayers. Inside you'll find more than 300 recipes and tips that offer convenience when it comes to setting a satisfying supper on the table.

To make searching for recipes easier, this book is divided into three main sections: Slow Cookers, Stovetop Suppers and Oven Entrees. It's like having three books in one! Each section is broken into chapters such as beef, poultry, pork, soup and more.

Let's Talk Slow Cookers. *If you've never owned a slow cooker, here's an opportunity for you to discover the benefits of this simple kitchen appliance. Its convenience is unmatched because it does all the work for you— you don't even have to be at home while your favorite meals simmer to mouth-watering perfection. The affordable appliance is easy to use...just set it and forget it! In addition, slow cookers are economical because they take affordable cuts of meat, such as beef stew meat or chuck roast, and turn them into tender, delicious sensations.*

The variety of dishes in the Slow Cooker section ranges from tantalizing appetizers to comforting entrees. You'll even find delicious side dishes perfect for potlucks, as well as recipes for chill-chasing beverages and desserts. It's one section you'll turn to time and again.

Success with Stovetop Suppers. *This section is chock-full of one-pot meals you can throw together in a snap. Quick, easy and family-friendly, these dishes require little cleanup because they usually take advantage of a skillet or Dutch oven. There are also oodles of super-easy dinner ideas that are sure to satisfy. Consider Beef Burgundy Over Noodles (p. 121) and Oktoberfest Roast Pork (p. 143). Or for a fast meal ideal for company, give Creamy Prosciutto Pasta (p. 149) or Citrus Scallops (p. 158) a try.*

Easy Oven Entrees. *If hearty one-dish dinners are what you have in mind, then check out the final section of this heartwarming cookbook. It features stick-to-your-ribs oven specialties. You'll enjoy every casserole imaginable, such as baked pastas, as well as beef and pork roasts, quiche, pizza and so much more. These meal-in-one sensations make perfect family fare, and they are especially well suited for potlucks, church suppers, banquets and other covered-dish dinners.*

If you're looking for a break from meat-and-potato items, check out this section's Fish & Seafood chapter (p. 228). Here you'll find some interesting and unique recipes that offer new variations on tried-and-true classics, such as Crab Quiche (p. 237) and Seafood Lasagna (p. 235).

Every recipe has been tested for accuracy and flavor by the Taste of Home Test Kitchen staff. You'll also notice that recipes with a lighter flair include Nutrition Facts and Diabetic Exchanges. These heart-smart delights are marked with an asterisk so you can find them easily.

So what are you waiting for? Set your slow cooker, grab your favorite skillet or preheat your oven and get ready to dig in! After one bite, you'll realize just how easy it is to make heartwarming dinner-table memories every day of the week.

SENIOR EDITOR/BOOKS: Mark Hagen
EDITOR: Krista Lanphier
ART DIRECTOR: Gretchen Trautman
LAYOUT DESIGNERS: Nancy Novak, Kathy Crawford
CONTENT PRODUCTION SUPERVISOR: Julie Wagner
PROOFREADER: Linne Bruskewitz
EDITORIAL ASSISTANT: Barb Czysz

RECIPE ASSET SYSTEM: Coleen Martin (manager), Sue Jurack (specialist)

FOOD DIRECTOR: Diane Werner
TEST KITCHEN MANAGER: Karen Scales
RECIPE EDITORS: Mary King, Christine Rukavena
HOME ECONOMISTS: Tina Johnson, Marie Parker, Annie Rundle
TEST KITCHEN ASSISTANT: Rita Krajcir

STUDIO PHOTOGRAPHERS: Rob Hagen (senior), Lori Foy, Dan Roberts, Jim Wieland
FOOD STYLISTS: Sarah Thompson (senior), Kaitlyn Besasie, Tamara Kaufman
SET STYLISTS: Jennifer Bradley Vent (senior), Stephanie Marchese (senior), Dee Dee Jacq, Melissa Haberman
PHOTO STUDIO COORDINATOR: Kathy Swaney

VICE PRESIDENT, EXECUTIVE EDITOR/BOOKS: Heidi Reuter Lloyd
CREATIVE DIRECTOR/CREATIVE MARKETING: James Palmen
CREATIVE DIRECTOR: Ardyth Cope
CHIEF MARKETING OFFICER: Lisa Karpinski
SENIOR VICE PRESIDENT, EDITOR IN CHIEF: Catherine Cassidy
PRESIDENT, FOOD & ENTERTAINING: Suzanne M. Grimes
PRESIDENT AND CHIEF EXECUTIVE OFFICER: Mary G. Berner

©2008 Reiman Media Group, Inc.
5400 S. 60th Street,
Greendale WI 53129

International Standard Book Number (10): 0-89821-605-2
International Standard Book Number (13): 978-0-8982-605-9

For other Taste of Home books and products, visit *www.shoptasteofhome.com.*

FRONT COVER
Pizza in a Pot (p. 36);
Photographed by Grace Natoli Sheldon;
Food Styled by Tamara Kaufman; and
Set Styled by Jenny Bradley Vent.

BACK COVER
Pot Roast with Mushroom Gravy (p. 29); Apricot Chicken and Snow Peas (p. 133); and Pork Roast Supper (p. 209).

table of contents

Slow Cooker

Stovetop Suppers

Oven Entrees

SLOW COOKER

Soups & Sandwiches

 25

 18

 10

Soups and sandwiches are longtime favorites on tables from coast to coast. Slowly simmered for hours, soups satisfy hungry appetites and chase away the chills, and slow cookers turn meat into tender fillings for robust sandwiches. You'll enjoy the comfort of a hearty family meal with the specialties in this chapter.

- In a large skillet, saute onions in butter until tender. Stir in flour. Gradually stir in 1 cup water. Bring to a boil; cook and stir for 2 minutes or until thickened. Transfer to a 5-qt. slow cooker.

- Add the broth, potatoes, potato flakes, bacon, pepper, salt, basil, thyme and remaining water. Cover and cook on low for 6-8 hours or until potatoes are tender. Stir in cream; heat through. Garnish with cheese and green onions.

Yield: 10 servings.

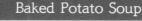
Baked Potato Soup

Barbara Bleigh
COLONIAL HEIGHTS, VIRGINIA

The only thing that beats the comforting flavor of this thick and hearty potato soup is possibly the idea that it simmers on its own all day in a slow cooker.

Baked Potato Soup

PREP: 35 min. ■ COOK: 6 hours

2 large onions, chopped	1/2 pound sliced bacon, cooked and crumbled
3 tablespoons butter	3/4 teaspoon pepper
2 tablespoons all-purpose flour	1/2 teaspoon salt
2 cups water, *divided*	1/2 teaspoon dried basil
4 cups chicken broth	1/8 teaspoon dried thyme
2 medium potatoes, peeled and diced	1 cup half-and-half cream
1-1/2 cups mashed potato flakes	1/2 cup shredded cheddar cheese
	2 green onions, sliced

When preparing bacon for Baked Potato Soup, use a kitchen shears to cut the slices so they cook faster. The handy scissors can also be used to snip the cooked bacon into small crumbles. And to speed up meal prep, keep a supply of cooked and crumbled bacon in the freezer. The crumbles are great in salads or soups.

Hearty Goose Soup

Loretta Fenrich
BARNEY LAKE, WASHINGTON

After my son went goose hunting, I had to cook what he brought home. So I got ingredients together and came up with this chunky soup. It's chock-full of pasta and vegetables.

Hearty Goose Soup

PREP: 15 min. ■ **COOK:** 5 hours

2-1/4 cups cubed uncooked goose
  1 pound red potatoes, cubed
  1 large onion, chopped
  1 each medium green, sweet yellow and red pepper, chopped
  2 medium carrot, cut into 1/2-inch slices
  1 cup water
  3 garlic cloves, minced
  2 teaspoons dried basil
Salt and pepper to taste
  1 can (15 ounces) tomato sauce
  1 can (14-1/2 ounces) Italian stewed tomatoes
  2 cups uncooked elbow macaroni

■ In a 5-qt. slow cooker, combine goose, potatoes, onion, peppers, carrots, water, garlic, basil, salt and pepper. Cover and cook on high for 4 hours or until meat juices run clear and vegetables are tender.

■ Stir in tomato sauce and tomatoes; cook 1 hour. Just before serving, cook macaroni according to package directions; drain. Stir into soup.

Yield: 13 servings (about 3 quarts).

French Onion Soup

Kris Ritter
PITTSBURGH, PENNSYLVANIA

It's hard to believe something this delightful came from a slow cooker! Topped with a slice of French bread and provolone cheese, individual servings are sure to be enjoyed by everyone at your dinner table.

PREP: 15 min.
COOK: 8 hours

  1 large sweet onion, thinly sliced (about 4 cups)
1/4 cup butter, cubed
  2 cans (14-1/2 ounces *each*) beef broth
  2 tablespoons sherry *or* additional beef broth
1/2 teaspoon pepper
  4 slices French bread (1/2 inch thick), toasted
  4 slices provolone cheese

■ Place onion and butter in a 1-1/2-qt. slow cooker coated with cooking spray. Cover and cook on low for 6 hours or until onion is tender. Stir in the broth, sherry and pepper. Cover and cook 2-3 hours longer or until heated through.

■ Ladle soup into ovenproof bowls. Top each with a slice of toast and cheese. Broil 4-6 in. from the heat for 2-3 minutes or until cheese is melted. Serve immediately.

Yield: 4 servings.

Chicken Chili

Slow-Cooked Chowder

Pam Leonard
ABERDEEN, SOUTH DAKOTA
Busy weeknights often leave little time for cooking. That's why this slow cooker recipe is a favorite. I just combine the ingredients, flip a switch and forget it! It's a standby in my house during the hectic holiday season.

PREP: 10 min.
COOK: 6 hours

> 5 cups water
> 5 teaspoons chicken bouillon granules
> 8 medium potatoes, cubed
> 2 medium onions, chopped
> 1 medium carrot, thinly sliced
> 1 celery rib, thinly sliced
> 1/4 cup butter, cubed
> 1 teaspoon salt
> 1/4 teaspoon pepper
> 1 can (12 ounces) evaporated milk
> 1 tablespoon minced fresh parsley

■ In a 5-qt. slow cooker, combine the first nine ingredients. Cover and cook on high for 1 hour. Reduce heat to low; cover and cook for 5-6 hours or until vegetables are tender. Stir in milk and parsley; heat through.

Yield: 12 servings (3 quarts).

Chicken Chili

PREP: 10 min. ■ **COOK:** 5 hours

> 1-1/2 pounds boneless skinless chicken breasts, cut into 1/2-inch cubes
> 1 cup chopped onion
> 3 tablespoons vegetable oil
> 1 can (15 ounces) cannellini *or* white kidney beans, rinsed and drained
> 1 can (14-1/2 ounces) diced tomatoes, undrained
> 1 can (14-1/2 ounces) diced tomatoes with mild green chilies, undrained

> 1 cup frozen corn
> 1 teaspoon salt
> 1 teaspoon ground cumin
> 1 teaspoon minced garlic
> 1/2 teaspoon celery salt
> 1/2 teaspoon ground coriander
> 1/2 teaspoon pepper
> Sour cream and shredded cheddar cheese, optional

■ In a large skillet, saute chicken and onion in oil for 5 minutes or until chicken is browned. Transfer to a 5-qt. slow cooker. Stir in the beans, tomatoes, corn and seasonings. Cover and cook on low for 5 hours or until chicken is no longer pink. Garnish with sour cream and cheese if desired.

Yield: 6 servings.

Cannellini beans are large white kidney beans and are generally available dry and canned. Some canned products will list both cannellini beans and large white kidney beans on the label. If you don't have any on hand, substitute navy beans or great northern beans.

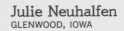

Julie Neuhalfen
GLENWOOD, IOWA

Three types of beans, taco seasoning, green chilies and plenty of flavor make this Southwestern take on chili a real success. Try serving it with a dollop of sour cream, a sprinkling of cheddar cheese and with corn chips on the side. It's perfect for any day of the year.

Hearty Taco Chili

PREP: 30 min. ■ **COOK:** 6 hours

2 pounds ground beef

1 can (16 ounces) kidney beans, rinsed and drained

1 can (15 ounces) pinto beans, rinsed and drained

1 can (15 ounces) black beans, rinsed and drained

1 can (14 ounces) hominy, rinsed and drained

1 can (10 ounces) diced tomatoes with green chilies, undrained

1 can (8 ounces) tomato sauce

1 small onion, chopped

1 envelope ranch salad dressing mix

1 envelope taco seasoning

1/2 teaspoon pepper

2 cans (14-1/2 ounces *each*) diced tomatoes, undrained

1 can (4 ounces) chopped green chilies

Corn chips, sour cream and shredded cheddar cheese, optional

■ In a large skillet, cook beef over medium heat until no longer pink; drain. Transfer to a 5-qt. slow cooker. Add the beans, hominy, tomatoes, tomato sauce, onion, salad dressing mix, taco seasoning and pepper.

■ In a blender, combine diced tomatoes and green chilies; cover and process until smooth. Add to the slow cooker. Cover and cook on low for 6 hours.

■ Serve with corn chips, sour cream and cheese if desired.

Yield: 11 servings.

Cooked ham imparts wonderful flavor to slow-cooked soups. Because it can be a tad salty, you might wish to consider omitting any extra salt a recipe may call for if you're adding ham to the dish. Once the soup is done cooking, salt can be added to taste.

Split Pea Soup

Heidi Schmidgall
HANCOCK, MINNESOTA

In less than half an hour, I can have the ingredients for my satisfying pea soup simmering away in my slow cooker. What a great treat to enjoy this soup on a chilly night.

PREP: 25 min.
COOK: 4 hours

1 package (16 ounces) dried green split peas

2 smoked ham hocks

2 quarts water

2 medium carrots, halved lengthwise and thinly sliced

1 medium onion, chopped

1 celery rib, thinly sliced

1 garlic clove, minced

1 bay leaf

1 teaspoon chicken bouillon granules

1 teaspoon dried thyme

3/4 teaspoon salt

1/2 teaspoon garlic salt

1/2 teaspoon dried basil

1/2 teaspoon dried marjoram

1/2 teaspoon pepper

■ In a 5-qt. slow cooker, combine all ingredients. Cover and cook on high for 4-5 hours or until peas are tender. Skim fat; discard bay leaf. When cool enough to handle, remove meat from bones; discard bones. Cut ham into small pieces and return to slow cooker; heat through.

Yield: 8 servings (2 quarts).

Kathy Rairigh
MILFORD, INDIANA
I've relied on this easily prepared soup on many occasions. Mom gave me the recipe, and we really love it. It offers the homemade flair we crave without all the work.

Home-Style Chicken Soup

Home-Style Chicken Soup

PREP: 15 min. ■ **COOK:** 6 hours 10 min.

- 1 can (14-1/2 ounces) chicken broth
- 1 can (14-1/2 ounces) diced tomatoes, undrained
- 1 cup cubed cooked chicken
- 1 can (8 ounces) mushroom stems and pieces, drained
- 1/4 cup sliced fresh carrot
- 1/4 cup sliced celery
- 1 bay leaf
- 1/8 teaspoon dried thyme
- 3/4 cup cooked egg noodles

■ In a 1-1/2-qt. slow cooker, combine the first eight ingredients. Cover and cook on low for 6 hours. Stir in noodles; cover and cook on high for 10 minutes. Discard bay leaf.

Yield: 4 servings.

Doubling a slow-cooked soup recipe? Doing so is easy, but keep in mind that you'll likely need a larger slow cooker. If the original recipe instructs you to cook any noodles or pasta in the simmering soup, it may be best to prepare the doubled amount of noodles on the stovetop instead. Then simply add the cooked noodles to the soup before serving.

Pulled Pork Subs

Denise Davis
PORTER, MAINE
Honey and ground ginger are the flavor boosters behind my no-stress sandwiches. A bottle of barbecue sauce ties it all together in a pinch.

PREP: 15 min.
COOK: 5 hours

- 1 small onion, finely chopped
- 1 boneless pork shoulder roast (2-1/2 pounds)
- 1 bottle (18 ounces) barbecue sauce
- 1/2 cup water
- 1/4 cup honey
- 6 garlic cloves, minced
- 1 teaspoon seasoned salt
- 1 teaspoon ground ginger
- 8 submarine buns, split

■ Place onion and roast in a 5-qt. slow cooker. Combine the barbecue sauce, water, honey, garlic, seasoned salt and ginger; pour over meat.

■ Cover and cook on high for 5-6 hours or until meat is tender. Remove meat; cool slightly. Shred meat with two forks and return to the slow cooker; heat through. Serve on buns. Cut sandwiches in half.

Yield: 16 servings.

Shredded Beef Sandwiches

- In a 4-cup measuring cup, combine the cola, Worcestershire sauce, garlic, vinegar, bouillon and seasonings; set aside. Cut roast in half. In a nonstick skillet, brown the meat in oil on all sides.

- Place onions in a 3-qt. slow cooker. Top with meat. Pour half of cola mixture over meat. Cover and cook on low for 8-10 hours or until meat is tender. Cover and refrigerate remaining cola mixture.

- Remove meat from cooking liquid and cool. Strain cooking liquid, reserving onions and discarding the liquid. When meat is cool enough to handle, shred with two forks. Return meat and onions to slow cooker. In a small saucepan, combine ketchup and reserved cola mixture; heat through. Pour over meat mixture and heat through. Serve on rolls.

Yield: 8 servings.

* **Nutrition Facts:** 1 serving (1/2 cup meat mixture with roll) equals 354 calories, 10 g fat (2 g saturated fat), 59 mg cholesterol, 714 mg sodium, 40 g carbohydrate, 2 g fiber, 26 g protein. **Diabetic Exchanges:** 3 lean meat, 2-1/2 starch.

Marie Elaine Basinger
CONNELLSVILLE, PENNSYLVANIA

Cola is the secret ingredient in this delicious slow-cooked beef. Coated with a well-seasoned sauce, the tender meat is wonderful for all sort of occasions and get-togethers.

Shredded Beef Sandwiches*

PREP: 30 min. + cooling ■ **COOK:** 8-1/4 hours

3/4 cup cola	1/4 teaspoon cayenne pepper
1/4 cup Worcestershire sauce	1 boneless beef rump roast (2 pounds)
2 garlic cloves, minced	2 teaspoons canola oil
1 tablespoon white vinegar	2 medium onions, chopped
1 teaspoon reduced-sodium beef bouillon granules	1/2 cup ketchup
1/2 teaspoon chili powder	8 kaiser rolls
1/2 teaspoon ground mustard	

For a fast, crunchy and colorful sandwich topper, consider picking up a bag of shredded cabbage (coleslaw) on the way home from work.

Colorful Minestrone*

Tiffany Anderson-Taylor
GULFPORT, FLORIDA

Butter squash, a leek and fresh kale make my minestrone different from most others. Not only do ingredients like this help keep the fat grams down, but they create a lovely blend of flavors.

PREP: 40 min. ■ COOK: 7-1/2 hours

- 3 slices deli ham, chopped
- 1 tablespoon olive oil
- 1 medium leek (white portion only), thinly sliced
- 1 small onion, chopped
- 2 garlic cloves, minced
- 2 quarts water
- 1 can (28 ounces) diced tomatoes, undrained
- 1 medium butternut squash, peeled, seeded and cubed
- 2 medium carrots, coarsely chopped
- 2 celery ribs, chopped
- 2 cups fresh baby spinach, cut into thin strips
- 1 cup fresh kale, trimmed and cut into thin strips
- 1 medium potato, peeled and cubed
- 1 tablespoon minced fresh rosemary
- 1 teaspoon salt

Pepper to taste

- 1 can (15 ounces) white kidney *or* cannellini beans, rinsed and drained

■ In a small skillet, saute ham in oil for 1 minute. Stir in the leek, onion and garlic; saute 2 minutes longer or until vegetables are tender. Transfer ham mixture to a 5-qt. slow cooker. Stir in the water, vegetables, rosemary, salt and pepper.

■ Cover and cook on low for 7-8 hours or until vegetables are tender. Stir in beans; cover and cook 30 minutes longer.

Yield: 10 servings (3-1/2 quarts).

*Nutrition Facts: 1-1/2 cups equals 134 calories, 2 g fat (trace saturated fat), 3 mg cholesterol, 477 mg sodium, 26 g carbohydrate, 7 g fiber, 5 g protein. **Diabetic Exchanges:** 2 vegetable, 1 starch.

Chunky Chili

PREP: 15 min.
COOK: 5 hours

- 1 pound ground turkey *or* beef
- 1 medium onion, chopped
- 2 medium tomatoes, cut up
- 1 can (16 ounces) kidney beans, rinsed and drained
- 1 can (15 ounces) chili beans, undrained
- 1 can (15 ounces) tomato sauce
- 1 cup water
- 1 can (4 ounces) chopped green chilies
- 1 tablespoon chili powder
- 2 teaspoons salt
- 1 teaspoon ground cumin
- 3/4 teaspoon pepper

Sour cream and sliced jalapenos, optional

■ In a large skillet, cook turkey and onion over medium heat until meat is no longer pink; drain. Transfer to a 3-1/2-qt. slow cooker.

■ Stir in the tomatoes, beans, tomato sauce, water, chilies, chili powder, salt, cumin and pepper. Cover and cook on low for 5-6 hours or until heated through. Garnish with sour cream and jalapenos if desired.

Yield: 6-8 servings (2 quarts).

To easily remove the middle ribs from kale, fold the large leaves in half and simply tear or cut the leafy part away from the rib.

Jolene Britten
GIG HARBOR, WASHINGTON

My family (especially my dad) loves chili. After experimenting with several recipes, I came up with my own version that uses ground turkey and is conveniently prepared in a slow cooker. The green chilies, chili powder and cumin add just the right touch of spicy flavor.

Mary Jo O'Brien
HASTINGS, MINNESOTA

I make this thick soup for our annual St. Patrick's Day party, and there's never any leftovers. Using the slow cooker means I can set the soup on the buffet table without worrying about it getting cold.

Slow-Cooked Potato Soup

Slow-Cooked Potato Soup

PREP: 30 min. ■ **COOK:** 5 hours

5-1/2 cups cubed peeled potatoes, *divided*

2-3/4 cups water

1/3 cup butter, cubed

1-1/3 cups cubed fully cooked ham

2 celery ribs, chopped

2/3 cup chopped onion

3/4 teaspoon garlic powder

3/4 teaspoon paprika

1/8 teaspoon pepper

1/2 pound process cheese (Velveeta), cubed

2/3 cup sour cream

Milk, optional

■ Place 4-1/2 cups of the potatoes in a saucepan; add water. Bring to a boil. Reduce heat; cover and cook for 15-20 minutes or until tender. Remove from the heat (do not drain). Mash potatoes; stir in butter.

■ In a 3-qt. slow cooker, combine the ham, celery, onion, garlic powder, paprika, pepper and remaining cubed potatoes. Stir in the mashed potatoes; top with cheese. Cover and cook on low for 5-6 hours or until potatoes and other vegetables are tender. Stir in the sour cream until blended. Thin soup with milk if desired.

Yield: 6 servings.

Chipotle Beef Sandwiches*

Jessica Ring
MADISON, WISCONSIN

A jar of chipotle salsa makes it easy to spice up beef sirloin for my mouth-watering sandwiches. Keep this no-stress recipe in mind the next time you have to feed a hungry crowd.

PREP: 25 min.
COOK: 7 hours

1 large sweet onion, halved and thinly sliced

1 boneless beef sirloin tip roast (3 pounds)

1 jar (16 ounces) chipotle salsa

1/2 cup beer *or* nonalcoholic beer

1 envelope beefy onion soup mix

10 kaiser rolls, split

■ Place onion in a 5-qt. slow cooker. Cut roast in half; place over onion. Combine the salsa, beer and soup mix. Pour over top. Cover and cook on low for 7-8 hours or until meat is tender.

■ Remove roast. Shred meat with two forks and return to the slow cooker; heat through. Using a slotted spoon, spoon shredded meat onto each roll.

Yield: 10 servings.

✱ Nutrition Facts: 1 sandwich equals 362 calories, 9 g fat (3 g saturated fat), 72 mg cholesterol, 524 mg sodium, 37 g carbohydrate, 2 g fiber, 31 g protein. **Diabetic Exchanges:** 3 lean meat, 2-1/2 starch.

Shredded Venison Sandwiches

- Cut venison roast in half; place in a 5-qt. slow cooker. In a large bowl, combine the ketchup, brown sugar, mustard, lemon juice, soy sauce, Liquid Smoke if desired and seasonings. Pour over venison. Cover and cook on high for 4-1/2 to 5 hours or until meat is tender.

- Remove the roast; set aside to cool. Strain sauce and return to slow cooker. Shred meat, using to two forks; stir into sauce and heat through. Using a slotted spoon, spoon meat mixture onto each bun.

Yield: 14-18 servings.

Ruth Setterlund
FREYBURG, MAINE

My husband hunts for deer every November, so I'm always looking for new recipes for venison. The whole family loves these well-seasoned slow-cooker sandwiches.

Shredded Venison Sandwiches

PREP: 5 min. ■ COOK: 4-1/2 hours

1 boneless venison roast (4 pounds)	2 teaspoons celery salt
1-1/2 cups ketchup	2 teaspoons pepper
3 tablespoons brown sugar	2 teaspoons Worcestershire sauce
1 tablespoon ground mustard	1 teaspoon onion powder
1 tablespoon lemon juice	1 teaspoon garlic powder
1 tablespoon soy sauce	1/8 teaspoon ground nutmeg
1 tablespoon Liquid Smoke, optional	3 drops hot pepper sauce
	14 to 18 hamburger buns, split

For a leaner meat, consider venison, which is quite lean by its nature. Trimmed of fat, a 3-ounce portion roasted venison provides about 135 calories, 26 grams of protein and 3 grams of fat. That's only 1 gram of fat per ounce of meat. When venison is ground up and processed, however, beef fat is often added to make up for its low-fat content to provide a more palatable product.

Tiffany Martinez,
ALISO VIEJO, CALIFORNIA

Preparing pork sirloin roast in the slow cooker makes it so moist and tender...it's just perfect for Pulled Pork Sandwiches. The meat shreds so easily, and the cumin and garlic add just the right flavor. The sourdough bread, chipotle mayonnaise, cheese and tomato make it complete.

Pulled Pork Sandwiches

PREP: 20 min. ■ **COOK:** 6 hours

1 boneless pork sirloin roast (2 pounds), trimmed	1/8 teaspoon pepper
1 cup barbecue sauce	16 slices sourdough bread
1/4 cup chopped onion	1 chipotle pepper in adobo sauce, chopped
2 garlic cloves, minced	3/4 cup mayonnaise
1/2 teaspoon ground cumin	8 slices cheddar cheese
1/4 teaspoon salt	2 plum tomatoes, thinly sliced

■ Place pork in a 3-qt. slow cooker. Combine the barbecue sauce, onion, garlic, cumin, salt and pepper; pour over pork. Cover and cook on low for 6-7 hours or until meat is tender. Remove meat. Shred with two forks and return to slow cooker; heat through.

■ Place bread on an ungreased baking sheet. Broil 4-6 in. from the heat for 2-3 minutes on each side or until golden brown.

■ Meanwhile, in a small bowl, combine chipotle pepper and mayonnaise; spread over toast. Spoon 1/2 cup meat mixture onto each of eight slices of toast. Top with cheese, tomatoes and remaining toast.

Yield: 8 servings.

After opening a can of chipotle peppers in adobo sauce, pour the rest of the can into a resealable freezer bag. Label the bag and set it in the freezer. The spicy peppers and zesty sauce add easy flair to lots of dishes.

Southwest Chicken Chili

Phyllis Beatty
CHANDLER, ARIZONA

Chicken thighs are a nice change-of-pace in this easy chili. I also add a smoked ham hock and fresh cilantro to add flavor and keep the dish interesting.

PREP: 15 min.
COOK: 6 hours

1-1/2 pounds boneless skinless chicken thighs, cut into 1-inch cubes
1 tablespoon olive oil
1 smoked ham hock
1 can (15-1/2 ounces) great northern beans, rinsed and drained
1 can (14-1/2 ounces) chicken broth
1 can (4 ounces) chopped green chilies
1/4 cup chopped onion
2 tablespoons minced fresh cilantro
1 teaspoon garlic powder
1 teaspoon ground cumin
1/2 teaspoon dried oregano
1/8 to 1/4 teaspoon crushed red pepper flakes
Sour cream, optional

■ In a large skillet, brown chicken in oil. Transfer to a 3-qt. slow cooker. Add the ham hock, beans, broth, chilies, onion and seasonings. Cover and cook on low for 6 to 8 hours or until ham is tender.

■ Remove ham bone; set aside until cool enough to handle. Remove meat from bone and cut into cubes. Discard bone. Return ham to slow cooker. Serve with sour cream if desired.

Yield: 5 servings.

- In a large skillet, cook beef and sausage over medium heat until no longer pink. Meanwhile, in a 3-qt. slow cooker, combine the tomatoes, tomato sauce, onion, red pepper, water, celery, broth, chili powder, Italian seasoning, sugar, garlic and salt.

- Drain beef mixture; add to the slow cooker. Cover and cook on low for 6 hours or until vegetables are tender.

- Add the beans, mushrooms, zucchini and parsley. Cover and cook on high for 30 minutes or until vegetables are tender. Serve with cheese if desired.

Yield: 6 servings.

Italian Chili

Taste of Home Test Kitchen
GREENDALE, WISCONSIN

By adding Italian seasoning and fresh veggies, our Test Kitchen put an Italian spin on traditional Southwestern-style chili and created this slow-simmered hearty dish.

Italian Chili

PREP: 20 min. ■ **COOK:** 6-1/2 hours

1 pound ground beef	1 tablespoon Italian seasoning
1/2 pound bulk Italian sausage	1 teaspoon sugar
1 can (28 ounces) diced tomatoes	1 teaspoon minced garlic
1 can (8 ounces) tomato sauce	1/2 teaspoon salt
1 cup chopped onion	1 can (16 ounces) kidney beans, rinsed and drained
1 cup chopped sweet red pepper	1 cup sliced fresh mushrooms
1 cup water	1 cup diced zucchini
1/2 cup chopped celery	3 tablespoons minced fresh parsley
1/4 cup beef broth	Shredded part-skim mozzarella cheese, optional
1 tablespoon chili powder	

For fast fixes at mealtime, keep a container in the freezer to hold ingredients for pots of chili. Fill it with leftover taco meat, extra sloppy joes and cooked poultry. You can also add tomato-based dishes such as spaghetti and marinara sauces. When the container is full, just add kidney beans, extra tomato sauce and meat if needed, then season it to taste.

Lori Hayes
VENICE, FLORIDA
I make this beef when I'm having a party so I don't have to spend the whole time in the kitchen. It smells so delicious!

Zesty Beef Subs

Zesty Beef Subs

PREP: 5 min. ■ **COOK:** 10 hours

> 1 boneless beef top round roast (4 pounds)
> 2 cups water
> 2 tablespoons Italian seasoning
> 1 teaspoon *each* salt, dried oregano, dried basil, garlic powder, dried parsley flakes and pepper
> 1 bay leaf
> 14 French rolls (5 inches long)

■ Cut roast in half; place in a 5-qt. slow cooker. Combine the water and seasonings; pour over roast. Cover and cook on low for 10-12 hours or until meat is very tender. Discard bay leaf. Remove meat and shred with a fork. Skim fat from cooking juices; return meat to slow cooker. Serve on rolls.

Yield: 14 servings.

Mix up suppertime standbys by serving Zesty Beef Subs tonight. Not only do the sandwiches feature unbeatable flavor due to a bevy of herbs and seasonings, but you can serve the juicy meat mixture however you'd like. Try stuffing the filling into pita bread or wrapping it up in flour tortillas.

Turkey Chili

Celesta Zanger
BLOOMFIELD HILLS, MICHIGAN
I've taken my mother's milder recipe for chili and made it thicker and more robust.

PREP: 20 min.
COOK: 6-1/2 hours

> 1 pound lean ground turkey
> 3/4 cup *each* chopped onion, celery and green pepper
> 1 can (28 ounces) diced tomatoes, undrained
> 1 jar (26 ounces) meatless spaghetti sauce
> 1 can (15-1/2 ounces) hot chili beans
> 1-1/2 cups water
> 1/2 cup frozen corn
> 2 tablespoons chili powder
> 1 teaspoon ground cumin
> 1/4 teaspoon pepper
> 1/8 to 1/4 teaspoon cayenne pepper
> 1 can (16 ounces) kidney beans, rinsed and drained
> 1 can (15 ounces) pinto beans, rinsed and drained
> Sour cream, optional

■ In a large nonstick skillet, cook the turkey, onion, celery and green pepper over medium heat until meat is no longer pink and vegetables are tender; drain. Transfer to a 5-qt. slow cooker. Add the tomatoes, spaghetti sauce, chili beans, water, corn and seasonings. Cover and cook on high for 1 hour.

■ Reduce heat to low; cook for 5-6 hours. Add kidney and pinto beans; cook 30 minutes longer. Garnish with sour cream if desired.

Yield: 13 servings.

Beef Vegetable Soup

Italian Meatball 'n' Bean Soup

Amanda Bowyer
CALDWELL, IDAHO

This is a taste sensation the whole family will love.

PREP: 30 min.
COOK: 5 hours

    1   egg
    3   tablespoons milk
  1/3   cup seasoned bread
        crumbs
    1   pound bulk Italian
        sausage
  1/2   pound ground turkey
    2   cans (14-1/2 ounces *each*)
        diced tomatoes
    1   can (15 ounces) white
        kidney *or* cannellini beans,
        rinsed and drained
    1   can (15 ounces) black
        beans, rinsed and drained
    1   can (8 ounces) tomato
        sauce
    1   cup water
    2   green onions, thinly sliced
    1   teaspoon Italian seasoning
    1   teaspoon dried minced
        garlic
  1/2   teaspoon crushed red
        pepper flakes

■ In a large mixing bowl, combine the egg, milk, and bread crumbs. Crumble sausage and turkey over mixture and mix well. Shape into 1-in. balls. In a large skillet, brown meatballs in batches; drain. Transfer meatballs to a 3-qt. slow cooker.

■ Stir in the remaining ingredients. Cover and cook on low for 5 hours or until meat is no longer pink.

Yield: *6 servings.*

Colleen Jubl
DAYTON, OHIO

Here's a slow-cooked meal-in-one just perfect for chilly winter nights. It's nice to come home to a hearty soup that's chock-full of good things and ready to eat.

Beef Vegetable Soup*

PREP: 10 min. ■ **COOK:** 4 hours

    1   pound lean ground beef
    1   medium onion, chopped
    2   garlic cloves, minced
    4   cups picante V8 juice
    2   cups coleslaw mix
    1   can (14-1/2 ounces) Italian
        stewed tomatoes
    1   package (10 ounces) frozen
        corn
    1   package (9 ounces) frozen
        cut green beans
    2   tablespoons Worcestershire
        sauce
    1   teaspoon dried basil
  1/4   teaspoon pepper

■ In a large nonstick skillet, cook the beef, onion and garlic over medium heat until meat is no longer pink; drain. Transfer to a 5-qt. slow cooker. Stir in the remaining ingredients. Cover and cook on high for 4-5 hours or until heated through.

Yield: *9 servings.*

✱Nutrition Facts: 1 cup equals 169 calories, 5 g fat (2 g saturated fat), 18 mg cholesterol, 578 mg sodium, 19 g carbohydrate, 3 g fiber, 14 g protein. **Diabetic Exchanges:** 1 starch, 1 lean meat, 1 vegetable.

Creamy Ham Chowder

Lee Bremson
KANSAS CITY, MISSOURI

You'll dig into satisfaction when this thick and creamy chowder is on the menu. Loaded with comforting flavor, it's sure to make friends and family think you labored for hours perfecting it.

PREP: 30 min. ■ **COOK:** 3-1/2 hours

4 cups cubed peeled potatoes	4 cups half-and-half cream
2 tablespoons chopped onion	2 cups (8 ounces each) shredded cheddar cheese
1/2 cup butter	3 cups cubed fully cooked ham
3/4 cup all-purpose flour	1 package (16 ounces) frozen broccoli cuts, thawed and drained
1/4 teaspoon salt	
1/4 teaspoon pepper	
Pinch ground nutmeg	
4 cups chicken broth	

■ Place potatoes in a large saucepan and cover with water. Bring to a boil. Reduce heat; cover and cook for 10-15 minutes or until tender.

■ Meanwhile, in a large saucepan, cook onion in butter over medium heat for 2 minutes. Stir in the flour, salt, pepper and nutmeg; gradually add broth. Bring to a boil; cook and stir for 2 minutes or until thickened. Stir in cream and cheese; transfer to a 5-qt. slow cooker. Drain potatoes; add to slow cooker. Stir in ham. Cover and cook on low for 3 hours.

■ Stir in broccoli. Cover and cook 30 minutes longer or until heated through and vegetables are tender.

Yield: 12 servings (about 3-1/2 quarts).

Perk up the flavor of dishes by selecting sharp cheddar when packaged shredded cheese is called for. If you will be shredding cheese at home from bulk cheddar, you can choose from mild, medium, sharp and extra-sharp varieties.

Halibut Chowder*

Donna Goutermont
JUNEAU, ALASKA

Try this great way to mix up dinner standbys. Mashed potato flakes thicken this easy chowder, and you can vary the chili powder and cayenne to fit your taste.

PREP: 20 min.
COOK: 5-1/2 hours

2 cups water
2 cups milk
2 medium potatoes, cubed
1 large onion, chopped
1 cup mashed potato flakes
1 can (8 ounces) tomato sauce
2 garlic cloves, minced
1 teaspoon celery salt
1 teaspoon dried parsley flakes
1/2 teaspoon ground mustard
1/4 teaspoon chili powder
1/4 teaspoon cayenne pepper
1 pound halibut fillets, cut into chunks
1 tablespoon butter

■ In a 3-qt. slow cooker, combine the first 12 ingredients. Cover and cook on low for 5 hours or until potatoes are tender. Add halibut and butter. Cover and cook 30-45 minutes longer or until the fish flakes easily with a fork.

Yield: 6 servings.

*Nutrition Facts: 1-1/4 cups equals 254 calories, 6 g fat (3 g saturated fat), 37 mg cholesterol, 534 mg sodium, 27 g carbohydrate, 2 g fiber, 21 g protein. **Diabetic Exchanges:** 3 very lean meat, 2 starch.

Curried Pumpkin Soup*

Debbie Flocco
NORRISTOWN, PENNSYLVANIA

Looking for something new to beat dinnertime doldrums? Try my pumpkin soup! A touch of curry powder lends an aromatic spiced appeal while whipping cream gives the soup its silky texture.

PREP: 20 min. ■ **COOK:** 6-1/2 hours

2-1/2 cups water
1 can (15 ounces) solid-pack pumpkin
2 medium tomatoes, quartered
1 medium potato, peeled and diced
1 medium onion, chopped
2 to 3 teaspoons curry powder
2 teaspoons chicken bouillon granules
1/2 teaspoon salt
1/8 teaspoon cayenne pepper
1/8 teaspoon pepper
1 cup milk
1/2 cup heavy whipping cream

■ In a 3-qt. slow cooker, combine the first 10 ingredients. Cover and cook on low for 5-1/2 to 6-1/2 hours or until vegetables are tender.

■ In a blender, process soup in batches until smooth. Return all to slow cooker. Stir in milk and cream. Cook on high for 30 minutes or until heated through.

Yield: 8 servings.

✳**Nutrition Facts:** 3/4 cup equals 121 calories, 7 g fat (4 g saturated fat), 24 mg cholesterol, 381 mg sodium, 13 g carbohydrate, 4 g fiber, 3 g protein. **Diabetic Exchanges:** 1 starch, 1 fat.

Choose the correct size slow cooker for your recipe. A slow cooker should be from half to three-quarters full. Unless the recipe instructs you to stir in or add ingredients, refrain from lifting the lid while the slow cooker is cooking. The loss of steam can mean an additional 15 to 30 minutes of cooking each time you lift the lid. Be sure the lid is sealed properly–not tilted or askew. The steam creates a seal.

Vegetable Bean Soup

PREP: 30 min.
COOK: 6 hours

2 cans (14-1/2 ounces *each*) petite diced tomatoes
1 can (16 ounces) kidney beans, rinsed and drained
1 can (15-1/4 ounces) whole kernel corn, drained
1 can (15 ounces) garbanzo beans *or* chickpeas, rinsed and drained
1 can (15 ounces) black beans, rinsed and drained
1 can (10 ounces) diced tomatoes and green chilies
1 can (8 ounces) tomato sauce
1 cup chopped green pepper
1 cup chopped zucchini
3/4 cup water
1/2 cup chopped onion
1/2 cup chopped celery
2 tablespoons chili powder
4 teaspoons dried oregano
2 garlic cloves, minced
1 teaspoon ground cumin
1 teaspoon pepper
1/2 teaspoon salt
2 bay leaves

■ In a 5-qt. slow cooker, combine all ingredients. Cover and cook on low for 6-8 hours or until vegetables are tender. Discard bay leaves before serving.

Yield: 7 servings.

Belinda Moran
WOODBURY, TENNESSEE

Kitchen staples and canned goods help me get this heartwarming soup on the table with very little preparation. Feel free to change the ingredients according to your tastes by adding a few of your favorite vegetables, or swap out some of the beans with the variety you like best.

Beef & Ground Beef

 29

 36

 32

For bringing out the rich, full-bodied flavor of beef nothing works better than a slow cooker. These stick-to-your-ribs recipes will satisfy even the heartiest of appetites and put dinner on the table with hardly any effort at all.

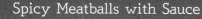
Spicy Meatballs with Sauce

■ In a bowl, combine the egg, croutons, onion, green pepper, garlic powder, cumin, oregano and pepper. Crumble beef or turkey and sausage over mixture and mix well. Shape into 1-in. balls. Place in a 5-qt. slow cooker.

■ In a large bowl, combine the cornstarch, sugar and broth until smooth; stir in the tomatoes, carrots, tomato paste, soup mix, garlic, basil and pepper flakes. Pour over meatballs. Cover and cook on low for 5-6 hours or until meat is no longer pink. Serve with pasta.

Yield: 8 servings (1 cup sauce with 5 meatballs).

Rosanne Bergman
ALTA LOMA, CALIFORNIA
I rely on Italian sausage to make my meatballs. Not only do they taste great, but they also cook to perfection in the slow cooker along with a homemade sauce!

Spicy Meatballs with Sauce

PREP: 30 min. ■ **COOK:** 5 hours

1 egg, beaten
3/4 cup crushed seasoned salad croutons
1/2 cup finely chopped onion
1/4 cup finely chopped green pepper
1 teaspoon garlic powder
1 teaspoon ground cumin
1 teaspoon dried oregano
1 teaspoon pepper
1 pound lean ground beef *or* turkey
1 pound bulk Italian sausage

SAUCE:
3 tablespoons cornstarch
1 tablespoon sugar
3/4 cup beef broth
2 cans (28 ounces *each*) crushed tomatoes
3 medium carrots, diced
1 can (6 ounces) tomato paste
1 envelope onion soup mix
3 garlic cloves, minced
1 teaspoon dried basil
1/2 teaspoon crushed red pepper flakes

Hot cooked pasta

Have fun at supper time by bringing a new pasta to the table. Try shells of different sizes or cook up some wagon wheels for a change of pace that's sure to get some attention.

Kathy Clark
BYRON, MINNESOTA

This recipe came with my first slow cooker. Today, I'm on my fourth slow cooker, and I still use the recipe on a very regular basis.

Stuffed Flank Steak

Stuffed Flank Steak*

PREP: 20 min. ■ COOK: 8 hours + 10 min. standing

1 beef flank steak (2 pounds)	1/4 cup minced fresh parsley
1 medium onion, chopped	1/4 cup egg substitute
1 garlic clove, minced	3/4 teaspoon poultry seasoning
1 tablespoon butter	1/2 teaspoon salt
1-1/2 cups soft bread crumbs (about 3 slices)	1/8 teaspoon pepper
1/2 cup chopped fresh mushrooms	1/2 cup beef broth
	2 teaspoons cornstarch
	4 teaspoons water

■ Flatten steak to 1/2-in. thickness; set aside. In a nonstick skillet, saute onion and garlic in butter until tender. Add the bread crumbs, mushrooms, parsley, egg substitute, poultry seasoning, salt and pepper; mix well. Spread over steak to within 1 in. of edge. Roll up jelly-roll style, starting with a long side; tie with kitchen string. Place in a 5-qt. slow cooker; add broth. Cover and cook on low for 8-10 hours.

■ Remove meat to a serving platter and keep warm. Skim fat from juices; pour into a small saucepan. Combine the cornstarch and water until smooth; stir into juices. Bring to a boil; cook and stir for 1-2 minutes or until thickened. Remove string before slicing steak; serve with gravy.

Yield: 8 servings.

✱ Nutrition Facts: 1 slice equals 230 calories, 11 g fat (5 g saturated fat), 62 mg cholesterol, 348 mg sodium, 6 g carbohydrate, 0.55 g fiber, 26 g protein. **Diabetic Exchanges:** 3 lean meat, 1/2 starch, 1/2 fat.

Pot Roast with Mushroom Gravy

PREP: 20 min.
COOK: 8 hours

- 1 pound small red potatoes, halved
- 2 cups fresh baby carrots
- 1 package (8 ounces) sliced fresh mushrooms
- 1 medium onion, cut into six wedges
- 2 celery ribs, cut into 1-inch pieces
- 1 boneless beef chuck roast (3 pounds)
- 1 can (14-1/2 ounces) reduced-sodium beef broth
- 1 can (10-1/2 ounces) mushroom gravy
- 1 package (1-1/2 ounces) beef stew seasoning mix

■ Place the potatoes, carrots, mushrooms, onion and celery in a 5-qt. slow cooker. Cut roast in half; place over vegetables. In a small bowl, combine the broth, gravy and seasoning mix; pour over roast.

■ Cover and cook on low for 8-9 hours or until meat is tender.

Yield: 8 servings.

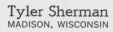

Tyler Sherman
MADISON, WISCONSIN

You just can't beat the comforting goodness of a pot roast...especially one that simmers extra slowly in its own juices during the day. Hearty vegetables like potatoes, carrots, mushrooms, celery and onion make it a great meal-in-one to come home to!

Slow-Cooked Meat Loaf

- In a small bowl, combine soup and water until blended. Pour half into a 1-1/2-qt. slow cooker. Cover and refrigerate remaining soup mixture.

- In a bowl, combine the egg, bread crumbs, Parmesan cheese, parsley, garlic powder, onion powder, salt if desired and pepper. Crumble beef over mixture and mix well. Shape into a loaf; place in slow cooker. Cover and cook on low for 5 hours or until a meat thermometer reads 160°.

- For gravy, place reserved soup mixture in a small saucepan; cook over low heat until heated through. Serve with the meat loaf and potatoes if desired.

Yield: 2 servings.

✻ **Nutrition Facts:** 1 serving (prepared with reduced-fat soup and egg substitute; calculated without optional ingredients) equals 354 calories, 15 g fat (6 g saturated fat), 79 mg cholesterol, 1,367 mg sodium, 22 g carbohydrate, 2 g fiber, 31 g protein. **Diabetic Exchanges:** 3 lean meat, 1-1/2 starch, 1-1/2 fat.

Ginger Cortese
HOLLSOPPLE, PENNSYLVANIA

My husband and I both work late, so it's great to come home to this classic dish served with mashed potatoes and a veggie side. It reminds me of supper at Mom's.

Slow-Cooked Meat Loaf*

PREP: 15 min. ■ COOK: 5 hours

1 can (10-3/4 ounces) condensed cream of celery soup, undiluted	1-1/2 teaspoons dried parsley flakes
1-1/4 cups water	1/2 teaspoon garlic powder
1 egg	1/4 teaspoon onion powder
1/4 cup dry bread crumbs	1/8 teaspoon salt, optional
2 tablespoons grated Parmesan cheese	1/8 teaspoon pepper
	1/2 pound lean ground beef
	Hot mashed potatoes, optional

Carol Mulligan
HONEOYE FALLS,
NEW YORK

I fixed this roast the first time I cooked for my husband-to-be over 20 years ago. He loves it today as much as he did then.

Sweet 'n' Tangy Pot Roast

Sweet 'n' Tangy Pot Roast*

PREP: 10 min. ■ **COOK:** 9 hours 30 min.

1 boneless beef chuck roast (3 pounds)	1 envelope brown gravy mix
1/2 teaspoon salt	2 teaspoons Dijon mustard
1/2 teaspoon pepper	1 teaspoon Worcestershire sauce
1 cup water	1/8 teaspoon garlic powder
1 cup ketchup	3 tablespoons cornstarch
1/4 cup red wine *or* beef broth	1/4 cup cold water

■ Cut meat in half and place in a 5-qt. slow cooker. Sprinkle with salt and pepper. In a bowl, combine the water, ketchup, wine or broth, gravy mix, mustard, Worcestershire sauce and garlic powder; pour over meat. Cover and cook on low for 9-10 hours or until meat is tender.

■ Combine cornstarch and cold water until smooth. Stir into slow cooker. Cover and cook on high for 30 minutes or until gravy is thickened. Remove meat from slow cooker. Slice and serve with gravy.

Yield: 8 servings.

＊**Nutrition Facts:** 3 ounces cooked beef with 1/2 cup gravy equals 249 calories, 8 g fat (3 g saturated fat), 89 mg cholesterol, 748 mg sodium, 13 g carbohydrate, 1 g fiber, 30 g protein. **Diabetic Exchanges:** 3 lean meat, 1 starch.

When looking for beef chuck roast, keep in mind that some grocery stores may label the roast as arm roast or chuckwagon roast.

Hobo Meatball Stew

Margery Bryan
MOSES LAKE, WASHINGTON

Potatoes, carrots, onion and peas do a fine job of jazzing up ground beef in this no-fuss dinner. Best of all, I can assemble it in the afternoon and it's ready for supper that night.

PREP: 20 min.
COOK: 5 hours

1 pound ground beef
1-1/2 teaspoons salt *or* salt-free seasoning blend, *divided*
1/2 teaspoon pepper, *divided*
4 medium potatoes, peeled and cut into chunks
4 medium carrots, cut into chunks
1 large onion, cut into chunks
1/2 cup water
1/2 cup ketchup
1-1/2 teaspoons cider vinegar
1/2 teaspoon dried basil
3/4 cup frozen peas

■ In a bowl, combine the beef, 1 teaspoon salt and 1/4 teaspoon pepper. Shape into 1-in. balls. In a large skillet over medium heat, brown meatballs on all sides; drain.

■ Place the potatoes, carrots and onion in a 3-qt. slow cooker; top with meatballs. Combine the water, ketchup, vinegar, basil, and remaining salt and pepper; pour over meatballs.

■ Cover and cook on high for 4-3/4 hours. Stir in peas; cook 15 minutes longer or until the vegetables are tender.

Yield: 4 servings.

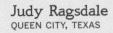

Judy Ragsdale
QUEEN CITY, TEXAS

This layered, Southwestern meal just can't be beat. It gets its spicy flavor from green chilies, chili powder and cumin. Using a slow cooker liner inside of the cooker makes it easier to lift and remove the meal so it can be cut into individual wedges.

Slow-Cooked Enchilada Dinner

PREP: 25 min. ■ **COOK:** 2 hours

- 1 pound lean ground beef
- 1 small onion, chopped
- 1 can (15 ounces) ranch-style beans, undrained
- 1 can (10 ounces) diced tomatoes with mild green chilies, undrained
- 1/4 cup chopped green pepper
- 1 teaspoon chili powder
- 1/2 teaspoon salt
- 1/2 teaspoon ground cumin
- 1/4 teaspoon pepper
- 1 cup (4 ounces) shredded Monterey Jack cheese
- 1 cup (4 ounces) shredded cheddar cheese
- 6 flour tortillas (6 inches)

■ In a large skillet, cook beef and onion over medium heat until meat is no longer pink; drain.

■ Stir in the beans, tomatoes, water, green pepper, chili powder, salt, cumin and pepper. In a small bowl, combine the cheeses; set aside.

■ In a 5-qt. slow cooker coated with cooking spray, place two tortillas side by side, overlapping if necessary. Layer with a third of the beef mixture and cheese. Repeat layers twice. Cover and cook on low for 2 to 2-1/2 hours or until heated through.

Yield: 6 servings.

To make the enchilada dinner extra special, top it with taco fixings, such as sour cream, green onion or even crushed corn chips. Or complete the meal with a spinach salad and refreshing limeade.

Mushroom Round Steak

Lois Hedke
SOUTH ROCKWOOD, MICHIGAN

This beef and noodle dish is light on ingredients but big on taste. Because of this, it's become one of our regular dinner staples. Sometimes I add a crisp salad to round out the menu.

PREP: 20 min.
COOK: 6 hours

- 1/2 medium green pepper, cut into 1/2-inch pieces
- 1/4 cup sliced onion
- 1 boneless beef top round steak (10 ounces), cut into two pieces
- 2/3 cup condensed cream of mushroom soup, undiluted
- 1/3 cup water
- 1-1/2 cups uncooked egg noodles

■ Place green pepper and onion in a 1-1/2-qt. slow cooker; top with beef. In a small bowl, combine soup and water; pour over meat. Cover and cook on low for 6-7 hours or until meat is tender.

■ Cook the noodles according to package directions; drain. Serve with round steak and gravy.

Yield: 2 servings.

Double-Onion Beef Brisket

Elaine Sweet
DALLAS, TEXAS

It's the slow simmering cooking method that makes my beef brisket so tender. It gets a wonderfully sweet-tangy flavor from chili sauce, cider vinegar and brown sugar.

PREP: 25 min. ■ **COOK:** 6 hours

1	fresh beef brisket (4 pounds)	3	medium onions, halved and sliced, *divided*
1-1/2	teaspoons kosher salt	3	celery ribs, chopped
1-1/2	teaspoons coarsely ground pepper	1	cup chili sauce
2	tablespoons olive oil	1/4	cup packed brown sugar
		1/4	cup cider vinegar
		1	envelope onion soup mix

■ Cut brisket in half; sprinkle all sides with salt and pepper. In a large skillet, brown brisket in oil; remove and set aside.

■ In the same skillet, saute onions for 1-2 minutes or until caramelized. Place half of the onions in a 5-qt. slow cooker; top with celery and brisket. Combine the chili sauce, brown sugar, vinegar and soup mix. Pour over brisket; top with remaining cooked onions.

■ Cover and cook on low for 6-7 hours or until meat is tender. Let stand for 5 minutes before slicing. Skim fat from cooking juices and serve with meat.

Yield: 10 servings.

Editor's Note: This is a fresh beef brisket, not corned beef.

Beef brisket tastes great, maybe even better, the day after it was cooked. Served over rye bread, it makes a great sandwich. Don't forget the dill pickle!

Spicy Beef Vegetable Stew*

Lynnette Davis
TULLAHOMA, TENNESSEE

This zesty beef stew is packed with flavor and comes together quickly. Try pairing it with warm corn bread, sourdough bread or French bread.

PREP: 10 min.
COOK: 8 hours

1	pound ground beef
1	cup chopped onion
1	jar (30 ounces) meatless spaghetti sauce
3-1/2	cups water
1	package (16 ounces) frozen mixed vegetables
1	can (10 ounces) diced tomatoes and green chilies
1	cup sliced celery
1	teaspoon beef bouillon granules
1	teaspoon pepper

■ In a large skillet, cook beef and onion over medium heat until meat is no longer pink; drain. Transfer to a 5-qt. slow cooker. Stir in the remaining ingredients. Cover and cook on low for 8 hours or until the vegetables are tender.

Yield: 12 servings.

✱ **Nutrition Facts:** 1 serving (prepared with lean ground beef, reduced-sodium spaghetti sauce and reduced-sodium bouillon) equals 159 calories, 7 g fat (0 saturated fat), 14 mg cholesterol, 159 mg sodium, 14 g carbohydrate, 0 fiber, 10 g protein. **Diabetic Exchanges:** 1-1/2 meat, 1 vegetable, 1/2 starch.

- Place roast and water in a 3-qt. slow cooker. Cover and cook on low for 8-9 hours or until meat is tender. Remove meat. When cool enough to handle, shred meat with two forks. Skim fat from cooking liquid; set aside 1/2 cup.

- In a large skillet, cook the tomatoes, green pepper, onion, garlic and bay leaf in oil for 18-22 minutes or until liquid is reduced to 2 tablespoons.

- Stir in the ketchup, jalapeno slices and juice, vinegar, salt, garlic salt and reserved cooking liquid. Bring to a boil. Stir in shredded beef; heat through. Discard bay leaf. Serve beef mixture on tortillas.

Yield: 8 servings.

Southwestern Beef Tortillas

Marie Rizzio
INTERLOCHEN, MICHIGAN

Beef chuck roast makes for a savory filling in these satisfying tortillas. Cooked to perfection in a slow cooker, it's treated to an effortless jalapeno-flavored sauce.

Southwestern Beef Tortillas

PREP: 25 min. ■ COOK: 8-3/4 hours

1 boneless beef chuck roast (2 pounds)	2 tablespoons canola oil
1/2 cup water	3/4 cup ketchup
4 large tomatoes, peeled and chopped	1/2 cup pickled jalapeno slices
1 large green pepper, thinly sliced	1 tablespoon juice from pickled jalapeno slices
1 medium onion, chopped	1 tablespoon cider vinegar
1 garlic clove, minced	1 teaspoon salt
1 bay leaf	1/8 teaspoon garlic salt
	8 flour tortillas (8 inches), warmed

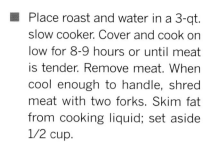

Minced garlic is available in jars in the produce department of most supermarkets. Typically, 1/2 teaspoon of jarred garlic equals one fresh garlic clove, minced. Jarred garlic can be slightly milder than fresh, but many cooks rely on the convenience it offers.

Pizza in a Pot

Dianna Cline
PHILIPPI, WEST VIRGINIA

Served with warm breadsticks or garlic toast, this is one dinner I know my family will always eagerly eat. It comes together in a pinch and simmers to perfection in a few hours.

Pizza in a Pot

PREP: 15 min. ■ **COOK:** 3 hours

1-1/2 pounds ground beef
1 medium green pepper, chopped
1 medium onion, chopped
1 can (15 ounces) tomato sauce
1 jar (14 ounces) pizza sauce

2 tablespoons tomato paste
3 cups spiral pasta, cooked and drained
2 packages (3-1/2 ounces *each*) sliced pepperoni
2 cups (8 ounces) shredded part-skim mozzarella cheese

■ In a large skillet, cook the beef, green pepper and onion over medium heat until meat is no longer pink; drain. Stir in the tomato sauce, pizza sauce and tomato paste.

■ In a 5-qt. slow cooker, layer the pasta, beef mixture, pepperoni and cheese. Cover and cook on low for 3-4 hours or until heated through.

Yield: 8 servings.

Rosemary Pot Roast*

PREP: 15 min.
COOK: 8 hours

1 boneless beef chuck steak (3/4 inch thick and 3/4 pound)
1 to 2 teaspoons canola oil
1/4 cup beef broth
1/4 cup tomato sauce
1/4 cup dry red wine *or* additional beef broth
2 tablespoons chopped onion
1 garlic clove, minced
1-1/2 teaspoons dried parsley flakes
1/4 teaspoon minced fresh rosemary
1/8 teaspoon salt
1/8 teaspoon pepper
1-1/2 teaspoons cornstarch
1 tablespoon water

■ In a large skillet, brown beef in oil on both sides. Transfer to a 1-1/2-qt. slow cooker. In a small bowl, combine the broth, tomato sauce, wine or additional broth, onion, garlic, parsley, rosemary, salt and pepper; pour over beef. Cover and cook on low for 8 hours or until meat is tender.

■ Remove beef and keep warm. In a small saucepan, combine cornstarch and water until smooth; stir in cooking juices. Bring to a boil; cook and stir for 2 minutes or until thickened. Serve with beef.

Yield: 2 servings.

* **Nutrition Facts:** 1 serving (calculated with 1 teaspoon oil) equals 354 calories, 19 g fat (7 g saturated fat), 111 mg cholesterol, 463 mg sodium, 6 g carbohydrate, 1 g fiber, 34 g protein. **Diabetic Exchanges:** 5 lean meat, 2 fat, 1 vegetable.

Marcia Schroeder
RIVER EDGE, NEW JERSEY

Come home to a comforting, ready-to-eat entree with this two-person delight. A neighbor originally shared the recipe, and I've served it often. Leftovers are so tender and tasty, you just might want to double this recipe to serve over noodles or in sandwiches the next day.

Butternut Beef Stew

Erin Lembke
MONROE, WASHINGTON

Butternut squash, chopped cabbage and a little adobo sauce make my beef stew refreshingly different from most. I love the fact that it simmers on its own all day long.

PREP: 30 min. ■ **COOK:** 7 hours

1-1/4	pounds beef stew meat, cut into 1-inch cubes
1	tablespoon canola oil
1-1/2	cups cubed peeled butternut squash
1	cup chopped cabbage
1/2	cup coarsely chopped sweet red pepper
1	celery rib with leaves, chopped
1	can (10 ounces) diced tomatoes with green chilies
1/4	cup packed brown sugar
1	can (14-1/2 ounces) beef broth
1	tablespoon adobo sauce
1	teaspoon dried oregano
1/4	teaspoon salt
1/8	teaspoon pepper

■ In a large skillet, brown meat in oil on all sides; drain. Transfer to a 3-qt. slow cooker. Stir in the squash, cabbage, red pepper and celery.

■ In a blender, combine tomatoes and brown sugar. Cover and process until blended. Pour over vegetables. Combine the broth, adobo sauce, oregano, salt and pepper; add to slow cooker.

■ Cover and cook on low for 7-8 hours or until meat and vegetables are tender. If desired, thicken pan juices.

Yield: 4 servings.

Butternut squash is extremely hard, and the peel can sometimes be difficult to remove. To make it easier to peel the squash, microwave on high for 1-3 minutes and use a vegetable peeler to remove the skin. It will come off without a problem.

Traditional Beef Stew*

Rosana Pape
HAMILTON, INDIANA

The aroma of this classic beef stew is irresistible, making it nearly impossible not to dig in the moment you walk through the door. It's a must-have recipe for anyone who relies on a slow cooker to set dinner on the table.

PREP: 15 min.
COOK: 8 hours

1	pound beef stew meat, cut into 1-inch cubes
1	package (16 ounces) fresh baby carrots
2	medium potatoes, cut into chunks
2	medium onions, cut into wedges
1	cup drained diced tomatoes
1	cup beef broth
1	celery rib, cut into 1/2-inch pieces
2	tablespoons quick-cooking tapioca
1	teaspoon Worcestershire sauce
1/4	teaspoon salt
1/4	teaspoon pepper

■ In a 3-qt. slow cooker, combine all the ingredients. Cover and cook on low for 8-10 hours or until meat and vegetables are tender.

Yield: 4 servings.

✱ **Nutrition Facts:** 1-1/2 cups equals 334 calories, 8 g fat (3 g saturated fat), 70 mg cholesterol, 611 mg sodium, 39 g carbohydrate, 6 g fiber, 26 g protein. **Diabetic Exchanges:** 3 very lean meat, 2 starch, 2 vegetable.

Meat Sauce for Spaghetti

Slow-Cooked Swiss Steak

Kathie Morris
REDMOND, OREGON

Here's an all-time classic that gets an update from the slow cooker. A can of creamed soup makes assembly a cinch, and celery and onion add a homey flavor.

PREP: 15 min.
COOK: 8 hours

- 3/4 cup all-purpose flour
- 1 teaspoon pepper
- 1/4 teaspoon salt
- 2 to 2-1/2 pounds boneless beef top round steak
- 1 to 2 tablespoons butter
- 1 can (10-3/4 ounces) condensed cream of mushroom soup, undiluted
- 1-1/3 cups water
- 1 cup sliced celery, optional
- 1/2 cup chopped onion
- 1 to 3 teaspoons beef bouillon granules
- 1/2 teaspoon minced garlic

- In a shallow bowl, combine the flour, pepper and salt. Cut steak into six serving-size pieces; dredge in flour mixture.

- In a large skillet, brown steak in butter. Transfer to a 3-qt. slow cooker. Combine the remaining ingredients; pour over steak. Cover and cook on low for 8-9 hours or until meat is tender.

Yield: 6 servings.

Mary Tallman
ARBOR VITAE, WISCONSIN
This is a thick, hearty sauce that turns ordinary spaghetti and garlic bread into a filling feast. When I'm in a hurry, I make this slow cooker recipe in an electric skillet instead.

Meat Sauce for Spaghetti

PREP: 30 min. ■ **COOK:** 8 hours

- 1 pound ground beef
- 1 pound bulk Italian sausage
- 1 can (28 ounces) crushed tomatoes, undrained
- 1 medium green pepper, chopped
- 1 medium onion, chopped
- 1 cup finely chopped carrots
- 1 cup water
- 1 can (8 ounces) tomato sauce
- 1 can (6 ounces) tomato paste
- 1 tablespoon brown sugar
- 1 tablespoon Italian seasoning
- 2 garlic cloves, minced
- 1/2 teaspoon salt
- 1/4 teaspoon pepper
- Hot cooked spaghetti

- In a large skillet, cook beef and sausage over medium heat until no longer pink; drain. Transfer to a 5-qt. slow cooker. Stir in the tomatoes, green pepper, onion, carrots, water, tomato sauce, tomato paste, brown sugar, Italian seasoning, garlic, salt and pepper. Cover and cook on low for 8-10 hours or until bubbly. Serve over spaghetti.

Yield: 9 servings.

Corned Beef and Cabbage

Tender Beef Over Noodles

PREP: 15 min.
COOK: 5-1/2 hours

- 1/2 to 3/4 pound beef stew meat
- 1/3 cup chopped onion
- 1 teaspoon canola oil
- 1 cup water, *divided*
- 1/3 cup ketchup
- 1 tablespoon brown sugar
- 1 tablespoon Worcestershire sauce
- 1/2 teaspoon paprika
- 1/4 teaspoon ground mustard
- 3 tablespoons all-purpose flour
- 1 cup uncooked egg noodles

■ In a small skillet, brown beef and onion in oil; drain. Transfer to a 1-1/2-qt. slow cooker.

■ Combine 1/2 cup water, ketchup, brown sugar, Worcestershire sauce, paprika and mustard; pour over the meat. Cover and cook on low for 5 hours or until meat is tender.

■ Combine the flour and remaining water until smooth; stir into meat mixture. Cook 30 minutes longer or until thickened. Meanwhile, cook noodles according to package directions; drain. Serve with beef.

Yield: 2 servings.

Karen Waters
LAUREL, MARYLAND

I first tried this fuss-free way to cook traditional corned beef and cabbage for St. Patrick's Day a few years ago. Now it's a regular in my menu planning.

Corned Beef and Cabbage

PREP: 15 min. ■ **COOK:** 8 hours

- 1 medium onion, cut into wedges
- 4 large red potatoes, quartered
- 1 pound baby carrots
- 3 cups water
- 3 garlic cloves, minced
- 1 bay leaf
- 2 tablespoons sugar
- 2 tablespoons cider vinegar
- 1/2 teaspoon pepper
- 1 corned beef brisket with spice packet (2-1/2 to 3 pounds), cut in half
- 1 small head cabbage, cut into wedges

■ Place the onion, potatoes and carrots in a 5-qt. slow cooker. Combine the water, garlic, bay leaf, sugar, vinegar, pepper and contents of spice packet; pour over vegetables. Top with brisket and cabbage.

■ Cover and cook on low for 8-9 hours or until meat and vegetables are tender. Discard bay leaf before serving.

Yield: 6-8 servings.

Olivia Gust
SALEM, OREGON

I like to cook beef stew meat with a slightly sweet red sauce made with ketchup, brown sugar, Worcestershire sauce and seasonings for fabulous flavor. To make the meal completely satisfying, I serve the stew over noodles and add a salad and garlic bread to the mix.

Poultry

45

48

55

It's a breeze to put your family's favorite chicken dinner on the table. Just try one of the chicken or turkey slow cooker recipes shared here. For a deliciously different supper, try the Sweet 'n' Sour Curry Chicken on page 50.

Stuffed Chicken Rolls

- ■ Flatten chicken to 1/8-in. thickness. Place ham and cheese on each breast. Roll up and tuck in ends; secure with a toothpick.

- ■ Combine the flour, Parmesan cheese, sage, paprika and pepper; coat chicken on all sides. Cover and refrigerate for 1 hour.

- ■ In a large skillet, brown chicken in oil over medium-high heat. Transfer to a 5-qt. slow cooker. Combine soup and broth; pour over chicken. Cover and cook on low for 4-5 hours. Remove toothpicks. Garnish with parsley if desired.

Yield: 6 servings.

Jean Sherwood
KENNETH CITY, FLORIDA

The wonderful aroma of this moist, delicious chicken sparks our appetites. The ham and cheese rolled inside is a tasty surprise...particularly for a slow-cooked dish.

Stuffed Chicken Rolls

PREP: 25 min. + chilling ■ **COOK:** 4 hours

6 large boneless skinless chicken breast halves	1/4 teaspoon paprika
6 slices fully cooked ham	1/4 teaspoon pepper
6 slices Swiss cheese	1/4 cup vegetable oil
1/4 cup all-purpose flour	1 can (10-3/4 ounces) condensed cream of chicken soup, undiluted
1/4 cup grated Parmesan cheese	
1/2 teaspoon rubbed sage	1/2 cup chicken broth
	Chopped fresh parsley, optional

To keep fresh parsley in the refrigerator for several weeks, wash the entire bunch in warm water, shake off all excess moisture, wrap it in paper toweling and seal it in a plastic bag. If you need longer storage time, just remove the paper towel and put the sealed bag in the freezer. Then simply break off and crumble the amount of parsley you need for your recipes.

Stephanie Wilson
HELIX, OREGON

I prefer main dishes that enable me to stay on my diet but still eat what the rest of the family enjoys. This stew gets rave reviews from my husband as well as our young children.

Southwest Turkey Stew

Southwest Turkey Stew*

PREP: 15 min. ■ **COOK:** 5 hours

1-1/2 pounds turkey tenderloins, cubed

2 teaspoons canola oil

1 can (15 ounces) turkey chili with beans, undrained

1 can (14-1/2 ounces) diced tomatoes

1 medium sweet red pepper, cut into 3/4-inch pieces

1 medium green pepper, cut into 3/4-inch pieces

3/4 cup chopped onion

3/4 cup salsa

3 garlic cloves, minced

1-1/2 teaspoons chili powder

1/2 teaspoon salt

1/2 teaspoon ground cumin

1 tablespoon minced fresh cilantro, optional

■ In a nonstick skillet, brown turkey in oil; transfer to a 3-qt. slow cooker. Stir in the chili, tomatoes, peppers, onion, salsa, garlic, chili powder, salt and cumin. Cover and cook on low for 5-6 hours or until turkey juices run clear. Garnish with cilantro if desired.

Yield: 6 servings.

✻ **Nutrition Facts:** 1-1/4 cups equals 238 calories, 4 g fat (1 g saturated fat), 65 mg cholesterol, 837 mg sodium, 17 g carbohydrate, 5 g fiber, 33 g protein. **Diabetic Exchanges:** 4 lean meat, 1 vegetable, 1/2 starch.

Chicken Cacciatore

PREP: 20 min.
COOK: 4 hours

1/3 cup all-purpose flour

1 broiler/fryer chicken (3 to 4 pounds), cut up

2 tablespoons canola oil

2 medium onions, cut into wedges

1 medium green pepper, cut into strips

1 jar (6 ounces) sliced mushrooms, drained

1 can (14-1/2 ounces) diced tomatoes, undrained

2 garlic cloves, minced

1/2 teaspoon salt

1/2 teaspoon dried oregano

1/4 teaspoon dried basil

1/2 cup shredded Parmesan cheese

■ Place flour in a large resealable plastic bag. Add chicken, a few pieces at a time, and shake to coat. In a large skillet, brown the chicken in oil on all sides. Transfer to a 5-qt. slow cooker.

■ Top with onions, green pepper and mushrooms. Combine the tomatoes, garlic, salt, oregano and basil; pour over vegetables. Cover and cook on low for 4-5 hours or until chicken and vegetables are tender. Serve with Parmesan cheese.

Yield: 6 servings.

If you don't have cilantro on hand to use as a garnish for Southwest Turkey Stew, try substituting another tasty garnish such as shredded cheese, chopped green onions, sour cream or crushed tortilla chips.

Denise Hollebeke
PENHOLD, ALBERTA

Here's an all-time favorite Italian dish made easy in the slow cooker! Dried herbs and fresh garlic give it an aromatic flavor. And green pepper, sliced mushrooms and diced tomatoes do a fine job of rounding out the juicy chicken entree.

Chicken Mushroom Stew

- Cut chicken into 1-in. cubes; brown in 1 tablespoon oil in a large skillet. Transfer to a 3-qt. slow cooker. In the same skillet, saute the mushrooms, onion, zucchini, green pepper and garlic in remaining oil until crisp-tender.

- Place in slow cooker. Add the tomatoes, tomato paste, water and seasonings. Cover and cook on low for 4 hours or until the vegetables are tender.

Yield: 6 servings.

Have an abundance of zucchini from your garden harvest? Chicken Mushroom Stew is a terrific solution. It uses 3 cups of zucchini, as well as plenty of tomatoes, green pepper and onion. Your family will rave about the fresh taste.

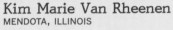

Kim Marie Van Rheenen
MENDOTA, ILLINOIS

The flavors blend beautifully in this pot of chicken, vegetables and herbs as it simmers in a slow cooker. Folks with busy schedules will love the convenient recipe.

Chicken Mushroom Stew

PREP: 20 min. ■ **COOK:** 4 hours

6 boneless skinless chicken breast halves (4 ounces *each*)	4 garlic cloves, minced
2 tablespoons vegetable oil, *divided*	3 medium tomatoes, diced
8 ounces fresh mushrooms, sliced	1 can (6 ounces) tomato paste
1 medium onion, diced	3/4 cup water
3 cups diced zucchini	2 teaspoons *each* dried thyme, oregano, marjoram and basil
1 cup diced green pepper	

Kathy Kittell
LENEXA, KANSAS

I was skeptical at first about fixing turkey in a slow cooker, but once I tasted this dish, I was hooked. With a little cornstarch to thicken the juices, the gravy is easily made. It's perfect for weeknight company!

Citrus Turkey Roast

Citrus Turkey Roast

PREP: 15 min. ■ **COOK:** 5-1/4 hours

1 frozen boneless turkey roast, thawed (3 pounds)	8 garlic cloves, peeled
1 tablespoon garlic powder	1 cup chicken broth, *divided*
1 tablespoon paprika	1/4 cup water
1 tablespoon olive oil	1/4 cup white wine *or* additional chicken broth
2 teaspoons Worcestershire sauce	1/4 cup orange juice
1/2 teaspoon salt	1 tablespoon lemon juice
1/2 teaspoon pepper	2 tablespoons cornstarch

■ Cut roast in half. Combine the garlic powder, paprika, oil, Worcestershire sauce, salt and pepper; rub over turkey. Place in a 5-qt. slow cooker. Add the garlic, 1/2 cup broth, water, wine or additional broth, orange juice and lemon juice. Cover and cook on low for 5-6 hours or until a meat thermometer reads 170°.

■ Remove turkey and keep warm. Discard garlic cloves. For gravy, combine cornstarch and remaining broth until smooth; stir into cooking juices. Cover and cook on high for 15 minutes or until thickened. Slice turkey; serve with gravy.

Yield: 12 servings.

Cornish Hens With Potatoes

Deborah Randall
ABBEVILLE, LOUISIANA

For a wonderful meal with only a fraction of the work, try my savory specialty. The slow-cooked game hens are simply delicious when served with green beans and a loaf of French bread.

PREP: 20 min.
COOK: 6-8 hours

4 Cornish game hens (20 ounces *each*)

2 tablespoons vegetable oil

4 large red potatoes, cut into 1/8-inch slices

4 bacon strips, cut into 1-inch pieces

Lemon-pepper seasoning and garlic powder to taste

Minced fresh parsley

■ In a large skillet, brown hens in oil. Place the potatoes in a 5-qt. slow cooker. Top with the hens and bacon. Sprinkle with lemon-pepper and garlic powder.

■ Cover and cook on low for 6-8 hours or until meat juices run clear and potatoes are tender. Thicken cooking juices if desired. Sprinkle the hens with parsley.

Yield: 4 servings.

Jane Bone
CAPE CORAL, FLORIDA

I like to give an Italian treatment to chicken by slow-cooking it in a zesty tomato sauce and serving it over spaghetti. It's a great main course for company because it frees up your time to spend with guests. Toss together a green salad, and you're ready to eat.

Mushroom Chicken Cacciatore

PREP: 20 min. ■ COOK: 4 hours

4 boneless skinless chicken breast halves (about 1-1/2 pounds)

2 tablespoons vegetable oil

1 can (15 ounces) tomato sauce

2 cans (4 ounces *each*) sliced mushrooms, drained

1 medium onion, chopped

1/4 cup red wine *or* chicken broth

2 garlic cloves, minced

1-1/4 teaspoons dried oregano

1/2 teaspoon dried thyme

1/8 to 1/4 teaspoon salt

1/8 teaspoon pepper

Hot cooked spaghetti

■ In a large skillet, brown chicken in oil on both sides. Transfer to a 3-qt. slow cooker. In a bowl, combine the tomato sauce, mushrooms, onion, wine or broth, garlic, oregano, thyme, salt and pepper; pour over chicken. Cover and cook on low for 4-5 hours or until a meat thermometer reads 170°. Serve over spaghetti.

Yield: 4 servings.

For fluffier rice to serve with Red Pepper Chicken, remove the saucepan from the heat after the cooking time is complete and let the rice stand for 5 to 10 minutes. Then just fluff the rice with a fork before serving it. Keep in mind that it's best not to lift the lid to peek at the rice while it's cooking.

Red Pepper Chicken

Piper Spiwak
VIENNA, VIRGINIA

Chicken breasts are treated to a bevy of black beans, red peppers and tomatoes in my Southwestern supper. We love the colorful dinner over rice that I prepare in chicken broth.

PREP: 15 min.
COOK: 6 hours

4 boneless skinless chicken breast halves

1 can (15 ounces) black beans, rinsed and drained

1 jar (15 ounces) roasted red peppers, undrained

1 can (14-1/2 ounces) Mexican stewed tomatoes, undrained

1 large onion, chopped

1/2 teaspoon salt

Pepper to taste

Hot cooked rice

■ Place the chicken in a 3-qt. slow cooker. In a bowl, combine the beans, red peppers, tomatoes, onion, salt and pepper. Pour over the chicken. Cover and cook on low for 6 hours or until chicken is no longer pink. Serve over rice.

Yield: 4 servings.

Carol Conrad
EDMONTON, ALBERTA
A little mango chutney goes a long way in adding a tangy twist to chicken. I even add some curry powder to this dish for extra flair.

Sweet 'n' Sour Curry Chicken

Sweet 'n' Sour Curry Chicken

PREP: 15 min. ■ **COOK:** 4 hours

1 pound boneless skinless chicken breasts, cut into 1-inch pieces	1 large onion, sliced
	1/2 cup mango chutney
1 can (14-1/2 ounces) stewed tomatoes, cut up	2 tablespoons cornstarch
	1-1/2 teaspoons curry powder
1 large green pepper, cut into 1-inch pieces	1/4 cup water

■ In a 3-qt. slow cooker, combine the chicken, tomatoes, green pepper, onion and chutney. In a small bowl, combine the cornstarch, curry powder and water until smooth; stir into chicken mixture.

■ Cover and cook on low for 4 hours or until chicken juices run clear.

Yield: 4 servings.

To cut the chicken wings into three sections for Barbecue Chicken Wings, place a wing on a cutting board. With a sharp knife, cut between the joint at the top of the tip end. (If you'd like to make use of the tips instead of discarding them, use them to make chicken broth.) Take the remaining wing and cut between the joints. Then continue preparing the recipe as directed.

Barbecue Chicken Wings

Jean Ann Herritt
CANTON, OHIO

I got this spicy recipe from a friend but altered the ingredient amounts to adjust the hotness of the sauce. Make sure everyone has extra napkins...this main dish is messy to eat but oh, so good!

PREP: 20 min.
BAKE: 40 min.

3	pounds whole chicken wings
2	cups ketchup
1/2	cup honey
2	tablespoons lemon juice
2	tablespoons vegetable oil
2	tablespoons soy sauce
2	tablespoons Worcestershire sauce
1	tablespoon paprika
4	garlic cloves, minced
1-1/2	teaspoons curry powder
1/2	teaspoon pepper
1/8	teaspoon hot pepper sauce

■ Cut chicken wings into three sections; discard the wing tips. Place wings in a greased 15-in. x 10-in. x 1-in. baking pan. Bake at 350° for 35-40 minutes or until juices run clear.

■ In a large bowl, combine the remaining ingredients. Pour 1/2 cup into a 3-qt. slow cooker. Drain chicken wings; add to slow cooker. Drizzle with the remaining sauce. Cover and cook on low for 1 hour, basting occasionally.

Yield: 10 servings.

Editor's Note: Uncooked chicken wing sections (wingettes) may be substituted for whole chicken wings.

Stuffed Sweet Peppers

■ Cut the tops off peppers; chop the tops and set aside. Discard stems and seeds; set pepper cups aside. Reserve 3/4 cup spaghetti sauce; pour the remaining sauce into a 5-qt. slow cooker. Combine the sausage, rice, feta cheese, onion, tomato, parsley, olives, garlic powder, salt, Italian seasoning, red pepper flakes and reserved chopped peppers and spaghetti sauce. Spoon into pepper cups; place in slow cooker. Cover and cook on low for 4-5 hours or until peppers are tender.

Yield: 5 servings.

Judy Earl
SARASOTA, FLORIDA
When I got married in 1970, slow cookers were all the rage, and if you ask me, they've never gone out of style. I've relied on this zesty, slow-cooked main dish for years.

Stuffed Sweet Peppers

PREP: 15 min. ■ COOK: 4 hours

3 medium sweet red peppers	1/4 cup chopped tomato
2 medium sweet yellow peppers	1/4 cup minced fresh parsley
1 jar (14 ounces) spaghetti sauce, *divided*	2 tablespoons sliced ripe olives
3/4 pound Italian turkey sausage links	1/4 to 1/2 teaspoon garlic powder
3/4 cup uncooked instant rice	1/2 teaspoon salt
1/2 cup crumbled feta cheese	1/2 teaspoon Italian seasoning
1/2 cup chopped onion	1/2 teaspoon crushed red pepper flakes

Italian seasoning

is sold in the spice aisle of most grocery stores. A basic blend might contain marjoram, thyme, savory, rosemary, sage, oregano and basil. If you're out of this seasoning, try mixing up your own. Don't have all of the ingredients? You can blend just a few with good results. Substitute 1/8 teaspoon each of basil, thyme, rosemary and oregano for 1/2 teaspoon of Italian seasoning.

Sunday Chicken Supper

Ruthann Martin
LOUISVILLE, OHIO

This convenient slow-cooker dish makes a hearty meal-in-one that's special any day of the week. With a 6-hour cook time, you can even start it late in the morning.

Sunday Chicken Supper

PREP: 15 min. ■ **COOK:** 6 hours

2	small carrots, cut into 2-inch pieces
1/2	medium onion, chopped
1/2	celery rib, cut into 2-inch pieces
1	cup cut fresh green beans (2-inch pieces)
2	small red potatoes, halved
2	bone-in chicken breast halves (7 ounces *each*), skin removed
2	bacon strips, cooked and crumbled
3/4	cup hot water
1	teaspoon chicken bouillon granules
1/4	teaspoon salt
1/4	teaspoon dried thyme
1/4	teaspoon dried basil
	Pinch pepper

■ In a 3-qt. slow cooker, layer the first seven ingredients in the order listed. Combine the water, bouillon, salt, thyme, basil and pepper; pour over the top. Do not stir. Cover and cook on low for 6-8 hours or until vegetables are tender and meat thermometer reads 170°. Remove chicken and vegetables. Thicken cooking juices for gravy if desired.

Yield: 2 servings.

Chicken, Bean and Rice Nachos

Barbara Schweitzer
CHESAPEAKE, VIRGINIA

You can't go wrong with this slow-cooked sensation! Tender shredded chicken is matched up with black beans, Mexicorn, rice and cheese, then served with tortilla chips. When you're craving nachos but need more than a snack, this makes one zesty dinner.

PREP: 15 min.
COOK: 5 hours

1-1/2	pounds boneless skinless chicken breasts
1	jar (16 ounces) salsa
1	can (15 ounces) black beans, rinsed and drained
1	can (7 ounces) Mexicorn, drained
1	package (8 ounces) cream cheese, cubed
3	cups cooked rice
3/4	cup shredded Mexican cheese blend
	Tortilla chips

■ Place chicken in a 3-qt. slow cooker. Combine the salsa, beans and corn; pour over chicken. Cover and cook on low for 5-6 hours or until chicken is tender. Shred chicken with two forks and return to cooker. Stir in cream cheese. To serve, place rice in serving bowls; top with the chicken mixture and cheese blend. Serve with tortilla chips.

Yield: 6 servings.

Ann Johnson
DUNN,
NORTH CAROLINA

*Sweet red and green
pepper strips add
attractive color to
this delicious
chicken. Put it in the
slow cooker and it's
ready to eat when
you get home.*

Sweet Pepper Chicken

Sweet Pepper Chicken

PREP: 10 min. ■ **COOK:** 4 hours

- 6 bone-in chicken breast halves, skin removed
- 1 tablespoon vegetable oil
- 2 cups sliced fresh mushrooms
- 1 medium onion, halved and sliced
- 1 medium green pepper, julienned
- 1 medium sweet red pepper, julienned
- 1 can (10-3/4 ounces) condensed cream of chicken soup, undiluted
- 1 can (10-3/4 ounces) condensed cream of mushroom soup, undiluted
- Hot cooked rice

■ In a large skillet, brown chicken in oil on both sides. Transfer to a 5-qt. slow cooker. Top with mushrooms, onion and peppers. Combine the soups; pour over vegetables. Cover and cook on low for 4-5 hours or until a meat thermometer reads 170°. Serve with rice.

Yield: 6 servings.

Simple Chicken Stew

Amy Dulling
ROCKWOOD, TENNESSEE

*This comforting stew was one of
my husband's experiments that
became one of our standard
Sunday dinners. Try it and I bet it
becomes a staple for you, too.*

PREP: 20 min.
COOK: 6 hours

- 1 can (10-3/4 ounces) condensed cream of chicken soup, undiluted
- 1 cup water
- 1/2 pound boneless skinless chicken breasts, cut into cubes
- 1 large potato, peeled and cut into 3/4-inch cubes
- 2 medium carrots, cut into 1/4-inch slices
- 1/2 cup sliced fresh mushrooms
- 1/4 cup chopped onion
- 1 teaspoon chicken bouillon granules
- 1/4 teaspoon poultry seasoning

■ In a 3-qt. slow cooker, combine all ingredients. Cover and cook on low for 6-7 hours or until vegetables are tender.

Yield: 2 servings.

After handling uncooked poultry, always use hot soapy water to wash your hands and anything else (such as knives, cutting boards and countertops) that has come into contact with the uncooked poultry. This will help prevent contamination with other foods.

Sweet-and-Sour Chicken

Mrs. Dorothy Hess
HARTWELL, GEORGIA

Who would believe that this stir-fry-like chicken supper came from a slow cooker? I found that adding the onions, pineapple and snow peas later in the process keeps them from becoming overcooked.

PREP: 15 min. ■ **COOK:** 3 hours 20 min.

1-1/4 pounds boneless skinless chicken breasts, cut into 1-inch strips
1 tablespoon vegetable oil
Salt and pepper to taste
1 can (8 ounces) pineapple chunks
1 can (8 ounces) sliced water chestnuts, drained
2 medium carrots, sliced
2 tablespoons soy sauce
4 teaspoons cornstarch
1 cup sweet-and-sour sauce
1/4 cup water
1-1/2 teaspoons ground ginger
3 green onions, cut into 1-inch pieces
1-1/2 cups fresh or frozen snow peas
Hot cooked rice

■ In a large skillet, saute chicken in oil for 4-5 minutes; drain. Sprinkle with salt and pepper. Drain pineapple, reserving juice; set pineapple aside. In a 5-qt. slow cooker, combine the chicken, water chestnuts, carrots, soy sauce and pineapple juice. Cover and cook on low for 3 hours or until chicken juices run clear.

■ In a small bowl, combine the cornstarch, sweet-and-sour sauce, water and ginger until smooth. Stir into the slow cooker. Add onions and reserved pineapple; cover and cook on high for 15 minutes or until thickened. Add peas; cook 5 minutes longer. Serve with rice.

Yield: *5 servings.*

Out of the broth needed for your recipe? Simply dissolve one bouillon cube or 1 teaspoon of granules in 1 cup of boiling water. This mixture may be substituted for 1 cup of broth in any recipe.

Lemon Chicken Breasts*

PREP: 20 min.
COOK: 4 hours

6 boneless skinless chicken breast halves (5 ounces *each*)
1 cup chicken broth, *divided*
1/4 cup lemon juice
3 tablespoons Dijon mustard
3 garlic cloves, minced
2 tablespoons butter, melted
1/4 teaspoon dried rosemary, crushed
3 tablespoons cornstarch
Hot cooked rice
1/2 cup slivered almonds, toasted
3 tablespoons minced fresh parsley

■ Place chicken in a 3-qt. slow cooker. Combine 3/4 cup broth, lemon juice, mustard, garlic, butter and rosemary; pour over chicken. Cover and cook on low for 4-5 hours or until chicken juices run clear. Remove the chicken; keep warm.

■ Pour cooking liquid into a small saucepan; bring to a boil. Combine cornstarch and remaining broth; gradually stir into the saucepan. Bring to a boil; cook and stir for 2 minutes or until thickened. Serve chicken with rice and sauce. Sprinkle with almonds and parsley.

Yield: *6 servings.*

✱ **Nutrition Facts:** 1 chicken breast half with 1/3 cup sauce equals 268 calories, 12 g fat (4 g saturated fat), 89 mg cholesterol, 440 mg sodium, 9 g carbohydrate, 1 g fiber, 31 g protein. **Diabetic Exchanges:** 4 very lean meat, 2 fat, 1/2 starch.

Kathy Evans
LACEY, WASHINGTON

Who says an easy dinner can't taste delicious? Dijon mustard, rosemary and lemon juice season chicken breasts wonderfully well in this fuss-free recipe. For an elegant and impressive finish, sprinkle on some toasted almonds and fresh parsley.

Other Entrees

70

59

75

Slow cookers aren't just for meat and poultry anymore! Check out all of the new and delicious meals you can create, such as lamb chops, seafood, ribs, lasagna and even breakfast staples. Regardless of your taste, you won't be disappointed!

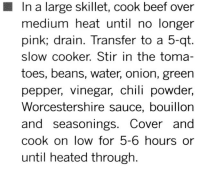

- In a large skillet, cook beef over medium heat until no longer pink; drain. Transfer to a 5-qt. slow cooker. Stir in the tomatoes, beans, water, onion, green pepper, vinegar, chili powder, Worcestershire sauce, bouillon and seasonings. Cover and cook on low for 5-6 hours or until heated through.

- Stir in macaroni; cover and cook 20-30 minutes longer or until macaroni is tender.

Yield: 12 servings.

*Nutrition Facts: 1 cup equals 223 calories, 4 g fat (2 g saturated fat), 19 mg cholesterol, 741 mg sodium, 34 g carbohydrate, 7 g fiber, 15 g protein. **Diabetic Exchanges:** 2 vegetable, 1-1/2 starch, 1 lean meat.

Spicy Goulash

Melissa Polk
WEST LAFAYETTE, INDIANA
Ground cumin, chili powder and a can of Mexican diced tomatoes jazz up my goulash recipe. Even the elbow macaroni is prepared in the slow cooker!

Spicy Goulash*

PREP: 25 min. ■ **COOK:** 5 hours

- 1 pound ground beef
- 4 cans (14-1/2 ounces *each*) Mexican diced tomatoes, undrained
- 2 cans (16 ounces *each*) kidney beans, rinsed and drained
- 2 cups water
- 1 medium onion, chopped
- 1 medium green pepper, chopped
- 1/4 cup red wine vinegar

- 2 tablespoons chili powder
- 1 tablespoon Worcestershire sauce
- 2 teaspoons beef bouillon granules
- 1 teaspoon dried basil
- 1 teaspoon dried parsley flakes
- 1 teaspoon ground cumin
- 1/4 teaspoon pepper
- 2 cups uncooked elbow macaroni

To top off each serving of Spicy Goulash in a special and tasty way, simply add a dollop of sour cream and then a sprinkling of minced fresh herbs. Try cilantro, basil or parsley.

Sandra McKenzie
BRAHAM, MINNESOTA

Chops are without a doubt the cut of lamb we like best. I usually simmer them on low for hours in a slow cooker. The aroma is irresistible.

Slow-Cooked Lamb Chops

Slow-Cooked Lamb Chops

PREP: 10 min. ■ COOK: 4 hours

1 medium onion, sliced	1/8 teaspoon pepper
1 teaspoon dried oregano	8 lamb loin chops (about 1-3/4 pounds)
1/2 teaspoon dried thyme	
1/2 teaspoon garlic powder	2 garlic cloves, minced
1/4 teaspoon salt	

■ Place onion in a 3-qt. slow cooker. Combine the oregano, thyme, garlic powder, salt and pepper; rub over the lamb chops. Place chops over onion. Top with garlic. Cover and cook on low for 4-6 hours or until the meat is tender.

Yield: 4 servings.

Round out your dinner of Thai Shrimp and Rice with a tropical fruit bowl of banana slices, pineapple chunks and mango. If you like, top the fruit with whipped cream and a sprinkling of coconut. Either way, you'll have a terrific Thai-flavored meal.

Thai Shrimp And Rice

PREP: 30 min.
COOK: 3 hours 20 min.

2 cans (14-1/2 ounces *each*) chicken broth

2 cups uncooked converted rice

1 large carrot, shredded

1 medium onion, chopped

1/2 cup *each* chopped sweet red and green pepper

1/2 cup water

1/2 cup coconut milk

1/3 cup lime juice

1/4 cup flaked coconut

1/4 cup *each* raisins and golden raisins

8 garlic cloves, minced

1 tablespoon grated lime peel

1 tablespoon minced fresh gingerroot

1 teaspoon salt

1 teaspoon *each* ground coriander and cumin

1/2 teaspoon cayenne pepper

1 pound cooked medium shrimp, peeled and deveined

1/2 cup fresh snow peas, cut into thin strips

■ In a 5-qt. slow cooker, combine chicken broth, rice, vegetables, water, milk, lime juice, coconut, raisins, garlic, lime peel, ginger and seasonings.

■ Cover and cook on low for 3 hours or until rice is tender. Stir in shrimp and peas. Cover and cook 20 minutes longer or until heated through.

Yield: 8 servings.

Paula Marchesi
LENHARTSVILLE, PENNSYLVANIA

Raisins and coconut milk add a lovely hint of sweetness to this Thai dish, and freshly grated lime peel and minced gingerroot give it a wonderful aroma and flavor. The meal-in-one features enough shrimp and snow peas to add a fun flair to weeknight menus.

Jambalaya

- In a 4-qt. slow cooker, combine the sausage, chicken, broth, tomatoes, celery, tomato paste, garlic and seasonings. Cover and cook on low for 6-7 hours or until chicken juices run clear.

- Stir in shrimp and rice. Cover and cook 15 minutes longer or until heated through.

Yield: 12 servings.

***Nutrition Facts:** 1 cup equals 228 calories, 11 g fat (4 g saturated fat), 95 mg cholesterol, 693 mg sodium, 12 g carbohydrate, 1 g fiber, 18 g protein. **Diabetic Exchanges:** 2 lean meat, 1 starch, 1 fat.

Sherry Huntwork
GRETNA, NEBRASKA

Sausage, chicken and shrimp keep this dish hearty and satisfying. Made easy with canned items and other kitchen staples, it's perfect for casual get-togethers.

Jambalaya*

PREP: 20 min. ■ COOK: 6-1/4 hours

1	pound smoked Polish sausage, cut into 1/2-inch slices
1/2	pound boneless skinless chicken breasts, cut into 1-inch cubes
1	can (14-1/2 ounces) beef broth
1	can (14-1/2 ounces) diced tomatoes, undrained
2	celery ribs, chopped
1/3	cup tomato paste
4	garlic cloves, minced
1	tablespoon dried parsley flakes
1-1/2	teaspoons dried basil
1	teaspoon cayenne pepper
1/2	teaspoon salt
1/2	teaspoon dried oregano
1	pound cooked medium shrimp, peeled and deveined
2	cups cooked rice

For best flavor, keep dried herbs and ground spices for up to 6 months. They may be used if they are older, but the flavors might not be as intense. Store dried herbs and ground spices in a cool, dry place.

Betty Helton
MELBOURNE, FLORIDA

I rely on a can of cranberry sauce to create a sweet addition to my tender pork entree. Orange juice and ground cloves season the main course nicely as it simmers.

Cranberry Pork Tenderloin

Cranberry Pork Tenderloin

PREP: 10 min. ■ **COOK:** 5 hours

1 pork tenderloin (1 pound)	1 tablespoon brown sugar
1 can (16 ounces) whole-berry cranberry sauce	1 teaspoon ground mustard
	1/4 to 1/2 teaspoon ground cloves
1/2 cup orange juice	2 tablespoons cornstarch
1/4 cup sugar	3 tablespoons cold water

■ Place the tenderloin in a 3-qt. slow cooker. Combine the cranberry sauce, orange juice, sugars, mustard and cloves; pour over pork. Cover and cook on low for 5-6 hours or until a meat thermometer reads 160°.

■ Remove pork and keep warm. In a small bowl, combine cornstarch and cold water until smooth; gradually stir into cranberry mixture. Cover and cook on high for 15 minutes longer or until thickened. Serve with pork.

Yield: 4 servings.

Country-style ribs are meaty and come from the rib end of the pork loin. Baby back ribs come from the blade and center section of the pork loin and are smaller than spareribs, which are curved ribs from the belly and are the least meaty of the ribs. St. Louis-style ribs are spareribs with the breastbone removed.

Barbecue Country Ribs

Rebecca Knode
MECHANICSBURG, PENNSYLVANIA

A homemade sauce makes these lip-smacking ribs a success whenever I prepare them! I like the fact that I can whip up such a great dinner without much hands-on time in the kitchen.

PREP: 15 min.
COOK: 6 hours

4 pounds boneless country-style pork ribs
1 bottle (12 ounces) chili sauce
1 cup ketchup
1/2 cup packed brown sugar
1/3 cup balsamic vinegar
2 tablespoons Worcestershire sauce
2 teaspoons onion powder
1 teaspoon salt
1 teaspoon garlic powder
1 teaspoon chili powder
1 teaspoon pepper
1/2 teaspoon hot pepper sauce, optional
1/4 teaspoon Liquid Smoke, optional

■ Place the ribs in a 5-qt. slow cooker. Combine chili sauce, ketchup, brown sugar, balsamic vinegar, Worcestershire sauce, seasonings, hot pepper sauce and Liquid Smoke if desired; pour over ribs.

■ Cover and cook on low for 6-7 hours or until meat is tender.

Yield: 10 servings.

Dan Kelmenson
WEST BLOOMFIELD, MICHIGAN

Looking to switch up your slow-cooker staples? Consider this lamb entree. A terrific meal-in-one, it certainly adds flair to dinnertime doldrums. A splash of lemon juice and zesty lemon peel complement the flavors of fresh spinach and feta cheese.

Lamb with Orzo

PREP: 30 min. ■ **COOK:** 8 hours

- 1 bone-in lamb shoulder roast (3-1/2 pounds)
- 3 tablespoons lemon juice
- 3 garlic cloves, minced
- 2 teaspoons dried oregano
- 2 teaspoons grated lemon peel
- 1/4 teaspoon salt
- 1 package (16 ounces) orzo pasta
- 2 packages (9 ounces *each*) fresh spinach, torn, *divided*
- 1 cup (4 ounces) crumbled feta cheese, *divided*

■ Cut roast in half. Place in a 5-qt. slow cooker; drizzle with lemon juice. Sprinkle with garlic, oregano, lemon peel and salt. Cover and cook on low for 8-10 hours or until meat is tender.

■ Cook orzo according to package directions. Remove lamb from slow cooker. When cool enough to handle, remove meat from bones; discard bones. Cut meat into bite-size pieces; set aside. Skim fat from the cooking juices if necessary; return 1 cup cooking juices to the slow cooker. Add one package spinach. Cook on high for 5-10 minutes or until the spinach is wilted.

■ Drain orzo; add to spinach mixture. Stir in lamb and half of feta cheese. To serve, arrange remaining spinach on individual plates. Top with lamb mixture. Sprinkle with remaining feta cheese.

Yield: *9 servings.*

To cook pasta more evenly, prevent it from sticking together and avoid boil-overs, cook it in a large kettle or Dutch oven. Unless you have a very large kettle, don't cook more than 2 pounds of pasta at a time.

Pork Chops With Fruit

Marian Platt
SEQUIM, WASHINGTON

This recipe came from a good friend, and it's been a big hit whenever I've served it. With rice pilaf and a green salad, a quick meal for two is ready without much effort.

PREP: 5 min.
COOK: 4 hours

- 2 bone-in center-cut pork loin chops (12 ounces *each*)
- 1 cup mixed dried fruit
- 1/3 cup unsweetened pineapple juice
- 1/4 cup dark corn syrup
- 1/4 teaspoon salt
- 1/4 teaspoon curry powder
- 1 teaspoon cornstarch
- 1 tablespoon cold water

■ Place pork chops in a 1-1/2-qt. oval or 3-qt. slow cooker. In a bowl, combine the dried fruit, pineapple juice, corn syrup, salt and curry powder; pour over chops. Cover and cook on low for 4 to 4-1/2 hours or until meat is tender.

■ With a slotted spoon, remove the meat and fruit to a serving platter and keep warm. In a small saucepan, combine the cornstarch and cold water until smooth; stir in the cooking juices. Bring to a boil; cook and stir for 2 minutes or until thickened. Serve over pork chops and fruit.

Yield: *2 servings.*

Honey-Glazed Ham

Slow Cooker Cranberry Pork

Joyce Turley
SLAUGHTERS, KENTUCKY

You can put this roast in the slow cooker and then forget about it, knowing it will be moist and tender when you get home after a day of work. The fruity sauce complements the meat so well!

PREP: 10 min.
COOK: 6 hours

- 1 boneless rolled pork loin roast (3 to 4 pounds), halved
- 2 tablespoons vegetable oil
- 1 can (16 ounces) whole-berry cranberry sauce
- 3/4 cup sugar
- 3/4 cup cranberry juice
- 1 teaspoon ground mustard
- 1 teaspoon pepper
- 1/4 teaspoon ground cloves
- 1/4 cup cornstarch
- 1/4 cup cold water

Salt to taste

- ■ In a Dutch oven, brown roast in oil on all sides over medium-high heat. Transfer to a 5-qt. slow cooker. Combine the cranberry sauce, sugar, cranberry juice, ground mustard, pepper and cloves; pour over roast.

- ■ Cover and cook on low for 6-8 hours or until a meat thermometer reads 160°. Remove roast and keep warm.

- ■ In a saucepan, combine the cornstarch, water and salt until smooth; stir in cooking juices. Bring to a boil; cook and stir for 2 minutes or until thickened. Serve with roast.

Yield: 9-12 servings.

Jacquie Stolz
LITTLE SIOUX, IOWA

Here's an easy solution to feeding a large group. The simple ham is perfect for holiday dinners where time in the kitchen is as valuable as space in the oven.

Honey-Glazed Ham

PREP: 10 min. ■ **COOK:** 4-1/2 hours

- 1 boneless fully cooked ham (4 pounds)
- 1-1/2 cups ginger ale
- 1/4 cup honey
- 1/2 teaspoon ground mustard
- 1/2 teaspoon ground cloves
- 1/4 teaspoon ground cinnamon

Sour cream, optional

- ■ Cut ham in half; place in a 5-qt. slow cooker. Pour ginger ale over ham. Cover and cook on low for 4-5 hours or until a meat thermometer reads 140° and ham is heated through.

- ■ Combine the honey, mustard, cloves and cinnamon; stir until smooth. Spread over the ham; cook 30 minutes longer. Garnish ham with the sour cream if desired.

Yield: 14 servings.

Barb Keith
EAU CLAIRE,
WISCONSIN

Here's a recipe that combines slow cooking with brunch. It's a wonderful treat to take to a covered dish event or a morning get-together.

Hash Brown Egg Brunch

Hash Brown Egg Brunch

PREP: 20 min. ■ **COOK:** 4 hours

1 package (32 ounces) frozen shredded hash brown potatoes	1-1/2 cups (6 ounces) shredded cheddar cheese
1 pound bacon strips, cooked and crumbled	12 eggs
1 medium onion, chopped	1 cup milk
1 medium green pepper, chopped	1/2 teaspoon salt
	1/2 teaspoon pepper

■ Layer a third of the potatoes, bacon, onion, green pepper and cheese in a 5-qt. slow cooker coated with cooking spray. Repeat layers twice. In a large bowl, whisk the eggs, milk, salt and pepper; pour over top.

■ Cover and cook on high for 30 minutes. Reduce heat to low; cook for 3-1/2 to 4 hours or until a thermometer reads 160°.

Yield: 10 servings.

Cut prep work in the morning by cooking and crumbling a pound of bacon ahead of time and storing it in the freezer. That way, you'll get your Hash Brown Egg Brunch into the slow cooker faster,

Peachy Spareribs

Jeanne Brino
WOODBURY, MINNESOTA

Canned peaches make a delightful addition to the sauce I use to flavor my spareribs. Served over rice, these sweet-tangy ribs make a sensational meal any time of the year.

PREP: 10 min.
COOK: 5-1/2 hours

    4 pounds pork spareribs
    1 can (15-1/4 ounces) sliced peaches, undrained
 1/2 cup packed brown sugar
 1/4 cup ketchup
 1/4 cup white vinegar
    2 tablespoons soy sauce
    1 garlic clove, minced
    1 teaspoon salt
    1 teaspoon pepper
    2 tablespoons cornstarch
    2 tablespoons cold water
Hot cooked rice

■ Cut ribs into serving-size pieces. In a large skillet, brown ribs on all sides; drain. Transfer to a 5-qt. slow cooker. Combine peaches, brown sugar, ketchup, vinegar, soy sauce, garlic, salt and pepper; pour over ribs. Cover and cook on low for 5-1/2 to 6 hours or until meat is tender.

■ Remove pork and peaches; keep warm. Pour cooking juices into a small saucepan and skim fat. Combine cornstarch and water until smooth; stir into cooking juices. Bring to a boil; cook and stir for 1-2 minutes or until thickened. Serve with pork and rice.

Yield: 8 servings.

Vegetarian Tortilla Lasagna

Connie McDowell
GREENWOOD, DELAWARE

You won't miss the meat in this savory delight. The layered main course is as tasty as it is impressive. Serve warm wedges alongside tortilla chips or a green salad.

PREP: 20 min. ■ **COOK:** 3 hours

- 1 can (14-1/2 ounces) diced tomatoes with basil, oregano and garlic
- 1 cup chunky salsa
- 1 can (6 ounces) tomato paste
- 1/2 teaspoon ground cumin
- 2 cans (15-1/2 ounces *each*) hominy, rinsed and drained
- 1 can (15 ounces) black beans, rinsed and drained
- 3 flour tortillas (10 inches)
- 2 cups (8 ounces) shredded Monterey Jack cheese
- 1/4 cup sliced ripe olives

- ■ Cut four 20-in. x 9-in. strips of heavy-duty foil; fold each lengthwise into thirds. Crisscross strips so they resemble spokes of a wheel; place on the bottom and up the sides of a round 5-qt. slow cooker. Coat strips with cooking spray.

- ■ In a large bowl, combine the tomatoes, salsa, tomato paste and cumin. Stir in hominy and beans. Place one tortilla onto bottom of slow cooker. Top with a third of the hominy mixture and cheese. Repeat layers twice. Sprinkle with olives. Cover and cook on low for 3 to 3-1/2 hours or until heated through.

- ■ Using foil strips as handles, remove the lasagna to a platter. Let stand for 5 minutes before cutting into wedges.

Yield: 8 servings.

Placing strips of heavy-duty foil inside the slow cooker creates handles that allow you to easily remove Vegetarian Tortilla Lasagna after cooking. Try using foil handles for other layered slow-cooker recipes or for slow-cooked meat loaves.

Cranberry-Apricot Pork Roast with Potatoes

PREP: 15 min.
COOK: 5 hours

- 1 boneless whole pork loin roast (3 pounds)
- 4 medium potatoes, peeled and quartered
- 1 can (16 ounces) whole-berry cranberry sauce
- 1 can (15 ounces) apricot halves, drained
- 1 medium onion, quartered
- 1/2 cup chopped dried apricots
- 1 tablespoon sugar
- 1/2 teaspoon ground mustard
- 1/4 teaspoon cayenne pepper

- ■ Cut pork roast in half. Place potatoes in a 5-qt. slow cooker. Add the pork. In a blender, combine the cranberry sauce, apricots, onion, dried apricots, sugar, mustard and cayenne pepper. Cover and process for 30 seconds or until almost smooth. Pour over pork.

- ■ Cover and cook on low for 5-6 hours or until a meat thermometer reads 160° and pork is tender.

- ■ Transfer the pork to a platter and potatoes to a bowl. Pour cooking juices into a pitcher; serve with meat and potatoes.

Yield: 8 servings.

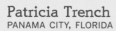

Patricia Trench
PANAMA CITY, FLORIDA

Here's a delightful meal-in-one that makes weeknight dining a snap. The fresh and dried apricots blend well with the whole-berry cranberry sauce for a delightful sweet-and-tart taste. Cayenne pepper adds just the right touch of zing to this easy-to-make meat-and-potatoes meal.

- In a bowl, combine the egg, bread crumbs, water chestnuts, soy sauce, ginger and garlic. Crumble ground venison and sausage over the mixture and mix well. Shape into 1-in. balls. In a skillet over medium heat, brown meatballs in batches in 2 teaspoons oil, adding 1 teaspoon oil if needed. Transfer meatballs to a 3-qt. slow cooker.

- In the same skillet, saute the mushrooms in 1 teaspoon oil until tender. Stir in the broth and 1 cup cold water. Pour over the meatballs. Cover and cook on low for 4-5 hours or until a meat thermometer reads 160°.

- Remove meatballs and mushrooms with a slotted spoon; keep warm. Strain the cooking juices into a saucepan. Combine cornstarch and remaining water until smooth; add to saucepan. Bring to a boil; cook and stir for 2 minutes or until thickened. Serve over the meatballs, mushrooms and noodles.

Yield: 8-10 servings.

Venison Meatballs

Geraldine Mennear
MASTIC, NEW YORK

These meatballs feature a savory blend of ground venison and pork sausage...plus it has water chestnuts for crunch. Even my co-workers, who normally don't like game meat, enjoy it.

Venison Meatballs

PREP: 30 min. ■ COOK: 4 hours

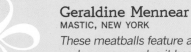

1 egg, lightly beaten	3 to 4 teaspoons vegetable oil, *divided*
1 cup soft bread crumbs	1/2 pound fresh mushrooms, sliced
1 can (8 ounces) water chestnuts, drained and finely chopped	1 can (14-1/2 ounces) chicken broth
1/4 cup soy sauce	1-1/4 cups cold water, *divided*
2 teaspoons ground ginger	3 tablespoons cornstarch
1 garlic clove, minced	Hot cooked noodles
1 pound ground venison	
1 pound bulk pork sausage	

To make soft bread crumbs, tear fresh or slightly stale bread apart with a fork. Or use a blender or food processor to break the bread into fluffy crumbs. Pile them gently (do not pack) into a measuring cup.

LaVerne Parkin
MANITOWOC,
WISCONSIN

These ribs get a touch of sweetness from brown sugar and apricot preserves. It's one slow-cooked recipe that you will surely enjoy time and again.

Pork Baby Back Ribs

Pork Baby Back Ribs

PREP: 10 min. ■ COOK: 6 hours

1 rack pork baby back ribs (2-1/2 pounds)
2 tablespoons canola oil
1 medium onion, thinly sliced
1/2 cup apricot preserves

1/3 cup beef broth
3 tablespoons white vinegar
2 tablespoons Worcestershire sauce
1 tablespoon brown sugar

■ Cut the ribs into five servings. In a Dutch oven, brown ribs in oil in batches. Place onion in a 5-qt. slow cooker; top with ribs. In a bowl, combine the remaining ingredients. Pour over ribs.

■ Cover and cook on low for 6-7 hours or until meat is tender.

Yield: 5 servings.

Slow Cooker Oatmeal

Brandy Schaefer
GLEN CARBON, ILLINOIS

It's wonderful to prepare this oatmeal whenever I have time. Store leftovers in the refrigerator and just reheat a serving in the microwave on busy mornings.

PREP: 10 min.
COOK: 3 hours

2 cups milk
1 cup old-fashioned oats
1 cup chopped peeled tart apple
1/2 cup raisins
1/4 cup packed brown sugar
1/4 cup chopped walnuts
1 tablespoon butter, melted
1/2 teaspoon ground cinnamon
1/4 teaspoon salt

■ In a 1-1/2-qt. slow cooker coated with cooking spray, combine all ingredients. Cover and cook on low for 3-4 hours or until liquid is absorbed and oatmeal is tender.

Yield: 4 servings.

Old-fashioned oats and quick-cooking oats can be used interchangeably in many recipes, but make sure to use the old-fashioned variety for Slow Cooker Oatmeal. Old-fashioned oats will hold up best during slow cooking and yield the right texture.

Dorothy Jordan
COLLEGE STATION, TEXAS

Here's a jambalaya-type dish that comes together in the slow cooker. It's a wonderful way to warm up cold winter nights and works equally well for casual get-togethers or family dinners. For extra pizzazz, top with sour cream or shredded cheese, or try it with a loaf of crusty bread.

Spicy Beans with Turkey Sausage

PREP: 25 min. ■ COOK: 5 hours

1 pound smoked turkey sausage, halved lengthwise and cut into 1/2-inch slices

1 can (16 ounces) kidney beans, rinsed and drained

1 can (15-1/2 ounces) great northern beans, rinsed and drained

1 can (15 ounces) black beans, rinsed and drained

1-1/2 cups frozen corn

1-1/2 cups salsa

1 large green pepper, chopped

1 large onion, chopped

1/2 to 1 cup water

3 garlic cloves, minced

1 teaspoon ground cumin

■ In a 5-qt. slow cooker, combine all ingredients. Cover and cook on low for 5-6 hours or until meat is tender. Stir before serving.

Yield: 6 servings.

Do you have leftover cooked rice in the fridge? Spoon some into each bowl before adding a helping of Spicy Beans with Turkey Sausage. The rice will perfectly complement this jambalaya-like main dish.

Tangy Venison Stroganoff

Ellen Spes
CARO, MICHIGAN

For an incredible supper, I like to coat tender chunks of venison and chopped onion with a silky sour cream sauce, and prepare it all in my slow cooker.

PREP: 10 min.
COOK: 3-1/4 hours

1-1/2 pounds boneless venison steak, cubed

1 medium onion, sliced

1 can (10-1/2 ounces) condensed beef broth, undiluted

1 tablespoon Worcestershire sauce

1 tablespoon ketchup

1 teaspoon curry powder

1/2 teaspoon ground ginger

1/2 teaspoon salt

1/4 teaspoon pepper

4-1/2 teaspoons cornstarch

1/2 cup sour cream

2 tablespoons prepared horseradish

Hot cooked noodles

■ Place venison and onion in a 3-qt. slow cooker. Combine the next seven ingredients; pour over venison. Cover and cook on high for 3 to 3-1/2 hours or until meat is tender. Combine the cornstarch, sour cream and horseradish; mix well. Gradually stir into venison mixture. Cover and cook 15 minutes longer or until sauce is thickened. Serve over noodles.

Yield: 4 servings.

- In a 5-qt. slow cooker, combine the potatoes, carrots, spaghetti sauce, mushrooms, minced garlic, turmeric, cayenne and salt. Cover and cook on low for 4-1/2 to 5 hours or until the potatoes are tender.

- Stir in the water, scallops and shrimp. Cover and cook for 15-20 minutes or until scallops are opaque and shrimp turn pink.

Yield: 9 servings.

*Nutrition Facts: 1 serving (1 cup) equals 261 calories, 4 g fat (1 g saturated fat), 93 mg cholesterol, 958 mg sodium, 35 g carbohydrate, 5 g fiber, 22 g protein. **Diabetic Exchanges:** 3 very lean meat, 2 starch, 1 vegetable.

Spicy Seafood Stew

Bonnie Marlow
OTTOVILLE, OHIO

When you're in the mood for seafood but also for something that has a little kick to it, look no further than this zippy stew. It spices up shrimp and scallops with turmeric and cayenne.

Spicy Seafood Stew*

PREP: 30 min. ■ **COOK:** 4-3/4 hours

2 pounds potatoes, peeled and diced

1 pound carrots, sliced

1 jar (26 ounces) spaghetti sauce

2 jars (6 ounces *each*) sliced mushrooms, drained

1-1/2 teaspoons minced garlic

1-1/2 teaspoons ground turmeric

1 teaspoon cayenne pepper

3/4 teaspoon salt

1-1/2 cups water

1 pound sea scallops

1 pound uncooked medium shrimp, peeled and deveined

Feel free to peel and dice the potatoes for Spicy Seafood Stew the night before. Just place the diced potatoes in water and store them in the refrigerator.

Peachy Pork Chops

Bonnie Morrow
SPENCERPORT, NEW YORK

I played around with many variations of this recipe until I came up with one that was just right. The warm peaches make an excellent side dish for the pork.

Peachy Pork Chops

PREP: 15 min. ■ **COOK:** 5 hours

2 bone-in center-cut pork loin chops (7 ounces *each*)

2 teaspoons canola oil

1 can (8-1/4 ounces) sliced peaches

1 can (8 ounces) tomato sauce

1/2 cup water

1 teaspoon reduced-sodium soy sauce

1/8 teaspoon dried rosemary, crushed

1/8 teaspoon dried thyme

1/8 teaspoon dried basil

Dash to 1/8 teaspoon cayenne pepper

■ In a small skillet, brown pork chops in oil; drain. Transfer to a 1-1/2-qt. slow cooker.

■ Drain peaches, reserving juice. In a bowl, combine the tomato sauce, water, soy sauce, rosemary, thyme, basil, cayenne and reserved peach juice; pour over pork. Top with peaches. Cover and cook on low for 5 hours or until pork is tender.

Yield: 2 servings.

Chili Casserole

Marietta Slater
THAYER, MISSOURI

Even people who try to bypass casseroles can't stay away from this zesty meat-and-rice dish. The seasonings make it irresistible and the slow cooker makes it a snap to prepare!

PREP: 15 min.
COOK: 7 hours

1 pound bulk pork sausage

2 cups water

1 can (15-1/2 ounces) chili beans, undrained

1 can (14-1/2 ounces) diced tomatoes, undrained

3/4 cup uncooked long grain rice

1/4 cup chopped onion

1 tablespoon chili powder

1 teaspoon Worcestershire sauce

1 teaspoon prepared mustard

3/4 teaspoon salt

1/8 teaspoon garlic powder

1 cup (4 ounces) shredded cheddar cheese

■ In a skillet, cook sausage until no longer pink; drain. Transfer to a 3-qt. slow cooker. Add the next 10 ingredients; stir well. Cover and cook on low for 7 hours or until rice is tender. Stir in cheese during the last 10 minutes of cooking time.

Yield: 6 servings.

Italian Shrimp 'n' Pasta

Karen Scaglione
NANUET, NEW YORK

This dish is always a hit! The shrimp, orzo, tomatoes and cayenne pepper remind me of a Creole favorite, but the Italian seasoning adds a different twist.

Italian Shrimp 'n' Pasta

PREP: 10 min. ■ **COOK:** 7 hours 20 min.

1 pound boneless skinless chicken thighs, cut into 2-inch x 1-inch strips	1 tablespoon sugar
	1/2 teaspoon salt
2 tablespoons vegetable oil	1/2 teaspoon Italian seasoning
1 can (28 ounces) crushed tomatoes	1/8 to 1/4 teaspoon cayenne pepper
2 celery ribs, chopped	1 bay leaf
1 medium green pepper, cut into 1-inch pieces	1/2 cup uncooked orzo pasta *or* other small pasta
1 medium onion, coarsely chopped	1 pound cooked medium shrimp, peeled and deveined
2 garlic cloves, minced	

■ In a large skillet, brown chicken in oil; transfer to a 3-qt. slow cooker. Add the next 11 ingredients; mix well. Cover and cook on low for 7-8 hours or until chicken juices run clear. Discard bay leaf. Stir in the pasta; cover and cook on high for 15 minutes or until pasta is tender. Stir in shrimp; cover and cook for 5 minutes or until shrimp are heated through.

Yield: *6-8 servings.*

Old-Fashioned Pork Chops

PREP: 20 min.
COOK: 5 hours

- 1/2 cup all-purpose flour
- 1-1/2 teaspoons ground mustard
- 1/2 teaspoon garlic salt
- 1/2 teaspoon pepper
- 6 boneless pork loin chops (5 ounces *each*)
- 2 tablespoons canola oil
- 1 can (10-1/2 ounces) condensed chicken with rice soup, undiluted
- 1 medium onion, quartered
- 1-1/2 teaspoons dried parsley flakes

■ In a large resealable plastic bag, combine the flour, mustard, garlic salt and pepper. Add the pork, a few pieces at a time, and shake to coat.

■ In a large skillet, brown chops in oil on each side. Transfer to a 3-qt. slow cooker. Top with the soup, onion and parsley. Cover and cook on low for 5-6 hours or until pork is tender.

Yield: *6 servings.*

The outer ribs

of celery may be peeled with a vegetable peeler to remove some of the thicker strings before chopping. If you like, save celery leaves for use in soups or as garnishes.

Loy Acerra Crane
JACKSON, TENNESSEE

Tender chops simmer to fork-tender perfection in this classic dish. The savory sauce comes together easily with a can of soup, an onion and a few parsley flakes. I serve this regularly for an easy weeknight meal, but it goes over well for a company dinner, too.

Side Dishes

80

79

86

Need a potluck side dish to bring to a social function or family gathering? Let a slow cooker do the job for you! Not only will it cook recipes such as baked beans and applesauce to perfection, it'll keep the dish warm during the event.

- Place sweet potatoes in a 3-qt. slow cooker coated with cooking spray. Combine the brown sugar, coconut, pecans, vanilla, salt and cinnamon; sprinkle over sweet potatoes. Drizzle with butter.

- Cover and cook on low for 5-6 hours or until potatoes are tender, sprinkling with marshmallows during last 5 minutes of cooking time.

Yield: 6 servings.

Sweet potatoes

are available year-round, but their peak season is in November. Be sure to buy the moist, orange-fleshed variety, sometimes called "yams." Sweet potatoes with yellow flesh tend to be starchier and drier than others.

Coconut-Pecan Sweet Potatoes

Rebecca Clark
WARRIOR, ALABAMA

Taking advantage of a slow cooker is one way to free up time when preparing a big meal. Consider this no-fuss side dish the next time you're planning a large menu.

Coconut-Pecan Sweet Potatoes

PREP: 20 min. ■ **COOK:** 5 hours

2 pounds sweet potatoes, peeled and cut into 3/4-inch cubes

1/4 cup packed brown sugar

2 tablespoons flaked coconut

2 tablespoons chopped pecans, toasted

1 teaspoon vanilla extract

1/2 teaspoon salt

1/4 teaspoon ground cinnamon

1 tablespoon butter, melted

1/2 cup miniature marshmallows

Tonya Vowels
VINE GROVE, KENTUCKY

Cream cheese and a can of cheese soup turn ordinary sliced potatoes into a rich side that's a perfect accompaniment to almost any meal.

Au Gratin Garlic Potatoes

Au Gratin Garlic Potatoes

PREP: 10 min. ■ **COOK:** 6 hours

1/2	cup milk	
1	can (10-3/4 ounces) condensed cheddar cheese soup, undiluted	
1	package (8 ounces) cream cheese, cubed	
1	garlic clove, minced	

1/4 teaspoon ground nutmeg
1/8 teaspoon pepper
2 pounds potatoes, peeled and sliced
1 small onion, chopped

Paprika, optional

■ In a saucepan, heat milk over medium heat until bubbles form around side of saucepan. Remove from the heat. Add the soup, cream cheese, garlic, nutmeg and pepper; stir until smooth.

■ Place the potatoes and onion in a 3-qt. slow cooker. Pour the milk mixture over the potato mixture; mix well. Cover and cook on low for 6-7 hours or until potatoes are tender. Sprinkle with paprika if desired.

Yield: 6-8 servings.

Spanish Hominy

PREP: 15 min.
COOK: 6 hours

4 cans (15-1/2 ounces *each*) hominy, rinsed and drained
1 can (14-1/2 ounces) diced tomatoes, undrained
1 can (10 ounces) diced tomatoes and green chilies, undrained
1 can (8 ounces) tomato sauce
3/4 pound sliced bacon, diced
1 large onion, chopped
1 medium green pepper, chopped

■ In a 5-qt. slow cooker, combine hominy, tomatoes and tomato sauce. In a large skillet, cook the bacon until crisp; remove with a slotted spoon to paper towels. Drain, reserving 1 tablespoon drippings.

■ In the same skillet, saute onion and green pepper in drippings until tender. Stir onion mixture and bacon into hominy mixture. Cover and cook on low for 6-8 hours or until heated through.

Yield: 12 servings.

Grating your own nutmeg is easy, and the wonderfully aromatic flavor it imparts to a dish is worth it. No need for special equipment–just run the whole nutmeg over the small holes of a grater. Stored in an airtight container, whole nutmeg will keep indefinitely.

Donna Brockett
KINGFISHER, OKLAHOMA

Here's a recipe that I received from a good friend of mine who is a fabulous cook. The colorful side dish gets its zesty taste from spicy canned tomatoes with green chilies. Plus, bacon gives it hearty flavor that always satisfies big appetites.

Stuffing from the Slow Cooker

Hearty Wild Rice

Mrs. Garnet Pettigrew
COLUMBIA CITY, INDIANA

My father-in-law made this hearty casserole in the oven. I switched it to the slow cooker so I wouldn't need to keep an eye on it. Try it and you'll see how nicely it complements most any dinner.

PREP: 15 min.
COOK: 5 hours

- 1 pound ground beef
- 1/2 pound bulk pork sausage
- 6 celery ribs, diced
- 2 cans (10-1/2 ounces *each*) condensed beef broth, undiluted
- 1-1/4 cups water
- 1 medium onion, chopped
- 1 cup uncooked wild rice
- 1 can (4 ounces) mushroom stems and pieces, drained
- 1/4 cup soy sauce

■ In a large skillet, cook beef and sausage over medium heat until no longer pink; drain.

■ Transfer to a 5-qt. slow cooker. Add the celery, broth, water, onion, rice, mushrooms and soy sauce; mix well. Cover and cook on high for 1 hour. Reduce heat to low; cover and cook for 4 hours or until rice is tender.

Yield: 10-12 servings.

Mrs. Donald Seiler
MACON, MISSISSIPPI

If you're hosting Thanksgiving dinner this year, add this simple, slow-cooked stuffing to your menu to ease entertaining. The recipe comes in handy when you run out of oven space.

Stuffing from the Slow Cooker

PREP: 30 min. ■ **COOK:** 3 hours

- 1 cup chopped onion
- 1 cup chopped celery
- 1/4 cup butter
- 6 cups cubed day-old white bread
- 6 cups cubed day-old whole wheat bread
- 1 teaspoon salt
- 1 teaspoon poultry seasoning
- 1 teaspoon rubbed sage
- 1/2 teaspoon pepper
- 1 can (14-1/2 ounces) reduced-sodium chicken broth *or* vegetable broth
- 1/2 cup egg substitute

■ In a small nonstick skillet over medium heat, cook onion and celery in butter until tender. In a large bowl, combine the bread cubes, salt, poultry seasoning, sage and pepper. Stir in onion mixture. Combine broth and egg substitute; add to bread mixture and toss to coat.

■ Transfer to a 3-qt. slow cooker coated with cooking spray. Cover and cook on low for 3-4 hours or until heated through.

Yield: 12 servings.

Tara Branham
AUSTIN, TEXAS

I usually prepare these potatoes when I'm having guests for dinner. Using the slow cooker leaves plenty of room on my stove for the other dishes.

Lemon Red Potatoes

Lemon Red Potatoes

PREP: 5 min. ■ **COOK:** 2-1/2 hours

1-1/2 pounds medium red potatoes

1/4 cup water

1/4 cup butter, melted

1 tablespoon lemon juice

3 tablespoons minced fresh parsley

1 tablespoon snipped fresh chives

Salt and pepper to taste

■ Cut a strip of peel from around the middle of each potato. Place potatoes and water in a 3-qt. slow cooker. Cover and cook on high for 2-1/2 to 3 hours or until tender (do not overcook); drain.

■ In a small bowl, combine the butter, lemon juice, parsley and chives. Pour over the potatoes and toss to coat. Season with salt and pepper.

Yield: 6 servings.

When making the Lemon Red Potatoes, it's easy to change the flavor profile to suit your needs. For a Greek-style potato, replace the chives with chopped oregano and add 1 teaspoon of grated lemon peel. For Italian potatoes, use chopped basil instead of chives and add a pinch of red pepper flakes. For potatoes with a Mexican flair, substitute the parsley with cilantro and use green onion instead of chives.

All-Day Apple Butter

Betty Ruenholl
SYRACUSE, NEBRASKA

I make several batches of this simple and delicious apple butter to freeze in jars. Depending on the sweetness of the apples used, you can adjust the sugar to taste.

PREP: 20 min.
COOK: 11 hours

5-1/2 pounds apples, peeled and finely chopped

4 cups sugar

2 to 3 teaspoons ground cinnamon

1/4 teaspoon ground cloves

1/4 teaspoon salt

■ Place apples in a 3-qt. slow cooker. Combine sugar, cinnamon, cloves and salt; pour over apples and mix well. Cover and cook on high for 1 hour. Reduce heat to low; cover and cook for 9-11 hours or until thickened and dark brown, stirring occasionally (stir more frequently as it thickens to prevent sticking).

■ Uncover and cook on low 1 hour longer. If desired, stir with a wire whisk until smooth. Spoon the butter into freezer containers, leaving 1/2-in. headspace. Cover and refrigerate or freeze.

Yield: 4 pints.

Jolene Walters
NORTH MIAMI, FLORIDA

Not only does this French-style recipe make a phenomenal side dish with just about any meaty main course, but you can also serve it with sliced French bread for a warm but easy appetizer. Try it in the summer with your garden-fresh vegetables.

Ratatouille

PREP: 45 min. ■ COOK: 4 hours

- 1 large eggplant, peeled and cut into 1-inch cubes
- 2 teaspoons salt, *divided*
- 3 medium tomatoes, chopped
- 3 medium zucchini, halved lengthwise and sliced
- 2 medium onions, chopped
- 1 large green pepper, chopped
- 1 large sweet yellow pepper, chopped
- 1 can (6 ounces) pitted ripe olives, drained and chopped
- 1 can (6 ounces) tomato paste
- 1/2 cup minced fresh basil
- 2 garlic cloves, minced
- 1/2 teaspoon pepper
- 2 tablespoons olive oil

■ Place eggplant in a colander over a plate; sprinkle with 1 teaspoon salt and toss. Let stand for 30 minutes. Rinse and drain well. Transfer to a 5-qt. slow cooker coated with cooking spray.

■ Stir in the tomatoes, zucchini, onions, green and yellow peppers, olives, tomato paste, basil, garlic, pepper and remaining salt. Drizzle with oil. Cover and cook on high for 3-4 hours or until vegetables are tender.

Yield: 10 servings.

Ratatouille (pronounced ra-tu-TOO-ee), can be served hot, cold or at room temperature. This popular, classic dish from the South of France is as versatile as it is delicious. If you want to take full advantage of the bright beautiful colors of summer produce, it's okay to substitute summer squash for some of the zucchini or to use orange or red sweet bell peppers instead of, or in conjunction with, the green and yellow peppers.

Lazy-Day Cranberry Relish

June Formanek
BELLE PLAINE, IOWA

When I'm busy preparing to feed a crowd, I often turn to this four-ingredient ruby-red condiment. I think that it's especially delicious served with turkey.

PREP: 5 min. + chilling
COOK: 6 hours

- 2 cups sugar
- 1 cup orange juice
- 1 teaspoon grated orange peel
- 4 cups fresh *or* frozen cranberries

■ In a 1-1/2 qt. slow cooker, combine sugar, orange juice and peel; stir until sugar is dissolved. Add the cranberries. Cover and cook on low for 6 hours. Mash the mixture. Chill several hours or overnight.

Yield: 10-12 servings (3 cups).

Tamara Ellefson
FREDERIC, WISCONSIN

I prepare this comforting side dish with all of my holiday meals. It's more moist than corn pudding made in the oven, plus the cream cheese is a nice addition.

Corn Spoon Bread

Corn Spoon Bread

PREP: 15 min. ■ **COOK:** 3 hours

1 package (8 ounces) cream cheese, softened	1/4 teaspoon ground nutmeg
1/3 cup sugar	Dash pepper
1 cup milk	2-1/3 cups frozen corn, thawed
1/2 cup egg substitute	1 can (14-3/4 ounces) cream-style corn
2 tablespoons butter, melted	1 package (8-1/2 ounces) corn bread/muffin mix
1 teaspoon salt	

■ In a large mixing bowl, beat cream cheese and sugar until smooth. Gradually beat in milk. Beat in the egg substitute, butter, salt, nutmeg and pepper until blended. Stir in corn and cream-style corn. Stir in corn bread mix just until moistened. Pour into a greased 3-qt. slow cooker. Cover and cook on high for 3-4 hours or until center is almost set.

Yield: 8 servings.

Apples range in flavor from tart to sweet, with some being better suited for baking purposes than others. Here are a few varieties of apple that are recommended for the Cranberry-Stuffed Apples: Cortland, Empire, Golden Delicious, Granny Smith, Jonathan, Pink Lady or Rome Beauty.

Cranberry-Stuffed Apples*

Graciela Sandvigen
ROCHESTER, NEW YORK

Looking for a change-of-pace dinner addition? Consider my stuffed apples. Cinnamon, nutmeg and walnuts add a homey autumn flavor, but the slow cooker does most of the work for me!

PREP: 10 min.
COOK: 4 hours

- 5 medium apples
- 1/3 cup fresh *or* frozen cranberries, thawed and chopped
- 1/4 cup packed brown sugar
- 2 tablespoons chopped walnuts
- 1/4 teaspoon ground cinnamon
- 1/8 teaspoon ground nutmeg
- Whipped cream *or* vanilla ice cream, optional

■ Core apples, leaving bottoms intact. Peel top third of each apple; place in a 5-qt. slow cooker. Combine the cranberries, brown sugar, walnuts, cinnamon and nutmeg; spoon into apples. Cover and cook on low for 4-5 hours or until apples are tender. Serve with whipped cream or ice cream if desired.

Yield: 5 servings.

*Nutrition Facts: 1 apple (calculated without whipped cream or ice cream) equals 136 calories, 2 g fat (trace saturated fat), 0 cholesterol, 6 mg sodium, 31 g carbohydrate, 4 g fiber, 1 g protein. **Diabetic Exchanges:** 1 starch, 1 fruit.

Four-Bean Medley

Susanne Wasson
MONTGOMERY, NEW YORK

This bean side dish always draws compliments. Because it's easy to fix ahead and simmers in the slow cooker, it's convenient to take to potlucks and church meals.

Four-Bean Medley

PREP: 40 min. ■ **COOK:** 6 hours

- 8 bacon strips, diced
- 2 medium onions, quartered and sliced
- 3/4 cup packed brown sugar
- 1/2 cup cider vinegar
- 1 teaspoon salt
- 1 teaspoon ground mustard
- 1/2 teaspoon garlic powder
- 1 can (16 ounces) baked beans, undrained
- 1 can (16 ounces) kidney beans, rinsed and drained
- 1 can (15 ounces) butter beans, rinsed and drained
- 1 can (14-1/2 ounces) cut green beans, drained

■ In a large skillet, cook bacon until crisp. Drain, reserving 2 tablespoons drippings; set bacon aside. Saute onions in drippings until tender. Stir in brown sugar, vinegar, salt, mustard and garlic powder.

■ Simmer, uncovered, for 15 minutes or until onions are golden brown. Place the beans in a 3-qt. slow cooker. Add onion mixture and bacon; stir to combine. Cover and cook on low for 6-7 hours or until heated through. Serve with a slotted spoon.

Yield: 8-10 servings.

Banana Applesauce

Judy Batson
TAMPA, FLORIDA

Thanks to my slow cooker, it's a breeze to create homemade applesauce! Banana, raisins and a splash of citrus flavor make my sauce different than most.

PREP: 20 min.
COOK: 3 hours

- 8 medium apples, peeled and cubed
- 1 medium ripe banana, thinly sliced
- 1 cup raisins
- 3/4 cup orange juice
- 1/2 cup packed brown sugar
- 1/4 cup honey
- 1/4 cup butter, melted
- 2 teaspoons pumpkin pie spice
- 1 small lemon
- 1 envelope instant apples and cinnamon oatmeal
- 1/2 cup boiling water

■ Place the apples, banana and raisins in a 3-qt. slow cooker coated with cooking spray. In a small bowl, combine the orange juice, brown sugar, honey, butter and pie spice; pour over apple mixture. Cut ends off lemon. Cut into six wedges and remove seeds. Transfer to slow cooker. Cover and cook on high for 3-4 hours or until apples are soft.

■ Remove and discard lemon. Mash apple mixture. In a small bowl, combine oatmeal and water. Let stand for 1 minute. Stir into applesauce.

Yield: 5-1/2 cups.

Squash Stuffing Casserole

Pamela Thorson
HOT SPRINGS, ARKANSAS
My friends just rave about this creamy dish. It's a snap to jazz up summer squash, zucchini and carrots with canned soup and stuffing mix.

Squash Stuffing Casserole

PREP: 15 min. ■ **COOK:** 4 hours

1/4 cup all-purpose flour
  1 can (10-3/4 ounces) condensed cream of chicken soup, undiluted
  1 cup (8 ounces) sour cream
  2 medium yellow summer squash, cut into 1/2-inch slices

  1 small onion, chopped
  1 cup shredded carrots
  1 package (8 ounces) stuffing mix
1/2 cup butter, melted

■ In a bowl, combine the flour, soup and sour cream until blended. Add the vegetables and gently stir to coat. Combine the stuffing mix and butter; sprinkle half into a 5-qt. slow cooker. Top with vegetable mixture and remaining stuffing mixture. Cover and cook on low for 4-5 hours or until vegetables are tender.

Yield: 8 servings.

Creamed Corn

Barbara Brizendine
HARRISONVILLE, MISSOURI
Five ingredients are all you'll need for my popular dinner accompaniment. It's wonderful no matter what the occasion is. Try it on a barbecue buffet or holiday menu.

PREP: 10 min.
COOK: 3 hours

  2 packages (one 16 ounces, one 10 ounces) frozen corn
  1 package (8 ounces) cream cheese, softened and cubed
1/4 cup butter, cubed
  1 tablespoon sugar
1/2 teaspoon salt

■ In a 3-qt. slow cooker coated with cooking spray, combine all ingredients. Cover and cook on low for 3 to 3-1/2 hours or until cheese is melted and corn is tender. Stir just before serving.

Yield: 5 servings.

A sprinkling of cheddar cheese and green onion will add a bit of fancy flavor to Creamed Corn. For extra zing, stir in 1 tablespoon of fresh chopped jalapeno pepper at the end.

Bob Malchow
MONON, INDIANA
This is one of my favorite recipes from my mother. With only seven ingredients, it's quick to assemble in the morning before I leave for work.

Mushroom Wild Rice

Mushroom Wild Rice

PREP: 5 min. ■ **COOK:** 7 hours

2-1/4 cups water
1 can (10-1/2 ounces) condensed beef consomme, undiluted
1 can (10-1/2 ounces) condensed French onion soup, undiluted

3 cans (4 ounces *each*) mushroom stems and pieces, drained
1/2 cup butter, melted
1 cup uncooked brown rice
1 cup uncooked wild rice

■ In a 3-qt. slow cooker, combine all ingredients. Cover and cook on low for 7-8 hours or until rice is tender.

Yield: 12-16 servings.

Wild rice, which is actually a long-grain marsh grass, is cooked like regular rice, but usually takes a bit longer. It's important to clean wild rice before using it. Place the rice in a bowl. Cover it with cold water, stir it a couple of times and set aside for 5 minutes. Any debris from the rice will float to the top of the water and can be poured off.

Michigan Bean Bake

Sondra Bergy
LOWELL, MICHIGAN
Ten minutes is all the time you'll need to get these tangy beans in the slow cooker. Just let them simmer all day long for a great-tasting side dish that simply can't be beat.

PREP: 10 min.
COOK: 8 hours

1 jar (48 ounces) great northern beans, rinsed and drained
1-1/2 pounds lean pork, cut into 1-inch cubes
1/2 teaspoon salt
1 bottle (14 ounces) ketchup
3 tablespoons prepared mustard
1-1/2 cups packed brown sugar
1/4 large sweet onion, chopped

■ Combine all ingredients; mix gently but well. Place in a 3-qt. slow cooker. Cover and cook on low for 8-10 hours. Or, place in a beanpot or baking dish. Bake at 325°, uncovered, for 5 to 6 hours; cover last hour. Or heat on low in slow cooker overnight.

Yield: 10-12 servings.

Rich Spinach Casserole

Vioda Geyer
UHRICHSVILLE, OHIO

I found this recipe in an old slow cooker cookbook. When I took the side dish to our church sewing circle, it was a big hit with everyone.

PREP: 10 min. ■ **COOK:** 2-1/2 hours

- 2 packages (10 ounces *each*) frozen chopped spinach, thawed and well drained
- 2 cups (16 ounces) 4% cottage cheese
- 1 cup cubed process cheese (Velveeta)
- 3/4 cup egg substitute
- 2 tablespoons butter, cubed
- 1/4 cup all-purpose flour
- 1/2 teaspoon salt

■ In a 3-qt. slow cooker, combine all ingredients; mix well. Cover and cook on low for 2-1/2 hours or until the cheese is melted.

Yield: 8 servings.

Scraping out the seeds and veins from bell peppers can get tricky without cutting them in half. A melon baller works as the perfect tool for this task. Use it to gently scrape out the insides of the pepper. It works like a charm.

Vegetable-Stuffed Peppers

PREP: 10 min.
COOK: 8-1/4 hours

- 2 cans (14-1/2 ounces *each*) diced tomatoes, undrained
- 1 can (16 ounces) kidney beans, rinsed and drained
- 1-1/2 cups cooked rice
- 2 cups (8 ounces) shredded cheddar cheese, *divided*
- 1 package (10 ounces) frozen corn, thawed
- 1/4 cup chopped onion
- 1 teaspoon Worcestershire sauce
- 3/4 teaspoon chili powder
- 1/2 teaspoon pepper
- 1/4 teaspoon salt
- 6 medium green peppers

■ In a large bowl, combine the tomatoes, kidney beans, rice, 1-1/2 cups cheese, corn, onion, Worcestershire sauce, chili powder, pepper and salt. Remove and discard tops and seeds of green peppers. Fill each pepper with about 1 cup vegetable mixture. Place in a 5-qt. slow cooker. Cover; cook on low for 8 hours.

■ Sprinkle with remaining cheese. Cover and cook for 15 minutes longer or until peppers are tender and cheese is melted.

Yield: 6 servings.

Sandra Allen
AUSTIN, TEXAS

Here's a family-favorite recipe that came with my slow cooker. By filling green peppers with a flavorful combination of cooked rice, kidney beans, corn and onions, I have a dish that can be used for either a side or a meatless entree.

Cheesy Sausage Gravy

P.J. Prusia
RAYMORE, MISSOURI

I truly appreciate the make-ahead convenience of slow-cooked dishes. Shared by a friend, this breakfast is one I've served to many overnight guests. They never fail to ask for the recipe.

PREP: 15 min. ■ **COOK:** 7 hours

1 pound bulk pork sausage	2 cans (10-3/4 ounces *each*) condensed cheddar cheese soup, undiluted
1/4 cup butter	6 hard-cooked eggs, chopped
1/4 cup all-purpose flour	1 jar (4-1/2 ounces) sliced mushrooms, drained
1/4 teaspoon pepper	Warm biscuits
2-1/2 cups milk	

■ In a large skillet, cook sausage over medium heat until no longer pink; drain and remove sausage. In the same skillet, melt butter. Stir in flour and pepper until smooth. Gradually whisk in milk. Bring to a boil; cook and stir for 2 minutes or until thickened and bubbly.

■ Stir in soup until blended. Stir in the eggs, mushrooms and sausage. Transfer to a 3-qt. slow cooker. Cover and cook on low for 7-8 hours. Stir; serve over biscuits.

Yield: 8 servings.

For the warm biscuits that accompany the Cheesy Sausage Gravy, you can rely on your own recipe, or simply pop open a can of refrigerated biscuit dough. Better yet, make them the night before, store in a resealable plastic bag and warm in the microwave the next morning.

Mushroom Potatoes

Linda Bernard
GOLDEN MEADOW, LOUISIANA

I jazzed up sliced potatoes with mushrooms, onions, canned soup and cheese to create this versatile dinner staple. With its comforting flavor, it's a nice accompaniment to most meats.

PREP: 25 min.
COOK: 6 hours

- 7 medium potatoes, peeled and thinly sliced
- 1 medium onion, sliced
- 4 garlic cloves, minced
- 2 green onions, chopped
- 1 can (8 ounces) mushroom stems and pieces, drained
- 1/4 cup all-purpose flour
- 2 teaspoons salt
- 1/2 teaspoon pepper
- 1/4 cup butter, cubed
- 1 can (10-3/4 ounces) condensed cream of mushroom soup, undiluted
- 1 cup (4 ounces) shredded Colby-Monterey Jack cheese

■ In a 3-qt. slow cooker, layer half of the potatoes, onion, garlic, green onions, mushrooms, flour, salt, pepper and butter. Repeat layers. Pour soup over the top. Cover and cook on low for 6-8 hours or until the potatoes are tender; sprinkle with cheese during the last 30 minutes of cooking time.

Yield: 8-10 servings.

Sausage Spanish Rice

Saucy Pork And Beans

Ginnie Busam
PEWEE VALLEY, KENTUCKY

Everyone enjoys the tangy sauce in my pork and beans, but they never guess the secret ingredient—a little cola. The recipe takes advantage of convenience foods as well as my slow cooker.

PREP: 15 min.
COOK: 3 hours

- 4 cans (15 ounces *each*) pork and beans
- 8 bacon strips, cooked and crumbled
- 1 medium onion, chopped
- 1 small green pepper, chopped
- 3/4 cup cola
- 1/2 cup packed brown sugar
- 1/2 cup spicy brown mustard
- 1/2 cup ketchup
- 1/2 cup barbecue sauce

■ In a 5-qt. slow cooker, combine all ingredients. Cover and cook on high for 3-4 hours or until heated through. Serve with a slotted spoon.

Yield: 12 servings.

Michelle McKay
GARDEN CITY, MICHIGAN

My husband and I both work the midnight shift, so I'm always on the lookout for slow-cooker recipes. This side dish couldn't be easier. We've even eaten it as a main course.

Sausage Spanish Rice

PREP: 5 min. ■ **COOK:** 5 hours

- 1 pound fully cooked kielbasa *or* Polish sausage, cut into 1/4-inch slices
- 2 cans (14-1/2 ounces *each*) diced tomatoes, undrained
- 2 cups water
- 1-1/2 cups uncooked converted rice
- 1 cup salsa
- 1 medium onion
- 1/2 cup chopped green pepper
- 1/2 cup chopped sweet red pepper
- 1 can (4 ounces) chopped green chilies
- 1 envelope taco seasoning

■ In a 3-qt. slow cooker, combine all ingredients; stir to blend. Cover and cook on low for 5-6 hours or until rice is tender.

Yield: 9 servings.

Snacks & Sweets

97

95

98

Bring out the party hats, because it's time to have a celebration using your slow cooker! The menu may include cheese fondue, chicken wings, artichoke dip, candy, cake or beverages. Regardless of what you serve, success never tasted so sweet!

Nutty Apple Streusel Dessert

- In a large bowl, toss apples with cinnamon, allspice and nutmeg. Place in a greased 3-qt. slow cooker. In a mixing bowl, combine milk, butter, sugar, eggs, vanilla and baking mix. Spoon over apples.

- For topping, combine biscuit mix and brown sugar in a bowl; cut in butter until crumbly. Add almonds; sprinkle over apples. Cover and cook on low for 6-7 hours or until the apples are tender. Serve with ice cream or whipped cream if desired.

Yield: 6-8 servings.

Jacki Every
ROTTERDAM, NEW YORK
Many people don't think of using a slow cooker to make dessert, but this down-home apple treat turns out scrumptious every time I prepare it.

Nutty Apple Streusel Dessert

PREP: 20 min. ■ BAKE: 6 hours

6 cups sliced peeled tart apples	2 eggs
1-1/4 teaspoons ground cinnamon	1 teaspoon vanilla extract
1/4 teaspoon ground allspice	1/2 cup biscuit/baking mix
1/4 teaspoon ground nutmeg	TOPPING:
3/4 cup milk	1 cup biscuit/baking mix
2 tablespoons butter, softened	1/3 cup packed brown sugar
3/4 cup sugar	3 tablespoons cold butter
	1/2 cup sliced almonds
	Ice cream *or* whipped cream, optional

When choosing

apples for Nutty Apple Streusel Dessert, select a tart variety such as Granny Smith, Rome Beauty or Jonathan. Do you have a family of sweet tooths? Stir a handful of peanut butter baking chips in with the apples.

Sunshine Chicken Wings

Ami Miller
PLAIN CITY, OHIO

Casual get-togethers get a flavorful boost when these finger-licking-good wings are on the buffet table. Served with white rice and a salad, they could even be a main course.

Sunshine Chicken Wings

PREP: 25 min. ■ BAKE: 45 min.

2	jars (12 ounces *each*) orange marmalade
3	cups ketchup
1	cup packed brown sugar
1	large onion, finely chopped
1/2	cup butter, cubed

3	tablespoons chili powder
3	tablespoons vinegar
1	tablespoon Worcestershire sauce
	Hot pepper sauce to taste
8	pounds whole chicken wings (about 40)

■ In a large saucepan, combine the first nine ingredients. Bring to a boil. Reduce heat; simmer, uncovered, for 15 minutes.

■ Meanwhile, cut chicken wings into three sections; discard wing tips. Dip wings into the sauce and place on two foil-lined 15-in. x 10-in. x 1-in. baking pans.

■ Bake at 350° for 45 minutes, reversing pans once during baking. Serve immediately or cover and refrigerate for up to 2 days before serving. Reheat in the oven, a slow cooker or electric roaster.

Yield: 15-20 servings.

Editor's Note: Uncooked chicken wing sections (wingettes) may be substituted for whole chicken wings.

Strawberry Rhubarb Sauce*

PREP: 15 min.
COOK: 4-1/4 hours

6	cups sliced fresh *or* frozen rhubarb, thawed
1	cup sugar
1/2	cup unsweetened apple juice
3	cinnamon sticks (3 inches)
1/2	teaspoon grated orange peel
1/4	teaspoon ground ginger
1	pint fresh strawberries, halved

Vanilla ice cream

■ Place the rhubarb, sugar, juice, cinnamon sticks, orange peel and ginger in a 3-qt. slow cooker. Cover and cook on low for 4-5 hours or until rhubarb is tender. Stir in the strawberries; cover and cook 15 minutes longer or until heated through. Discard cinnamon sticks. Serve with ice cream.

Yield: 4-1/2 cups.

✱ **Nutrition Facts:** 1/4 cup (calculated without ice cream) equals 60 calories, trace fat (trace saturated fat), 0 cholesterol, 2 mg sodium, 15 g carbohydrate, 1 g fiber, trace protein. **Diabetic Exchange:** 1 fruit.

Nancy Cowlishaw
BOISE, IDAHO

The perfect addition to vanilla ice cream, my colorful, fruity sauce features a delightful combination of rhubarb, apple and strawberry flavors. I also like to serve this delicious sauce over pancakes, French toast or even fresh, hot biscuits.

1. In a large bowl, combine the flour, 3/4 cup sugar, baking powder, salt, cinnamon and nutmeg. Combine the eggs, milk and oil; stir into dry ingredients just until moistened. Spread the batter evenly onto the bottom of a greased 5-qt. slow cooker.

2. In a large saucepan, combine the berries, water, orange peel and remaining sugar; bring to a boil. Remove from the heat; immediately pour over batter. Cover and cook on high for 2 to 2-1/2 hours or until a toothpick inserted into the batter comes out clean.

3. Turn cooker off. Uncover and let stand for 30 minutes before serving. Serve with whipped cream or ice cream if desired.

Yield: 6 servings.

Black and Blue Cobbler

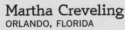

Martha Creveling
ORLANDO, FLORIDA

It never occurred to me that I could bake a cobbler in my slow cooker until I tried my favorite fruity dessert recipe in one. It turned out delicious!

Black and Blue Cobbler

PREP: 15 min. ■ **COOK:** 2 hours + standing

1 cup all-purpose flour
1-1/2 cups sugar, *divided*
1 teaspoon baking powder
1/4 teaspoon salt
1/4 teaspoon ground cinnamon
1/4 teaspoon ground nutmeg
2 eggs, lightly beaten
2 tablespoons milk
2 tablespoons vegetable oil

2 cups fresh *or* frozen blackberries
2 cups fresh *or* frozen blueberries
3/4 cup water
1 teaspoon grated orange peel
Whipped cream *or* vanilla ice cream, optional

If you are not sure that your baking powder is still fresh, test it before preparing your recipe. Mix 1 teaspoon baking powder and 1/3 cup hot water. If bubbling occurs, the baking powder is still fresh. Otherwise, it should be replaced.

Faye O'Bryan
OWENSBORO,
KENTUCKY

Before I retired, I took these yummy peanut butter bites to work for special occasions. They're so simple, however, that I still make them for holidays.

Crunchy Candy Clusters

Crunchy Candy Clusters

PREP: 15 min. ■ COOK: 1 hour

- 2 pounds white candy coating, broken into small pieces
- 1-1/2 cups peanut butter
- 1/2 teaspoon almond extract, optional
- 4 cups Cap'n Crunch cereal
- 4 cups crisp rice cereal
- 4 cups miniature marshmallows

■ Place candy coating in a 5-qt. slow cooker. Cover and cook on high for 1 hour. Add peanut butter. Stir in extract if desired. In a large bowl, combine the cereals and marshmallows. Stir in the peanut butter mixture until well coated. Drop by tablespoonfuls onto waxed paper. Let stand until set. Store at room temperature.

Yield: 6-1/2 dozen.

Crystallized, or candied, ginger is the root of the ginger plant that has been cooked in a sugar syrup. It's used mostly in fruit desserts, dips and sauces. Larger supermarkets carry candied ginger in the spice section.

Gingered Pears

Catherine Mueller
ST. PAUL, MINNESOTA

My slow cooker allows me to serve a heartwarming dessert without much effort. Topped with caramel sauce, these tender pears feature a surprise filling of nuts and brown sugar.

PREP: 35 min.
COOK: 4 hours

- 1/2 cup finely chopped candied *or* crystallized ginger
- 1/4 cup packed brown sugar
- 1/4 cup chopped pecans
- 1-1/2 teaspoons grated lemon peel
- 6 medium Bartlett *or* D'Anjou pears
- 2 tablespoons butter, cubed

Vanilla ice cream and caramel ice cream topping, optional

■ In a small bowl, combine the ginger, brown sugar, pecans and lemon peel. Using a melon baller or long-handled spoon, core pears to within 1/4-in. of bottom. Spoon ginger mixture into the center of each.

■ Place pears upright in a 5-qt. slow cooker. Top each with butter. Cover and cook on low for 4-5 hours or until pears are tender. Serve with ice cream and caramel topping if desired.

Yield: 6 servings.

Mary Spencer
WAUKESHA, WISCONSIN

Folks are sure to gather around this ooey-gooey, lightened-up dip whenever it's placed on any buffet table. With cheese, jalapenos and a hint of lemon, it's a treasure in our house. Best of all, it's much lighter in fat and calories than traditional artichoke dips.

Light Creamy Artichoke Dip*

PREP: 20 min. ■ **COOK:** 1 hour

- 2 cans (14 ounces *each*) water-packed artichoke hearts, rinsed, drained and coarsely chopped
- 1 package (8 ounces) reduced-fat cream cheese, cubed
- 1 carton (6 ounces) plain yogurt
- 1 cup (4 ounces) shredded part-skim mozzarella cheese
- 1 cup reduced-fat ricotta cheese
- 3/4 cup shredded Parmesan cheese, *divided*
- 1/2 cup shredded reduced-fat Swiss cheese
- 1/4 cup reduced-fat mayonnaise
- 2 tablespoons lemon juice
- 1 tablespoon chopped seeded jalapeno pepper
- 1 teaspoon garlic powder
- 1 teaspoon seasoned salt
- Tortilla chips

■ In a 3-qt. slow cooker, combine the artichokes, cream cheese, yogurt, mozzarella, ricotta, 1/2 cup Parmesan, Swiss, mayonnaise, lemon juice, jalapeno, garlic powder and seasoned salt. Cover and cook on low for 1 hour or until heated through. Sprinkle with remaining Parmesan cheese. Serve with tortilla chips.

Yield: 5 cups.

Editor's Note: When cutting hot peppers, disposable gloves are recommended. Avoid touching your face.

✱ Nutrition Facts: 1/4 cup (calculated without tortilla chips) equals 104 calories, 6 g fat (3 g saturated fat), 20 mg cholesterol, 348 mg sodium, 5 g carbohydrate, trace fiber, 7 g protein. **Diabetic Exchanges:** 1 fat, 1/2 starch.

When it comes to dippers for a savory dip, you have all sorts of choices. Consider tortilla chips, corn chips, fresh vegetables, breadsticks, crackers or pretzels.

Hot Cider With Orange Twists*

Catherine Allan
TWIN FALLS, IDAHO

I first tasted a steaming mug of this comforting beverage on a frigid evening, and knew I had to learn how to make it. It's still a family favorite on a wintry day.

PREP: 10 min.
COOK: 2 hours

- 2 quarts apple cider
- 1 cup pineapple juice
- 1 cup orange juice
- 1 tablespoon brown sugar
- 1 tablespoon lemon juice
- 1/8 teaspoon salt
- 8 whole cloves
- 4 unpeeled fresh orange slices (1/4 inch thick)
- 4 cinnamon sticks (3 inches)
- Additional orange slices and cinnamon sticks

■ In a 5-qt. slow cooker, combine the first six ingredients. Push two cloves through each orange slice. Push a cinnamon stick through the center of each orange slice; add to cider mixture. Cover and cook on low for 2-4 hours or until heated through. Discard the oranges, cloves and cinnamon sticks. Stir cider before serving. Use additional oranges and cinnamon sticks to make garnishes.

Yield: 2-1/2 quarts.

✱ Nutrition Facts: 1 serving (1 cup) equals 127 calories, trace fat (trace saturated fat), 0 cholesterol, 50 mg sodium, 32 g carbohydrate, trace fiber, trace protein. **Diabetic Exchange:** 2 fruit.

Bonnie Evans
NORCROSS, GEORGIA

The house smells great while this recipe is cooking. My husband and son enjoy this warm dessert most when I add a big scoop of vanilla ice cream.

Fudgy Peanut Butter Cake

Fudgy Peanut Butter Cake

PREP: 10 min. ■ **COOK:** 1-1/2 hours

3/4 cup sugar, *divided*	1 tablespoon vegetable oil
1/2 cup all-purpose flour	1/2 teaspoon vanilla extract
3/4 teaspoon baking powder	2 tablespoons baking cocoa
1/3 cup milk	1 cup boiling water
1/4 cup peanut butter	Vanilla ice cream

■ In a bowl, combine 1/4 cup sugar, flour and baking powder. In another bowl, combine the milk, peanut butter, oil and vanilla; stir into dry ingredients just until combined. Spread evenly into a 1-1/2-qt. slow cooker coated with cooking spray.

■ In a bowl, combine the cocoa and remaining sugar; stir in boiling water. Pour into slow cooker (do not stir). Cover and cook on high for 1-1/2 to 2 hours or until a toothpick inserted near the center of cake comes out clean. Serve warm with ice cream.

Yield: 4 servings.

To give Fudgy Peanut Butter Cake even more nut flavor and a little bit of crunch, too, top off each bowlful with a sprinkling of chopped peanuts.

Apricot-Apple Cider*

Ginnie Busam
PEWEE VALLEY, KENTUCKY

Dried apricots give this comforting cider a friendly taste twist. Cranberries, cinnamon, allspice and cloves make it a perfect way to chase away the chill from autumn and winter nights.

PREP: 20 min.
COOK: 3 hours

    8 cups unsweetened apple juice
    1 can (12 ounces) ginger ale
  1/2 cup dried apricots, halved
  1/2 cup dried cranberries
    2 cinnamon sticks (3 inches)
    1 tablespoon whole allspice
    1 tablespoon whole cloves

■ In a 5-qt. slow cooker, combine apple juice and ginger ale. Place the apricots, cranberries, cinnamon sticks, allspice and cloves on a double thickness of cheesecloth; bring up corners of cloth and tie with string to form a bag. Place in slow cooker. Cover and cook on high for 3-4 hours or until heated through. Discard spice bag.

Yield: 13 servings (2-1/2 quarts).

❋ Nutrition Facts: 3/4 cup equals 111 calories, trace fat (trace saturated fat), 0 cholesterol, 6 mg sodium, 28 g carbohydrate, 1 g fiber, trace protein. **Diabetic Exchange:** 2 fruit.

Beer Cheese Fondue

Sweet Sausage Puffs

Gloria Butler
PLAIN CITY, OHIO

Whenever I'm hosting friends or family, I reach for this slow-cooked hors d'oeuvre. The slow cooker keeps the puffs nice and toasty during the event.

PREP: 25 min.
BAKE: 15 min.

- 1/2 cup butter
- 1 cup packed brown sugar
- 2 tablespoons water
- 1/2 cup finely chopped pecans
- 1 tube (12 ounces) refrigerated flaky buttermilk biscuits
- 40 miniature smoked sausages

- For syrup, in a heavy saucepan, melt butter. Stir in the brown sugar and water. Bring to a boil. Stir in pecans. Remove from the heat; set aside.

- Flatten each biscuit into a 3-in. circle; cut into quarters. Place a sausage on each piece of dough; wrap dough around sausage and seal edge. Place seam side down in a greased 15-in. x 10-in. x 1-in. baking pan. Pour syrup over bundles.

- Bake at 375° for 15-20 minutes or until golden brown. Transfer to a chafing dish or slow cooker; cover and keep warm over low heat.

Yield: 40 appetizers.

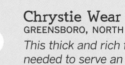

Chrystie Wear
GREENSBORO, NORTH CAROLINA

This thick and rich fondue originated in my kitchen when I needed to serve an appetizer in a pinch. Now it's a staple when I entertain guests.

Beer Cheese Fondue

PREP/TOTAL TIME: 15 min.

- 1 loaf (1 pound, about 20 inches) French bread, cubed
- 1/4 cup chopped onion
- 1 teaspoon minced garlic
- 1 tablespoon butter
- 1 cup beer *or* nonalcoholic beer
- 4 cups (16 ounces) shredded cheddar cheese
- 1 tablespoon all-purpose flour
- 2 to 4 tablespoons half-and-half cream

- Place bread cubes in a single layer in an ungreased 15-in. x 10-in. x 1-in. baking pan. Bake at 450° for 5-7 minutes or until lightly crisp, stirring twice.

- Meanwhile, in a small saucepan, saute onion and garlic in butter until tender. Stir in beer. Bring to a boil; reduce heat to medium-low. Toss cheese and flour; stir into saucepan until melted. Stir in 2 tablespoons cream.

- Transfer to a small ceramic fondue pot or slow cooker; keep warm. Add additional cream if fondue thickens. Serve with toasted bread cubes.

Yield: about 3 cups.

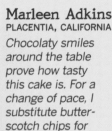

Marleen Adkins
PLACENTIA, CALIFORNIA
Chocolaty smiles around the table prove how tasty this cake is. For a change of pace, I substitute butterscotch chips for the chocolate.

Hot Fudge Cake

Hot Fudge Cake

PREP: 20 min. ■ **COOK:** 4 hours

1-3/4 cups packed brown sugar, *divided*
1 cup all-purpose flour
6 tablespoons baking cocoa, *divided*
2 teaspoons baking powder
1/2 teaspoon salt
1/2 cup milk
2 tablespoons butter, melted
1/2 teaspoon vanilla extract
1-1/2 cups semisweet chocolate chips
1-3/4 cups boiling water
Vanilla ice cream

■ In a bowl, combine 1 cup brown sugar, flour, 3 tablespoons cocoa, baking powder and salt. In another bowl, combine the milk, melted butter and vanilla extract; stir into dry ingredients just until combined. Spread evenly in a 3-qt. slow cooker coated with cooking spray. Sprinkle with chocolate chips.

■ In a bowl, combine the remaining brown sugar and cocoa; stir in boiling water. Pour over batter (do not stir). Cover and cook on high for 4 to 4-1/2 hours or until a toothpick inserted near the center of cake comes out clean. Serve warm with ice cream.

Yield: 6-8 servings.

Editor's Note: This recipe does not use eggs.

Ginger Tea Drink*

PREP: 15 min.
COOK: 2 hours

4 cups boiling water
15 individual green tea bags
4 cups white grape juice
1 to 2 tablespoons honey
1 tablespoon minced fresh gingerroot
Candied *or* crystallized ginger, optional

■ In a 3-qt. slow cooker, combine boiling water and tea bags. Cover and let stand for 10 minutes. Discard the tea bags. Stir in the remaining ingredients. Cover and cook on low for 2-3 hours or until heated through.

■ Strain if desired before serving warm. Garnish with candied ginger if desired.

Yield: 2 quarts.

*Nutrition Facts: 1 cup equals 82 calories, trace fat (trace saturated fat), 0 cholesterol, 8 mg sodium, 20 g carbohydrate, trace fiber, 1 g protein. **Diabetic Exchange:** 1 fruit.

Has the honey in your pantry crystallized? Place the jar in warm water and stir the honey until it is smooth. Or put the honey in a microwave-safe container and microwave on high, stirring every 30 seconds, until the crystals dissolve.

Alexandra Marcotty
CLEVELAND HEIGHTS, OHIO

Looking for something new and special to serve party guests? Let this soothing, warm green tea simmer in the slow cooker while you concentrate on preparing other dishes for the get-together. Everyone is sure to ask for this heartwarming recipe.

Cranberry Appetizer Meatballs

Jim Ulberg
ELK RAPIDS, MICHIGAN

A tangy, non-traditional sauce nicely coats these meatballs for a memorable party snack.

PREP: 25 min. ■ **BAKE:** 15 min.

2 eggs, beaten
1 cup dry bread crumbs
1/3 cup minced fresh parsley
1/3 cup ketchup
2 tablespoons finely chopped onion
2 tablespoons soy sauce
2 garlic cloves, minced
1/2 teaspoon salt
1/4 teaspoon pepper
2 pounds ground beef

CRANBERRY SAUCE:

1 can (16 ounces) whole-berry cranberry sauce
1 bottle (12 ounces) chili sauce
1 tablespoon brown sugar
1 tablespoon prepared mustard
1 tablespoon lemon juice
2 garlic cloves, minced

■ In a large bowl, combine the eggs, bread crumbs, parsley, ketchup, onion, soy sauce, garlic, salt and pepper. Crumble beef over mixture and mix well. Shape into 1-in. balls.

■ Place meatballs on a rack in a shallow baking pan. Bake, uncovered, at 400° for 15 minutes or until no longer pink. Transfer with a slotted spoon to a slow cooker.

■ Combine sauce ingredients in a saucepan; simmer for 10 minutes, stirring occasionally. Pour over meatballs. Serve warm.

Yield: about 7 dozen.

To make meatballs of equal size, lightly pat the meat mixture into a 1-inch-thick rectangle. Cut the rectangle into the same number of squares as the number of meatballs the recipe yields. Then gently roll each meat square into a ball.

Zesty Smoked Links

Jackie Boothman
LAGRANDE, OREGON

These flavorful sausages prepared in a slow cooker are great when entertaining. The men in my family can't resist these basic but satisfying snacks.

PREP: 5 min.
COOK: 35 min.

1 bottle (12 ounces) chili sauce
1 cup grape jelly
2 tablespoons lemon juice
2 packages (1 pound *each*) miniature smoked sausage links *and/or* hot dogs

■ In a large skillet, combine the chili sauce, jelly and lemon juice; cook over medium-low heat until jelly is melted. Stir in sausages. Reduce heat; cover and cook for 30 minutes or until heated through, stirring occasionally. Serve immediately or keep warm in a 1-1/2-qt. slow cooker.

Yield: about 32 servings.

Julie Barwick
MANSFIELD, OHIO

While growing up, I'd sit for hours reading cookbooks. I've carried that love of cooking with me through the years, and this appetizer has been a favorite.

Cheesy Pizza Fondue

Cheesy Pizza Fondue

PREP/TOTAL TIME: 30 min.

- 1/2 pound ground beef
- 1 medium onion, chopped
- 2 cans (15 ounces *each*) pizza sauce
- 1-1/2 teaspoons dried basil *or* dried oregano
- 1/4 teaspoon garlic powder
- 2-1/2 cups (10 ounces) shredded sharp cheddar cheese
- 1 cup (4 ounces) shredded part-skim mozzarella cheese

Breadsticks

- ■ In a heavy saucepan, cook beef and onion over medium heat until meat is no longer pink; drain. Stir in the pizza sauce, basil and garlic powder; mix well. Reduce heat to low. Add cheeses; stir until melted. Transfer to a slow cooker and keep warm over low heat. Serve with breadsticks.

Yield: about 5 cups.

Do your friends, family members or neighbors appreciate the ease of slow cooking? Give them a gift of Spiced Tea Mix. Just place a portion of the drink mix in a jar, write the preparation instructions on a tag and tie it onto the jar with a decorative ribbon.

Spiced Tea Mix

Deb McKinney
CEDAR FALLS, IOWA

For years, I've relied on this homespun mix to make a heartwarming punch. My parents always served steaming mugs of it at Thanksgiving. It was everyone's favorite...and still is today.

PREP: 10 min.
COOK: 4 hours

- 1 jar (21.1 ounces) orange breakfast drink mix
- 1 jar (6 ounces) sugar-free instant lemon ice tea mix
- 2/3 cup sweetened lemonade drink mix
- 2 teaspoons ground cinnamon
- 1 teaspoon ground cloves

ADDITIONAL INGREDIENTS FOR HOT SPICED PUNCH:
- 2 quarts apple juice *or* cider
- 1-1/2 cups cranberry juice
- 3 cinnamon sticks (3-1/2 inches)

- ■ In an airtight container, combine the first five ingredients. Store in a cool dry place for up to 6 months.

- ■ To prepare punch: In a 3-qt. slow cooker, combine the juices, 1/4 to 1/3 cup tea mix and cinnamon sticks. Cover and cook on low for 4 hours.

Yield: about 12 servings (6 ounces each).

Nella Parker
HERSEY, MICHIGAN

A handful of items and a few moments of prep work are all you'll need for this festive fondue. Not only does it take advantage of canned goods and other convenience items, but the slow cooker does most of the work for you and keeps things warm on the appetizer buffet.

Mexican Fondue

PREP: 15 min. ■ **COOK:** 1-1/2 hours

- 1 can (14-3/4 ounces) cream-style corn
- 1 can (14-1/2 ounces) diced tomatoes, drained
- 3 tablespoons chopped green chilies
- 1 teaspoon chili powder
- 1 package (16 ounces) process cheese (Velveeta), cubed

French bread cubes

■ In a 1-1/2-qt. slow cooker coated with cooking spray, combine the corn, tomatoes, green chilies and chili powder. Stir in cheese. Cover and cook on high for 1-1/2 hours, stirring every 30 minutes or until cheese is melted. Serve with bread cubes.

Yield: 4-1/2 cups.

Nutty Apples

Rosemary Franta
NEW ULM, MINNESOTA

I have handed out this recipe to more people than any other. It has a delicious nutty flavor. Mix it with vanilla or plain yogurt for a light snack or pour it over ice cream for a no-fuss dessert.

PREP: 5 min. ■ **COOK:** 3 hours

- 8 baking apples (about 3-1/2 pounds), peeled and sliced
- 1/2 to 1 cup chopped pecans
- 3/4 cup raisins
- 1/2 cup butter, melted
- 1/3 cup sugar
- 1/4 cup old-fashioned oats
- 2 tablespoons lemon juice
- 1/4 teaspoon ground cinnamon

Yogurt, optional

■ Combine all ingredients in a 1-1/2-qt. slow cooker. Cook on high heat for 3 hours until apples are tender, stirring occasionally. Serve warm with yogurt if desired.

Yield: 5 cups.

Hot Spiced Cranberry Punch

Geraldine Evans
HERMOSA, SOUTH DAKOTA

For a taste of the season, simmer up this sensational punch as fall changes over to winter. It's a great way to warm up.

PREP/TOTAL TIME: 25 min.

- 8 cups cranberry juice
- 2-2/3 cups water
- 1-1/3 cups sugar
- 16 whole cloves
- 1 teaspoon ground cinnamon
- 1/2 to 1 teaspoon ground nutmeg
- 2/3 cup orange juice
- 1/2 cup lemon juice

■ In a Dutch oven or large saucepan, combine the cranberry juice, water and sugar; bring to a boil over medium heat. Place the cloves on a double thickness of cheesecloth; bring up the corners of the cloth and tie with string to form a bag. Add the cinnamon, nutmeg and spice bag to the pan. Reduce heat and simmer, uncovered, for 20 minutes.

■ Discard the spice bag. Stir in the orange and lemon juices. Transfer to a slow cooker and keep warm.

Yield: 12 servings (3 quarts).

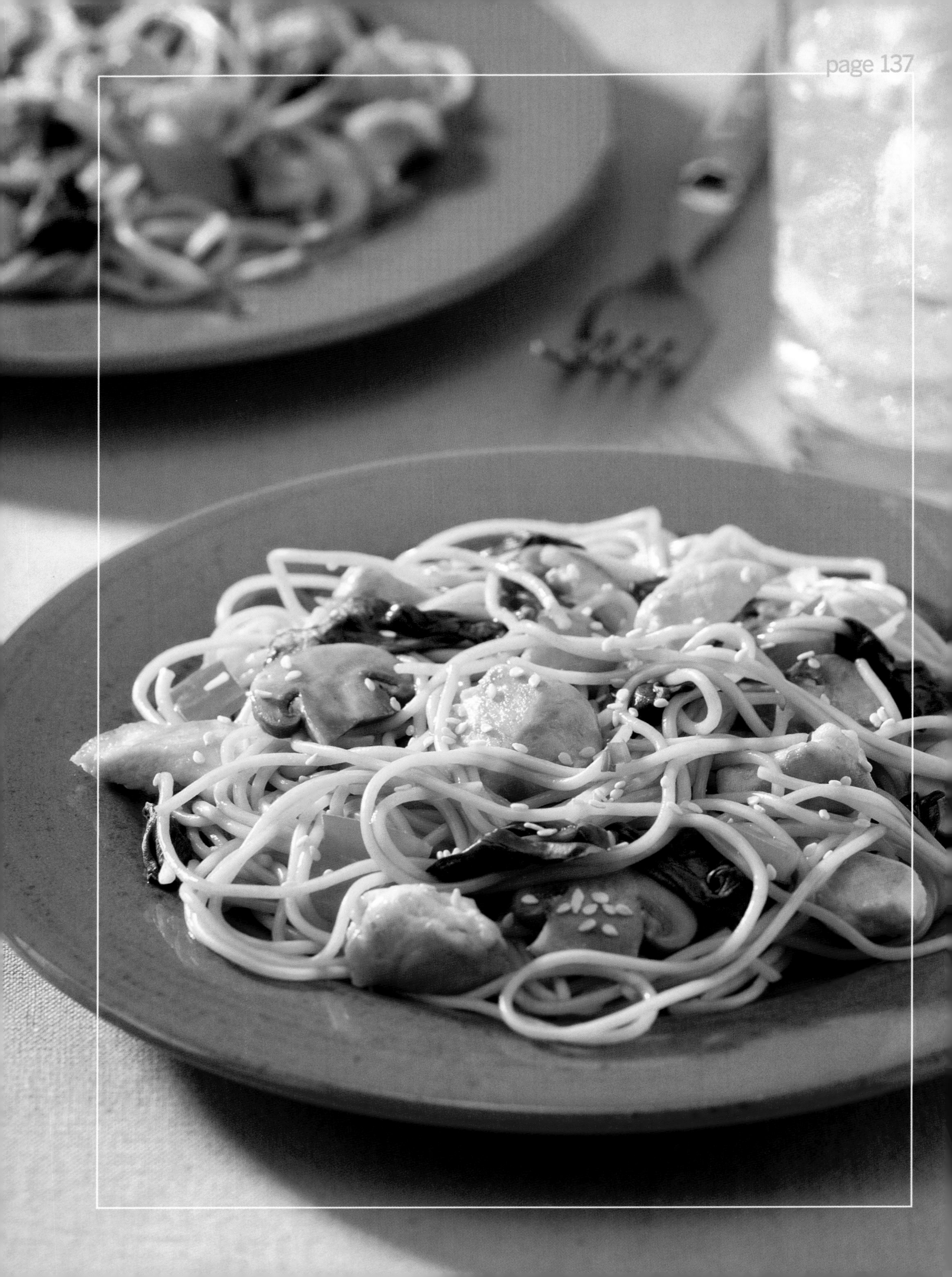

STOVETOP SUPPERS

Beef & Ground Beef

123

113

118

These quick and hearty one-pot beef and ground beef dishes, stews and skillet suppers mean less time in the kitchen and more time with your family. You might just find a new favorite, such as Barbecue Macaroni Beef on page 114.

Harvesttime Roast

- In a Dutch oven over medium heat, saute garlic in oil for 1 minute. Add the roast; brown on all sides.

- Combine vinegar, tomato juice, ketchup, sugar, salt and pepper; pour over roast. Cover and simmer for 2 hours. Add carrots and onions; cover and cook for 1 hour longer or until meat and vegetables are tender. Remove to a serving platter and keep warm.

- Skim fat from pan juices. Add enough water to the juices to measure 3 cups. Mix flour and cold water until smooth; stir into pan juices. Bring to a boil; cook and stir for 2 minutes or until thickened. Season with salt and pepper. Slice roast; serve with vegetables and gravy.

Yield: 14-16 servings.

Shirley Kidd
NEW LONDON, MINNESOTA

Fork-tender and robust, this pot roast is an old-fashioned, stick-to-your-ribs main dish. It's hard to believe how easy it is to make because it's so delicious.

Harvesttime Roast

PREP: 5 min. COOK: 3-1/4 hours

1 garlic clove, minced	2 teaspoons salt
2 tablespoons vegetable oil	1/4 teaspoon pepper
1 boneless beef rump roast (5 to 6 pounds)	8 medium carrots, cut into thirds
3 tablespoons cider vinegar	1/2 pound small whole onions
1/2 cup tomato juice	1/2 cup all-purpose flour
2 tablespoons ketchup	1 cup cold water
1 tablespoon sugar	Salt and pepper to taste

To determine how many people your boneless rump roast will feed, estimate that 1 pound of meat will yield 3 to 4 servings.

Jim Tusing
OKLAHOMA CITY,
OKLAHOMA

Back in the 1960s, we operated an inn in southern Indiana. Every week after the guests left, my wife and I would enjoy a leisurely dinner such as this.

Steak with Squash Medley

Steak with Squash Medley

PREP/TOTAL TIME: 30 min.

2 rib eye steaks (10 ounces *each*)

3 tablespoons olive oil, *divided*

1/2 cup chopped onion

1/2 cup chopped yellow summer squash

1/2 cup chopped zucchini

1/2 cup sliced okra, optional

1 garlic clove, minced

1/4 cup tomato sauce

3 tablespoons cider vinegar

1/2 teaspoon dried rosemary, crushed

1/2 teaspoon dried thyme

1/8 teaspoon pepper

■ In a skillet over medium heat, brown steaks on both sides in 2 tablespoons oil. Cook 8 minutes longer or until the meat reaches desired doneness (for medium-rare, a meat thermometer should read 145°; medium, 160°; well-done, 170°). Remove and keep warm.

■ Drain skillet. Saute onion, squash, zucchini, okra if desired and garlic in remaining oil for 6 minutes or until tender. Stir in the tomato sauce, vinegar, rosemary, thyme and pepper. Cook 3-4 minutes longer or until heated through. Serve over steaks.

Yield: 2 servings.

Okra, a summer vegetable, is a green ridged pod about 3 inches long. When buying it fresh, choose bright green, firm pods that are moist and without spots. If summer is over, check the freezer section of your grocery store.

Skillet Beef And Potatoes

PREP/TOTAL TIME: 25 min.

3 medium potatoes, halved and cut into 1/4-inch slices

1/3 cup water

1/2 teaspoon salt

1 pound boneless beef sirloin steak, cut into thin strips

2 teaspoons garlic pepper blend

1/2 cup chopped onion

3 tablespoons olive oil, *divided*

1-1/2 teaspoons minced fresh rosemary

■ Place potatoes, water and salt in a microwave-safe dish. Cover and microwave on high for 6-10 minutes or until tender; drain.

■ Season beef with pepper blend. In a large skillet, stir-fry beef and onion in 2 tablespoons oil for 5 minutes or until beef is no longer pink. Meanwhile, in another skillet, stir-fry potatoes in remaining oil for 5 minutes or until browned. Stir in beef mixture. Sprinkle with rosemary.

Yield: 4 servings.

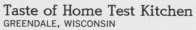

Taste of Home Test Kitchen
GREENDALE, WISCONSIN

Unpeeled potato slices, which are precooked in the microwave, speed up the cooking time for this one-dish meal. Convenient garlic pepper blend is a quick way to give the steaks bold flavor, and fresh rosemary adds a nice touch to the skillet supper.

Beef Stroganoff*

Rebecca Baird
SALT LAKE CITY, UTAH

You'd never guess this creamy, full-flavored Stroganoff is actually on the lighter side! It's very meaty and features a thick tomato sauce that lends it an impressive appearance.

PREP: 30 min. ■ **COOK:** 10 min.

1 pound beef tenderloin, cut into 1/4-inch strips	1/4 teaspoon salt
4 teaspoons canola oil, *divided*	1/8 teaspoon pepper
1/2 pound sliced fresh mushrooms	1 can (14 ounces) beef broth
1 large onion, thinly sliced	3 tablespoons apple juice
2 garlic cloves, minced	1 tablespoon tomato paste
1/3 cup all-purpose flour	1/2 teaspoon Worcestershire sauce
1/2 teaspoon dried basil	1/2 cup fat-free sour cream
	Dash ground nutmeg
	Hot cooked yolk-free noodles

■ In a large nonstick skillet or Dutch oven, brown beef in batches in 2 teaspoons oil over medium heat. Remove and keep warm. In the same skillet, saute the mushrooms, onion and garlic in remaining oil until tender.

■ Return meat to the pan. Sprinkle with flour, basil, salt and pepper; stir until blended. Add the broth, apple juice, tomato paste and Worcestershire sauce. Cook and stir over medium-low heat for 8-10 minutes or until meat is tender. Stir in sour cream and nutmeg until blended (do not boil). Serve over noodles.

Yield: 4 servings.

✱Nutrition Facts: 1 serving (1 cup beef mixture; calculated without noodles) equals 343 calories, 14 g fat (4 g saturated fat), 73 mg cholesterol, 583 mg sodium, 22 g carbohydrate, 2 g fiber, 30 g protein. **Diabetic Exchanges:** 3 lean meat, 1 vegetable, 1 fat, 1/2 starch, 1/2 fat-free milk.

What would Beef Stroganoff be without sour cream mixed into the sauce at the end? But watch out–if the heat is too high, the cream can curdle. To prevent this from happening, remove the skillet or Dutch oven from the heat first, then stir in the sour cream.

Barbecue Macaroni Beef

Rose Curten
MODOC, ILLINOIS

My husband's grandma made this meal for him when he was a little boy. Today, it's a regular around our house, which is fine with me, because it's easy to fix and so good. The veggies also add a nice crunch.

PREP/TOTAL TIME: 20 min.

1 pound ground beef

1 bottle (28 ounces) barbecue sauce

8 ounces elbow macaroni, cooked and drained

1 medium onion, chopped

1 medium green pepper, chopped

3 celery ribs, chopped

■ In a large skillet, cook beef over medium heat until no longer pink; drain. Stir in the barbecue sauce, macaroni, onion, green pepper and celery. Cook, uncovered, until heated through.

Yield: 4 servings.

Cantonese Beef

■ Drain the mandarin oranges, reserving juice; set oranges aside. In a Dutch oven, brown beef and onion in oil; drain. Stir in the water, soy sauce, ginger and reserved juice. Bring to a boil. Reduce heat; cover and simmer for 1 to 1-1/2 hours or until the beef is tender.

■ Add the celery, green pepper and water chestnuts. Cover and cook for 20-30 minutes or until vegetables are tender. Combine the cornstarch and cold water until smooth; stir into beef mixture. Bring to a boil; cook and stir for 2 minutes or until thickened. Stir in reserved oranges. Serve with rice.

Yield: 8 servings.

✳Nutrition Facts: 3/4 cup (calculated without rice) equals 233 calories, 10 g fat (3 g saturated fat), 71 mg cholesterol, 468 mg sodium, 13 g carbohydrate, 2 g fiber, 23 g protein. **Diabetic Exchanges:** 3 lean meat, 1 starch.

Michelle Harvey
NOBLESVILLE, INDIANA

This dish is always a big hit. I cook it in the oven instead of on the stovetop when I have time. For fun, pick up a package of fortune cookies from the ethnic aisle of the grocery store.

Cantonese Beef*

PREP: 20 min. ■ **COOK:** 1-1/2 hours

1 can (11 ounces) mandarin oranges	1/2 teaspoon ground ginger
2 pounds beef stew meat, cut into 1-inch cubes	4 celery ribs, sliced
1 small onion, sliced	1 small green pepper, julienned
1 tablespoon canola oil	1 can (8 ounces) sliced water chestnuts, drained
1-1/2 cups water	3 tablespoons cornstarch
1/3 cup reduced-sodium soy sauce	3 tablespoons cold water
	Hot cooked rice

One way to give this dish a restaurant-special look is to cut the celery ribs on the diagonal. With your knife perpendicular to the celery, turn the knife counterclockwise about 45°, then slice away.

Country Goulash Skillet

Lisa Neubert
SOUTH OGDEN, UTAH

I've found that basic recipes like this never go out of style. My homegrown onions, peppers and corn make every bite extra special.

PREP: 15 min.
COOK: 20 min.

- 1 pound ground beef
- 1 can (28 ounces) stewed tomatoes
- 1 can (10-3/4 ounces) condensed cream of mushroom soup, undiluted
- 2 cups fresh *or* frozen corn
- 1 medium green pepper, chopped
- 1 medium onion, chopped
- 1 tablespoon Worcestershire sauce
- 3 cups cooked elbow macaroni

- In a large skillet, cook beef over medium heat until no longer pink; drain. Stir in the tomatoes, soup, corn, green pepper, onion and the Worcestershire sauce. Bring to a boil. Reduce heat; cover and simmer for 20-25 minutes or until vegetables are tender. Stir in macaroni and heat through.

Yield: 6-8 servings.

Tracy Golder
BLOOMSBURG, PENNSYLVANIA

Speedy stovetop preparation and zippy flavor make this dish a dinnertime winner. Both children and adults give it a thumbs-up review.

Chili Mac Skillet

PREP/TOTAL TIME: 15 min.

- 1-1/4 cups uncooked elbow macaroni
- 1 pound ground beef
- 1 medium onion, chopped
- 1 medium green pepper, chopped
- 2 garlic cloves, minced
- 2 cans (14-1/2 ounces *each*) diced tomatoes, undrained
- 1 can (16 ounces) kidney beans, rinsed and drained
- 1 package (10 ounces) frozen corn, thawed
- 2 tablespoons chili powder
- 1/2 to 1 teaspoon salt
- 1/2 teaspoon ground cumin
- 1/2 cup shredded pepper Jack cheese

- Cook macaroni according to package directions.

- Meanwhile, in a large skillet, cook the beef, onion, green pepper and garlic over medium heat until meat is no longer pink and vegetables are tender; drain. Stir in the tomatoes, beans, corn, chili powder, salt and cumin. Bring to a boil. Reduce heat; cover and simmer for 15 minutes or until heated through.

- Drain the macaroni and add to skillet; stir to coat. Sprinkle with cheese.

Yield: 8 servings.

Tirzah Sandt
SAN DIEGO,
CALIFORNIA

This is the best shepherd's pie I've ever tasted. It's very quick to make, and I usually have most—if not all—of the ingredients ready at hand. Served with fresh fruit, it's a complete meal.

Skillet Shepherd's Pie

Skillet Shepherd's Pie

PREP/TOTAL TIME: 30 min.

1 pound ground beef	1/2 cup boiling water
1 cup chopped onion	1 tablespoon cornstarch
2 cups frozen corn, thawed	1/2 cup sour cream
2 cups frozen peas, thawed	3-1/2 cups mashed potatoes (prepared with milk and butter)
2 tablespoons ketchup	
1 tablespoon Worcestershire sauce	3/4 cup shredded cheddar cheese
2 teaspoons minced garlic	
1 teaspoon beef bouillon granules	

■ In a large skillet, cook beef and onion over medium heat until meat is no longer pink; drain. Stir in the corn, peas, ketchup, Worcestershire sauce and garlic. Reduce heat; cover and simmer for 5 minutes.

■ Meanwhile, in a small bowl, dissolve bouillon in boiling water. Combine cornstarch and sour cream until smooth; stir into beef mixture until blended. Add bouillon mixture. Bring to a boil. Reduce heat, cook and stir until thickened.

■ Spread mashed potatoes over the top; sprinkle with cheese. Cover and cook until potatoes are heated through and cheese is melted.

Yield: 6 servings.

Santa Fe Supper

Valerie Collier
CHARLESTON, SOUTH CAROLINA
This zesty skillet meal is a great way to bring a little variety to your dinnertime lineup. Green chilies spice up the rice, while salsa, zucchini, onion and cheddar cheese dress up the ground beef mixture.

PREP/TOTAL TIME: 30 min.

1 cup uncooked long grain rice

1 pound ground beef

2 small zucchini, cut into 1/4-inch slices

1 large onion, halved and sliced

1-1/2 cups chunky salsa, *divided*

1/4 teaspoon salt

1/4 teaspoon pepper

1 cup (4 ounces) shredded pepper Jack cheese

1 can (4 ounces) chopped green chilies, drained

1 cup (4 ounces) shredded cheddar cheese

■ Cook rice according to package directions. Meanwhile, in a large skillet, cook beef over medium heat until no longer pink; drain. Stir in the zucchini, onion, 1 cup salsa, salt and pepper; cook until vegetables are crisp-tender.

■ Add pepper Jack cheese and green chilies to the rice. Sprinkle the cheddar cheese over beef mixture; serve with the rice and remaining salsa.

Yield: 4 servings.

Olga Montecorboli
MANCHESTER, CONNECTICUT

Tender meat, lots of potatoes and carrots and a pleasant gravy make this meal-in-one satisfying and filling. Any leftover beef makes for excellent roast beef sandwiches the next day. Just be sure to slice the meat thin.

Home-Style Pot Roast*

PREP: 15 min. ■ COOK: 3-1/4 hours

1	beef eye round roast (2-1/2 pounds)	1/4	teaspoon pepper
6	tablespoons all-purpose flour, *divided*	16	small red potatoes (2 pounds), halved
1	tablespoon canola oil	4	medium carrots (3/4 pound), halved lengthwise and cut into 2-inch pieces
1-1/2	cups plus 1/3 cup water, *divided*	2	medium onions, quartered
1-1/2	cups dry red wine *or* reduced-sodium beef broth	1/2	teaspoon salt
2	teaspoons beef bouillon granules	1/2	teaspoon browning sauce, optional

■ Coat the roast with 2 tablespoons flour. In a large nonstick skillet, brown roast on all sides in oil over medium-high heat; drain. Add 1-1/2 cups water, wine or broth, bouillon and pepper. Bring to a boil. Reduce heat; cover and simmer for 2 hours.

■ Add the potatoes, carrots and onions; cover and simmer for 45 minutes or until meat and vegetables are tender. Remove meat and vegetables; keep warm.

■ Pour pan juices into a measuring cup; skim fat. In a saucepan, combine remaining flour and water until smooth. Stir in salt and browning sauce if desired. Gradually stir in 2 cups of pan juices. Bring to a boil; cook and stir for 2 minutes or until thickened. Serve with roast and vegetables.

Yield: 8 servings.

✱**Nutrition Facts:** 1 serving equals 341 calories, 9 g fat (3 g saturated fat), 82 mg cholesterol, 500 mg sodium, 32 g carbohydrate, 4 g fiber, 30 g protein. **Diabetic Exchanges:** 3 lean meat, 2 vegetable, 1-1/2 starch.

Browning sauce comes in a bottle and adds slight flavor and lovely color to any dish. Keep a bottle on hand for regular cooking needs.

Taco Supper In a Bowl

Linda Frisk
ROSEBURG, OREGON

This recipe is high on my family's list of favorites! It makes a hearty yet change-of-pace supper.

PREP: 20 min.
COOK: 70 min.

1-1/2	pounds ground beef
2	large onions, chopped
2	garlic cloves, minced
2	cans (28 ounces *each*) stewed tomatoes
4	cups water
1	can (28 ounces) kidney beans, drained
2	tablespoons canned chopped green chilies
1-1/2	teaspoons ground cumin
1	teaspoon dried oregano
1/2	teaspoon salt
1	package (15-1/2 ounces) tortilla chips
2	medium ripe avocados, peeled and chopped
8	cups shredded lettuce
4	cups shredded sharp cheddar cheese

Salsa

■ In a soup kettle or Dutch oven, cook the beef, onions and garlic over medium heat until meat is no longer pink; drain. Add the tomatoes, water, beans, chilies, cumin, oregano and salt. Bring to a boil. Reduce heat; simmer, uncovered, for 1 hour.

■ To serve, break tortilla chips into soup bowls; top with avocados and lettuce. Spoon soup over lettuce. Garnish with cheese and salsa.

Yield: 12-14 servings.

Mrs. Cort Smith
CORYDON, INDIANA
I have used this recipe for more than 30 years because it is delicious and so easy to make. You can mix it up in an electric skillet or on your stovetop in no time. Kids love the tangy tomato flavor and the crunch of the celery.

Busy Day Dinner

Busy Day Dinner

PREP: 15 min. ■ **BAKE:** 35 min.

1 pound ground beef, browned and drained

1 package (7 ounces) elbow macaroni, cooked and drained

1 cup finely chopped celery

1 cup chopped green pepper

1 cup finely chopped onion

2 cups thinly sliced carrots

1 can (28 ounces) tomatoes with liquid, chopped

1 can (8 ounces) tomato sauce

1 teaspoon salt

1/4 teaspoon pepper

1 teaspoon chili powder

■ Combine all ingredients in a saucepan. Bring to a boil over medium heat; reduce heat and simmer gently, covered, for 30 minutes. Add water if a thinner stew is desired.

Yield: 6 servings.

This dinner can be made even faster with a little preplanning and prep work. Next time you prepare it, just double (or triple) the amount of celery, pepper, onion and carrots and freeze. When you make the meal again, most of the prep work is done.

Sweet Potato Stew

Helen Vail
GLENSIDE, PENNSYLVANIA
Beef broth and herbs pair nicely with the sweet potatoes' subtle flavor in this hearty mainstay that's perfect for fall.

PREP: 5 min.
COOK: 35 min.

1 can (14-1/2 ounces) beef broth

3/4 pound lean ground beef

2 medium sweet potatoes, peeled and cut into 1/2-inch cubes

1 small onion, finely chopped

1/2 cup V8 juice

2 teaspoons golden raisins

1 garlic clove, minced

1/2 teaspoon dried thyme

Pinch cayenne pepper

■ In a large saucepan, bring the broth to a boil. Crumble beef into broth. Cover and cook for 3 minutes, stirring occasionally. Add the remaining ingredients; return to a boil. Reduce heat; simmer, uncovered, for 15 minutes or until meat is no longer pink and potatoes are tender.

Yield: 4 servings.

- In a Dutch oven or nonstick skillet, brown beef and onion in butter over medium heat. Add the mushrooms, wine or broth, 1/4 cup water, 2 tablespoons parsley, bay leaf, clove, salt and pepper. Bring to a boil. Reduce heat; cover and simmer for 1 hour or until beef is tender.

- Combine flour and remaining water until smooth; stir into beef mixture. Bring to a boil; cook and stir for 2 minutes or until thickened. Discard the bay leaf and clove. Stir in browning sauce if desired. Serve over noodles. Sprinkle with remaining parsley.

Yield: 2 servings.

*Nutrition Facts: 1-1/2 cups steak mixture equals 410 calories, 12 g fat (5 g saturated fat), 125 mg cholesterol, 403 mg sodium, 37 g carbohydrate, 2 g fiber, 33 g protein. **Diabetic Exchanges:** 3 lean meat, 2 starch, 1 vegetable, 1/2 fat.

Beef Burgundy over Noodles

Margaret Welder
MADRID, IOWA

I received this delightful recipe from my sister-in-law many years ago. The tender beef, mushrooms and flavorful sauce are delicious over noodles.

Beef Burgundy over Noodles*

PREP: 10 min. **COOK:** 1 hour 20 min.

1/2	pound boneless sirloin steak, cut into 1/4-inch strips
2	tablespoons diced onion
2	teaspoons butter
1-1/2	cups quartered fresh mushrooms
3/4	cup dry red wine *or* beef broth
1/4	cup plus 2 tablespoons water, *divided*

3	tablespoons minced fresh parsley, *divided*
1	bay leaf
1	whole clove
1/4	teaspoon salt
1/8	teaspoon pepper
1	tablespoon all-purpose flour
1/2	teaspoon browning sauce, optional
1-1/2	cups hot cooked egg noodles

Garlic mashed

potatoes taste just as great with Beef Burgundy as noodles. Just add one large garlic clove to the boiling potatoes as they cook. The garlic will turn soft and can be mashed with the potatoes.

Pepper Steak Stir-Fry*

Judy Brown
ROCKDALE, TEXAS

I make my own picante sauce for this beefy dish, but you can also use a store-bought brand if you'd like. My husband doesn't care for Asian food, but he likes this recipe with its hint of Mexican flair.

PREP: 20 min. ■ **COOK:** 10 min.

1 tablespoon cornstarch
1/2 cup water
1/2 cup picante sauce
2 tablespoons reduced-sodium soy sauce
2 teaspoons minced fresh gingerroot
1 pound boneless beef sirloin steak, cut into 1-inch strips

3 teaspoons canola oil, *divided*
1 medium green pepper, julienned
1 cup sliced fresh mushrooms
6 green onions, cut into 1/4-inch pieces
1 garlic clove, minced
Hot cooked rice, optional

■ In a bowl, combine the cornstarch and water until smooth. Stir in the picante sauce, soy sauce and ginger; set aside.

■ In a large nonstick skillet or wok, stir-fry meat in 2 teaspoons oil for 1-2 minutes. Remove meat with a slotted spoon and keep warm. Add the pepper, mushrooms, onions, garlic and remaining oil to the skillet. Stir-fry for 3 minutes.

■ Stir picante sauce mixture and add to skillet with meat. Bring to a boil; cook and stir for 1-2 minutes or until thickened and vegetables are crisp-tender. Serve with rice if desired.

Yield: 4 servings.

✱Nutrition Facts: One serving (1 cup stir-fry mixture, calculated without rice) equals 218 calories, 9 g fat (2 g saturated fat), 63 mg cholesterol, 614 mg sodium, 9 g carbohydrate, 1 g fiber, 23 g protein. **Diabetic Exchanges:** 3 lean meat, 1 vegetable.

For a refreshing spin to this stir-fry, add 1 to 2 tablespoons of freshly chopped cilantro at the very end, then top with chopped tomato. For flavorful rice, stir in shredded cheddar or Monterey Jack cheese.

Autumn Vegetable Beef Stew

PREP: 20 min.
COOK: 1-3/4 hours

1 teaspoon salt
1/4 teaspoon pepper
1/4 teaspoon paprika
1 pound round steak, cut into 1-inch cubes
1 tablespoon vegetable oil
1 tablespoon all-purpose flour
1-1/2 cups water
1 medium onion, chopped
1/2 cup tomato sauce
2 beef bouillon cubes
1/2 teaspoon caraway seeds
1 bay leaf
2 medium potatoes, peeled and cut into 1-inch cubes
2 medium turnips, peeled and cut into 1-inch cubes
2 medium carrots, cut into 1-inch slices

■ Combine salt, pepper and paprika; toss with beef. In a large saucepan over medium heat, brown beef in oil. Sprinkle with flour; stir well. Add water, onion, tomato sauce, bouillon, caraway seeds and bay leaf. Cover and simmer for 1 hour.

■ Add potatoes, turnips and carrots; cover and simmer 45 minutes or until the meat and vegetables are tender. Discard bay leaf.

Yield: 4 servings.

Martha Tonnies
FT. MITCHELL, KENTUCKY

This recipe was given to me by a dear friend many years ago. Served with homemade bread and a green salad, it makes an impressive meal. Even people who don't like turnips find they enjoy their distinctive flavor in this stick-to-your-ribs dinner.

Beef Skillet Supper

Stovetop Beef 'N' Shells*

Donna Roberts
SHUMWAY, ILLINOIS

I fix this 30-minute pasta supper when I'm pressed for time. It's as tasty as it is fast.

PREP/TOTAL TIME: 30 min.

- 4 ounces uncooked medium pasta shells
- 1 pound lean ground beef
- 1 medium onion, chopped
- 1 garlic clove, minced
- 1 can (15 ounces) crushed tomatoes
- 1 can (8 ounces) tomato sauce
- 1 teaspoon sugar
- 1/2 teaspoon salt
- 1/2 teaspoon pepper

- Cook pasta according to package directions. Meanwhile, in a large saucepan, cook the beef, onion and garlic over medium heat until meat is no longer pink; drain. Stir in the tomatoes, tomato sauce, sugar, salt and pepper. Bring to a boil. Reduce heat; simmer, uncovered, for 10-15 minutes. Drain pasta; stir into beef mixture and heat through.

Yield: 4 servings.

* **Nutrition Facts:** 1-1/4 cups equals 339 calories, 9 g fat (4 g saturated fat), 56 mg cholesterol, 772 mg sodium, 36 g carbohydrate, 4 g fiber, 29 g protein. **Diabetic Exchanges:** 3 lean meat, 3 vegetable, 1-1/2 starch.

Tabitha Allen
CYPRESS, TEXAS

Canned corn and tomato sauce put this cheesy pasta dinner on the fast track. Sometimes I make extra to ensure we have leftovers—they're great for lunch at work or school the next day.

Beef Skillet Supper

PREP/TOTAL TIME: 30 min.

- 1 package (8 ounces) medium egg noodles
- 1-1/2 pounds ground beef
- 1 medium onion, chopped
- 1 can (8 ounces) tomato sauce
- 1/2 cup water
- 1 can (11 ounces) Mexicorn, drained
- 1/2 teaspoon salt
- 1/4 teaspoon pepper
- 1 cup (4 ounces) shredded cheddar cheese

- Cook noodles according to package directions. Meanwhile, in a large skillet, cook beef and onion over medium heat until meat is no longer pink; drain. Add tomato sauce and water. Bring to a boil. Reduce heat; cover and cook for 8 minutes.

- Drain the noodles; add to beef mixture. Stir in the corn, salt and pepper. Sprinkle with cheese; cover and cook until heated through and cheese is melted.

Yield: 8-10 servings.

Tina
Schaubroeck
GREENCASTLE,
PENNSYLVANIA

Served with tortilla chips or taco shells, this easy and attractive one-dish meal is fun for everyone. And because it looks so festive, I put the skillet right on the table when we have company.

Taco Skillet

Taco Skillet

PREP/TOTAL TIME: 30 min.

- 1 pound ground beef
- 1 medium onion, chopped
- 1 can (16 ounces) refried beans
- 1 can (4 ounces) chopped green chilies
- 1/4 to 1/2 teaspoon garlic powder
- 3/4 cup sour cream
- 1/2 to 1 teaspoon ground cumin
- 1/2 to 1 teaspoon chili powder
- 1 medium tomato, seeded and chopped
- 1 can (2-1/4 ounces) sliced ripe olives, drained
- 1 small green pepper, chopped
- 1 cup (4 ounces) shredded Mexican cheese blend

Tortilla chips *or* taco shells, shredded lettuce and salsa

■ In a large skillet, cook beef and onion over medium heat until meat is no longer pink; drain. Stir in the beans, chilies and garlic powder; cook until heated through.

■ Combine the sour cream, cumin and chili powder; spread over beef mixture. Top with tomato, olives and green pepper. Sprinkle with cheese. Serve with tortilla chips or taco shells, lettuce and salsa.

Yield: 4-6 servings.

Almost Stuffed Peppers

Jan Roat
RED LODGE, MONTANA

For a quick way to enjoy an old favorite, I stir up stuffed green pepper ingredients in a skillet. The easy one-pan meal is requested so often I even make it when I'm not in a hurry.

PREP/TOTAL TIME: 25 min.

- 1 pound ground beef
- 2 cups water
- 1 can (14-1/2 ounces) diced tomatoes, undrained
- 1 large green pepper, cut into 1/4-inch slices
- 1 medium onion, thinly sliced
- 1-1/2 teaspoons salt
- 1/2 teaspoon Italian seasoning
- 1/2 teaspoon pepper
- 1-1/2 cups uncooked instant rice

■ In a large skillet, cook beef over medium heat until no longer pink; drain. Remove; set aside and keep warm.

■ In the same skillet, combine the water, tomatoes, green pepper, onion and seasonings; bring to a boil. Reduce heat; simmer, uncovered, until vegetables are tender. Stir in rice; cover and remove from the heat. Let stand for 5 minutes. Stir in beef; return to the heat and cook until heated through.

Yield: 4-6 servings.

Poultry

136

133

140

There's a meal to satisfy every member of your family in this collection of quick-cooking recipes that use versatile chicken or turkey. Best of all, the one-dish wonders cook up in a flash on the stovetop, so there's always time for a home-cooked dinner.

Stir-Fried Chicken and Rice Noodles

Kim Pettipas
OROMOCTO, NEW BRUNSWICK

This is a great dish to showcase rice noodles. Don't let the ingredients fool you. The stir-fry is very simple yet still features a mouth-watering Asian flair.

Stir-Fried Chicken And Rice Noodles

PREP: 25 min. **COOK:** 20 min.

2-1/2 teaspoons cornstarch

1/3 cup reduced-sodium soy sauce

1/4 cup white wine *or* reduced-sodium chicken broth

2 teaspoons sesame oil

1-1/2 pounds boneless skinless chicken breasts, cut into 1-inch cubes

1/2 cup reduced-sodium chicken broth

2 tablespoons sugar

1 tablespoon Worcestershire sauce

3/4 teaspoon chili powder

3 ounces uncooked Asian rice noodles

4 teaspoons canola oil, *divided*

3 cups fresh broccoli florets

2/3 cup chopped green onions

3 garlic cloves, minced

2 teaspoons minced fresh gingerroot

1/4 cup unsalted dry roasted peanuts

■ Combine the cornstarch, soy sauce, wine or broth and sesame oil until smooth. Pour 1/4 cup marinade into a large resealable plastic bag; add the chicken. Seal bag and turn to coat; refrigerate for 20 minutes. Add the broth, sugar, Worcestershire sauce and chili powder to remaining marinade; set aside.

■ Cook rice noodles according to package directions. Meanwhile, drain and discard marinade from chicken. In a large non-stick skillet or wok, stir-fry chicken in 2 teaspoons canola oil until juices run clear; remove and keep warm.

■ Stir-fry broccoli in remaining canola oil for 5 minutes. Add the onions, garlic and ginger; stir-fry 3-5 minutes longer or until broccoli is tender. Return chicken to the pan. Stir reserved broth mixture and stir into pan. Bring to a boil; cook and stir for 2 minutes or until thickened. Drain noodles; toss with chicken mixture. Garnish with peanuts.

Yield: 6 servings.

Rice noodles,

also called rice vermicelli, come in various shapes and thicknesses. Look for them in the ethnic aisle of your local supermarket.

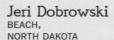

Jeri Dobrowski
BEACH,
NORTH DAKOTA

This meal has been a favorite since I discovered it in our church cookbook. I often make it with ground beef.

Spanish Rice Dinner

Spanish Rice Dinner

PREP: 5 min. **COOK:** 50 min.

1 pound ground turkey	1 tablespoon sugar
1-1/2 cups cooked long grain rice	1 teaspoon salt
1 can (14-1/2 ounces) stewed tomatoes	1 teaspoon Worcestershire sauce
1 can (14-1/2 ounces) cut green beans, drained	1/2 teaspoon ground mustard
1 tablespoon dried minced onion	1/4 teaspoon garlic powder
	1/8 teaspoon pepper
	1/8 teaspoon hot pepper sauce

■ In a large skillet, cook turkey over medium heat until no longer pink; drain. Stir in the remaining ingredients. Bring to a boil. Reduce heat; cover and simmer for 5-10 minutes or until heated through.

Yield: 4 servings.

Removing the bone from chicken breasts isn't difficult but is easy and economical. Insert a small boning knife between the ribs and breast meat. Pressing the knife along the bones, cut to remove the meat.

Basil Chicken Medley*

Susan Jansen
SMYRNA, GEORGIA

Everyone who's tried this dinner raves about it. I came up with the quick, colorful one-dish supper in my own kitchen. It's easy to put together when time is scarce.

PREP/TOTAL TIME: 25 min.

1 tablespoon olive oil
3 garlic cloves, minced
2 whole boneless, skinless chicken breasts (about 1-1/4 pounds), cut into 1-inch chunks
1 medium zucchini, cut into chunks
2 medium tomatoes, cut into chunks
1 tablespoon dried basil
2 tablespoons vinegar
1/4 teaspoon pepper
Cooked rice *or* pasta

■ Heat oil in a skillet; saute the garlic. Add chicken and cook until no longer pink; remove and keep warm. Combine zucchini, tomato, basil, vinegar and pepper; toss to coat vegetables well.

■ Add to skillet and stir-fry 3-5 minutes. Return chicken to skillet and heat through. Serve immediately over rice or pasta.

Yield: 4 servings.

*****Nutrition Facts:** 1/4 recipe (calculated without rice or pasta) equals 205 calories, 7 g fat (0 saturated fat), 73 mg cholesterol, 70 mg sodium, 8 g carbohydrate, 0 fiber, 28 g protein. **Diabetic Exchanges:** 3 lean meat, 1 vegetable.

Couscous Chicken Supper

Curried Chicken*

Karen McLaughlin
HAMILTON, ONTARIO

I season chicken and apples with curry powder and cinnamon for a great-tasting and quick meal.

PREP/TOTAL TIME: 30 min.

1/2 pound boneless skinless chicken breasts, cubed

2 medium tart apples, peeled and cubed

1 medium onion, chopped

2 garlic cloves, minced

3 tablespoons water

1 to 2 teaspoons curry powder

1/4 teaspoon ground cinnamon

1 tablespoon all-purpose flour

1 cup (8 ounces) reduced-fat sour cream

4 cups hot cooked rice

■ In a nonstick skillet, cook chicken until juices run clear; drain, remove and keep warm. In the same skillet, cook apples, onion and garlic in water until tender. Add cooked chicken and sprinkle with curry and cinnamon. Heat through.

■ Combine the flour and sour cream until smooth; stir into chicken mixture. Bring to a gentle boil; cook and stir for 2 minutes. Serve over rice.

Yield: 4 servings.

✱ **Nutrition Facts:** 1 serving (1 cup chicken mixture with 1 cup rice) equals 414 calories, 6 g fat (4 g saturated fat), 53 mg cholesterol, 80 mg sodium, 65 g carbohydrate, 4 g fiber, 22 g protein. **Diabetic Exchanges:** 3 starch, 2 lean meat, 1 fruit.

Taste of Home Test Kitchen
GREENDALE, WISCONSIN

Our home economists set out to prepare a meal-in-one featuring couscous...and they succeeded with this recipe that includes tender strips of chicken.

Couscous Chicken Supper

PREP: 10 min. **COOK:** 30 min.

1 medium yellow summer squash, chopped

1 medium sweet red pepper, chopped

1 medium green pepper, chopped

1 teaspoon dried rosemary, crushed

1/2 teaspoon salt

1/4 teaspoon pepper

4 tablespoons olive oil, *divided*

1 pound boneless skinless chicken breast halves

2 garlic cloves, minced

1-1/3 cups chicken broth

1 tablespoon dried minced onion

1 cup uncooked couscous

■ Place the squash and peppers in an ungreased 15-in. x 10-in. x 1-in. baking pan. Sprinkle with rosemary, salt and pepper. Drizzle with 2 tablespoons oil; gently stir to coat. Broil 4 in. from the heat for 10-15 minutes or until tender, stirring every 5 minutes.

■ Meanwhile, in a large skillet, cook chicken and garlic in remaining oil until chicken juices run clear; remove and keep warm. Add broth and onion to the skillet; bring to a boil. Stir in couscous. Cover and remove from the heat; let stand for 5 minutes. Fluff with a fork. Cut chicken into strips. Serve with couscous and vegetables.

Yield: 4 servings.

Chicken Chop Suey*

Arleen Gibson
SIMCOE, ONTARIO

This is my favorite stir-fry! It's versatile because you can change the meat or veggies to suit your taste...or make it according to what's in the refrigerator.

PREP: 15 min. + marinating **COOK:** 25 min.

3 tablespoons reduced-sodium soy sauce

1 tablespoon dark brown sugar

1 pound boneless skinless chicken breast, thinly sliced

3 medium onion, sliced

2 garlic cloves, minced

2 tablespoons canola oil

6 celery ribs with leaves, cut into 1/2-inch pieces

1/2 pound small fresh mushrooms

1 large green pepper, cut into 1-inch pieces

4-1/2 teaspoons cornstarch

1 cup water

2 cups canned bean sprouts

1 teaspoon salt

1/4 teaspoon pepper

Hot cooked rice, optional

- In a large resealable plastic bag, combine soy sauce and brown sugar; add the chicken. Seal bag and turn to coat; refrigerate for 20-30 minutes.

- In a large nonstick skillet or wok, stir-fry onions and garlic in oil until tender. Remove with a slotted spoon to a bowl. Add celery, mushrooms and green pepper to skillet; stir-fry 3-4 minutes or until crisp-tender. Remove with slotted spoon to bowl. Add chicken and marinade to skillet; stir-fry for 5-7 minutes or until chicken is no longer pink. Return the vegetables to skillet.

- Combine cornstarch and water until smooth; stir into chicken mixture. Bring to a boil; cook and stir for 2 minutes or until thickened. Add the bean sprouts, salt and pepper; cook and stir for 2 minutes or until heated through. Serve over rice if desired.

Yeild: 6 servings.

✱Nutrition Facts: 1 serving (1-1/2 cups chop suey, calculated without rice) equals 308 calories, 9 g fat (1 g saturated fat), 66 mg cholesterol, 822 mg sodium, 26 g carbohydrate, 5 g fiber, 32 g protein. **Diabetic Exchanges:** 4 vegetable, 3 lean meat, 1/2 starch.

Cranberry Turkey Stir-Fry*

PREP/TOTAL TIME: 25 min.

2 garlic cloves, minced

1 tablespoon canola oil

2 cups julienned carrots

2 cups uncooked turkey breast strips

2 cups julienned zucchini

1 cup canned bean sprouts

1 can (8 ounces) jellied cranberry sauce

1/3 cup apple juice

1/4 cup reduced-sodium soy sauce

1/4 cup cider vinegar

1 tablespoon cornstarch

1/4 cup cold water

4 cups hot cooked rice

- In a nonstick skillet or wok, stir-fry garlic in oil for 30 seconds. Add carrots; stir-fry for 2 minutes. Add turkey, zucchini and bean sprouts; stir-fry 3 minutes longer. Combine the cranberry sauce, apple juice, soy sauce and vinegar; stir into skillet. Bring to a boil.

- Combine cornstarch and cold water until smooth; gradually stir into skillet. Bring to a boil; cook and stir for 1-2 minutes or until thickened and bubbly and turkey juices run clear. Serve over rice.

Yield: 4 servings.

✱Nutrition Facts: 1 serving (1 cup turkey mixture with 1 cup rice) equals 530 calories, 10 g fat (2 g saturated fat), 55 mg cholesterol, 696 mg sodium, 83 g carbohydrate, 5 g fiber, 26 g protein. **Diabetic Exchanges:** 3 starch, 2 lean meat, 2 fruit, 1 vegetable.

Gwendolyn Roux
OCEANSIDE, CALIFORNIA

Soy sauce and cranberry sauce team up to give this pretty turkey stir-fry a sweet and savory flavor in just under half an hour. Try it the next time the kitchen clock is ticking and you need a quick fix. You could even serve it with pasta instead of the rice.

Orange-Ginger Chicken and Veggies

Nancy Johnson
TURAH, MONTANA

My colorful stir-fry is chock-full of tasty veggies, tender chicken chunks and a light, zippy sauce. Tangy oranges and crunchy cashews add extra pizzazz.

- Grate orange peel, reserving 1-1/2 teaspoons. Peel and section orange; set the orange sections aside. In a small bowl, combine cornstarch and ginger. Stir in the broth, soy sauce, chili sauce, hot pepper sauce and reserved grated orange peel until blended; set aside.

- In a large nonstick skillet or wok, stir-fry chicken and garlic in oil for 2-3 minutes or until lightly browned. Add the broccoli, peppers and carrot; stir-fry for 5 minutes or until the vegetables are crisp-tender. Stir broth mixture and add to the pan. Bring to a boil; cook and stir for 2 minutes or until thickened. Remove from the heat; stir in cashews and reserved oranges. Serve with rice.

Yield: 4 servings.

✳Nutrition Facts: 1 serving (1-1/2 cups stir-fry mixture with 3/4 cup rice) equals 467 calories, 12 g fat (2 g saturated fat), 67 mg cholesterol, 853 mg sodium, 56 g carbohydrate, 4 g fiber, 34 g protein. **Diabetic Exchanges:** 3 starch, 3 lean meat, 2 vegetable, 1/2 fat.

Orange-Ginger Chicken And Veggies*

PREP: 20 min. **COOK:** 20 min.

1 medium navel orange	2 garlic cloves, minced
4 teaspoons cornstarch	1 tablespoon vegetable oil
1/4 teaspoon ground ginger *or* 1 teaspoon grated fresh gingerroot	2 cups fresh broccoli florets
	1 medium sweet red pepper, julienned
1 cup reduced-sodium chicken broth	1 medium sweet yellow pepper, julienned
2 tablespoons reduced-sodium soy sauce	1/2 cup shredded carrot
2 tablespoons chili sauce	1/3 cup unsalted cashews
1/4 teaspoon hot pepper sauce	3 cups hot cooked rice
1 pound boneless skinless chicken breasts, cut into 1-inch pieces	

Cooking with

a wok is easy, but read the manufacturer's cleaning directions. Many suggest not using detergent for cleaning.

Lori Lockrey
WEST HILL, ONTARIO

I adore this easy meal-for-one. It's super simple and fast to make, plus it tastes great. Simply increase the recipe for a larger yield.

Apricot Chicken and Snow Peas

Pronto Pita Pizzas*

Debbi Smith
CROSSETT, ARKANSAS

Pita bread makes a terrific crust for my quick-to-fix individual pizzas. With the healthy ground turkey breast mixture on top, the pizzas can also be cut into quarters and served as appetizers.

PREP/TOTAL TIME: 25 min.

- 1 pound ground turkey breast
- 1 cup sliced fresh mushrooms
- 1/2 cup chopped onion
- 2 garlic cloves, minced
- 1 can (8 ounces) no-salt-added tomato sauce
- 1/2 teaspoon fennel seed
- 1/4 teaspoon dried oregano
- 4 pita breads, warmed
- 1/2 cup shredded part-skim mozzarella cheese

- In a skillet, brown the turkey; drain. Add mushrooms, onion and garlic; cook until tender. Stir in tomato sauce, fennel seed and oregano. Cover and simmer for 10-15 minutes or until heated through.

- Spread 1 cup of meat mixture onto each pita; sprinkle with the cheese. Serve immediately.

Yield: 4 servings.

＊Nutrition Facts: 1 serving equals 358 calories, 5 g fat (0 saturated fat), 63 mg cholesterol, 187 mg sodium, 41 g carbohydrate, 0 fiber, 38 g protein. **Diabetic Exchanges:** 4 very lean meat, 2 starch, 2 vegetable.

Apricot Chicken and Snow Peas

PREP/TOTAL TIME: 20 min.

- 1 small garlic clove, minced
- 1/2 teaspoon vegetable oil
- 1/4 pound boneless skinless chicken breast, cut into thin strips
- 1/2 cup fresh snow peas
- 3 tablespoons apricot preserves

- 2 tablespoons water
- 3/4 teaspoon sesame oil
- 1/2 teaspoon sesame seeds, toasted
- 1/2 teaspoon soy sauce
- 1/8 teaspoon Dijon mustard
- 1/8 teaspoon ground ginger

Hot cooked rice *or* pasta

- In a skillet, saute garlic in oil for 30 seconds. Add chicken; stir fry for 3 minutes. Stir in the snow peas, preserves, water, sesame oil, sesame seeds, soy sauce, mustard and ginger. Bring to a boil. Reduce heat; simmer, uncovered, for 5-7 minutes or until chicken juices run clear and vegetables are tender. Serve over rice.

Yield: 1 serving.

If the strings on snow peas bother you, just snap the end of the peel without removing it, then remove the string. Repeat with the other side of the pea pod.

Patricia Kile
NOKOMIS, FLORIDA

Dinners that come together on the stove are perfect when the kitchen clock is ticking. This chunky sauce, made easy with a can of tomato soup and leftover turkey, couldn't be more satisfying. It's a hearty change of pace from typical pasta dishes that feature a meat-based sauce.

Italian Turkey Skillet

PREP/TOTAL TIME: 20 min.

- 1 package (1 pound) linguine
- 3/4 cup sliced fresh mushrooms
- 1/2 cup chopped onion
- 1/2 cup chopped celery
- 1/2 cup chopped green pepper
- 2 tablespoons vegetable oil
- 2 cups cubed cooked turkey
- 1 can (14-1/2 ounces) diced tomatoes, drained
- 1 can (10-3/4 ounces) condensed tomato soup, undiluted
- 1 tablespoon Italian seasoning
- 1 tablespoon minced fresh parsley
- 1/4 teaspoon pepper
- 1/8 teaspoon salt
- 1 cup (4 ounces) shredded cheddar cheese, optional

■ Cook linguine according to package directions. Meanwhile, in a large skillet, saute the mushrooms, onion, celery and green pepper in oil over medium heat until tender. Stir in the turkey, tomatoes, soup, Italian seasoning, parsley, pepper and salt.

■ Drain linguine; stir into turkey mixture. Sprinkle with cheese if desired. Cover and cook for 3-4 minutes or until mixture is heated through and cheese is melted.

Yield: 8 servings.

Tomato Artichoke Chicken

Taste of Home Test Kitchen
GREENDALE, WISCONSIN

Preparing the pizza sauce early in the week sure saves time when it's used in this fast dinner. Tender chicken, roasted red peppers and marinated artichoke hearts put a flavorful spin on the red sauce that's served over fettuccine.

PREP/TOTAL TIME: 30 min.

- 1 jar (12 ounces) marinated quartered artichoke hearts
- 4 boneless skinless chicken breast halves
- 1 tablespoon olive oil
- 2 cups pizza sauce
- 1 jar (7 ounces) roasted sweet red peppers, drained and cut into strips
- Hot cooked fettuccine

■ Drain artichoke hearts, reserving 1/4 cup marinade. In a large skillet, brown chicken in oil. Add the pizza sauce, artichokes, red peppers and reserved artichoke marinade.

■ Bring to a boil. Reduce heat; cover and simmer for 8-10 minutes or until chicken juices run clear. Serve over fettuccine.

Yield: 4 servings.

Pecan Chicken A La King

Roxanne Kamberaj
WEST SENECA, NEW YORK

This is my favorite mainstay meal because it's fast, easy and very tasty. When I want to serve more than just my husband and me, I simply double or triple the recipe.

PREP/TOTAL TIME: 25 min.

- 1/4 cup chopped celery
- 2 tablespoons butter
- 1 teaspoon chicken bouillon granules
- 2 tablespoons all-purpose flour
- 1/8 to 1/4 teaspoon salt
- 1/8 teaspoon poultry seasoning
- 1-1/4 cups milk
- 1 cup cubed cooked chicken
- 1 tablespoon diced pimientos
- 1 teaspoon lemon juice
- 1/4 cup chopped pecans, *divided*
- Hot cooked rice

■ In a saucepan, saute celery in butter until tender. Add bouillon, stirring until dissolved. Stir in the flour, salt and poultry seasoning until blended. Gradually add milk, stirring until smooth. Bring to a boil over medium heat; cook and stir for 2 minutes or until thickened.

■ Add the chicken, pimientos, lemon juice and half of the pecans; cook until heated through. Serve over rice. Sprinkle with remaining pecans.

Yield: 2 servings.

Skillet Chicken And Vegetables

Sarah McClanahan
MANSFIELD, OHIO

Here's a meal I turn to often because my family loves the flavor! Various vegetables can be substituted for the peppers, mushrooms and zucchini, depending on what you have on hand.

PREP/TOTAL TIME: 20 min.

- 1 pound boneless skinless chicken breasts, cut into 1/2-inch strips
- 1 teaspoon garlic powder
- 1 teaspoon dried basil
- 1 tablespoon vegetable oil
- 1/2 pound fresh mushrooms, sliced
- 1 large zucchini, julienned
- 1 medium onion, chopped
- 1 medium green pepper, chopped
- 1 medium sweet red pepper, chopped
- 1 package (7 ounces) spaghetti
- 3/4 cup mayonnaise *or* salad dressing
- 4 tablespoons grated Parmesan cheese, *divided*

- In a large skillet, saute chicken, garlic and basil in oil for 4 minutes. Add mushrooms, zucchini, onion and peppers. Cook and stir for 5-7 minutes or until chicken juices run clear and the vegetables are crisp-tender. Meanwhile, cook spaghetti according to package directions.

- Stir mayonnaise and 3 tablespoons Parmesan cheese into chicken mixture. Drain spaghetti; top with chicken mixture. Sprinkle with remaining cheese.

Yield: 4 servings.

Theresa Stewart
NEW OXFORD, PENNSYLVANIA

Who would have thought that a chicken and stuffing dinner could be so easy. Canned peaches, brown sugar and a hint of allspice make it a lovely dinner when time is tight.

Chicken with Peach Stuffing

Chicken with Peach Stuffing

PREP/TOTAL TIME: 25 min.

- 1 can (15-1/4 ounces) sliced peaches
- 4 boneless skinless chicken breast halves (4 ounces *each*)
- 2 tablespoons vegetable oil
- 2 tablespoons butter
- 1 tablespoon brown sugar
- 1 tablespoon cider vinegar
- 1/8 teaspoon ground allspice
- 1 package (6 ounces) chicken stuffing mix

- Drain peaches, reserving syrup. Set aside eight peach slices for garnish; dice the remaining peaches. Add enough water to the syrup to measure 1 cup. Set peaches and syrup aside.

- In a large skillet, brown chicken in oil. Add the butter, brown sugar, vinegar, allspice and reserved syrup. Bring to a boil. Reduce heat; cover and simmer for 5 minutes. Add the dry stuffing mix and diced peaches. Remove from the heat; cover and let stand for 5 minutes. Serve with the peach slices.

Yield: 4 servings.

Chicken tenders are great to use instead of chicken breasts. They already come in convenient portion sizes, saving you time.

Sesame Chicken and Noodles

- Cook spaghetti according to package directions; drain. Toss with 1 tablespoon sesame oil; set aside. In a small bowl, combine the cornstarch, broth, soy sauce and vinegar until smooth; set aside.

- In a large skillet, stir-fry chicken, mushrooms, red pepper and garlic in remaining oil for 5-8 minutes or until the chicken is browned. Stir broth mixture and add to skillet. Bring to a boil; cook and stir for 2 minutes or until thickened and chicken is no longer pink. Add spinach; cover and cook for 2-3 minutes or until the spinach wilts. Add onions, sherry, ginger and spaghetti; cook for 2-3 minutes or until heated through. Sprinkle with sesame seeds.

Yield: 6 servings.

Taste of Home Test Kitchen
GREENDALE, WISCONSIN

Using sliced mushrooms and packaged cleaned baby spinach beats the clock when preparing this tasty dinner. Sprinkled on top, toasted sesame seeds add easy flavor and flair.

Sesame Chicken and Noodles

PREP/TOTAL TIME: 30 min.

8 ounces thin spaghetti

2 tablespoons sesame oil, *divided*

1 tablespoon cornstarch

1 cup chicken broth

1/4 cup soy sauce

1 tablespoon rice vinegar

1-1/2 pounds boneless skinless chicken breasts, cut into 1/2-inch cubes

1 package (8 ounces) sliced baby portobello mushrooms

1 medium sweet red pepper, chopped

1 teaspoon minced garlic

1 package (9 ounces) fresh baby spinach

1/2 cup chopped green onions

3 tablespoons sherry

2 teaspoons minced fresh gingerroot

1 tablespoon sesame seeds, toasted

When shopping

for baby portobello mushrooms, keep in mind that they are also known as "crimini" mushrooms.

Carol Roane
SARASOTA, FLORIDA

My family loves Asian food, so I came up with this quick-and-easy recipe to use up leftover chicken. You can also try it with any cooked pork or beef you might have on hand.

Szechuan Chicken Noodle Toss

Szechuan Chicken Noodle Toss*

PREP/TOTAL TIME: 20 min.

4 quarts water	2 garlic cloves, minced
6 ounces uncooked thin spaghetti	1/8 teaspoon crushed red pepper flakes
1 package (16 ounces) frozen stir-fry vegetable blend	1 tablespoon canola oil
1 tablespoon reduced-fat stick margarine	1/3 cup stir-fry sauce
1 pound boneless skinless chicken breasts, cut into 2-inch strips	3 green onions, chopped

■ In a Dutch oven, bring water to a boil. Add spaghetti; cook for 4 minutes. Add vegetables; cook 3-4 minutes longer or until spaghetti and vegetables are tender. Drain. Toss with margarine; set aside and keep warm.

■ In a nonstick skillet, stir-fry the chicken, garlic and red pepper flakes in oil until chicken is no longer pink. Add stir-fry sauce; heat through. Add onions and spaghetti mixture; toss to coat.

Yield: 4 servings.

Editor's Note: This recipe was tested with Parkay Light stick margarine.

✱Nutrition Facts: 1 serving (1-1/2 cups) equals 394 calories, 7 g fat (1 g saturated fat), 66 mg cholesterol, 831 mg sodium, 44 g carbohydrate, 5 g fiber, 35 g protein. **Diabetic Exchanges:** 3 lean meat, 2-1/2 starch, 1 vegetable.

Veggie Turkey Roll-Ups

PREP/TOTAL TIME: 30 min.

1/4 cup *each* julienned sweet red pepper, carrot, yellow summer squash and zucchini

4 uncooked turkey breast slices

2 tablespoons all-purpose flour

1/8 teaspoon paprika

1 tablespoon vegetable oil

1/4 cup water

3 tablespoons lemon juice

4-1/2 teaspoons white wine *or* additional water

2-1/4 teaspoons chicken bouillon granules

1/2 teaspoon dried basil

■ Combine the red pepper, carrot, summer squash and zucchini; spoon down the center of each turkey slice. Roll up and secure ends with toothpicks.

■ In a shallow bowl, combine flour and paprika; roll turkey in mixture until coated. In a skillet over medium heat, cook roll-ups in oil until golden brown.

■ In a bowl, combine the remaining ingredients; pour over the turkey. Cover and simmer for 3 minutes or until meat juices run clear and the vegetables are crisp-tender. Discard toothpicks from roll-ups; serve with the pan drippings.

Yield: 2 servings.

Gertrude Peischl
ALLENTOWN, PENNSYLVANIA

A medley of red pepper, carrot and yellow summer squash makes a colorful filling for these unique turkey breast roll-ups. Simmered in a light wine sauce, the no-stress bundles look like you fussed. Serve them with seasoned rice to quickly round out your menu.

- In a large resealable bag, combine the first seven ingredients. Cut chicken pieces into thirds; place in the bag and shake to coat.

- In a large nonstick skillet, melt butter. Brown chicken on all sides; remove and keep warm. Add onion, celery and mushrooms; cook until tender.

- Return chicken to the pan; add broth. Cover and simmer for 15 minutes. In a small bowl, whisk flour and milk until smooth. Add to pan; cook and stir for 2 minutes or until thickened and bubbly. Serve over noodles.

Yield: 4 servings.

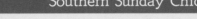

Southern Sunday Chicken

Maurine Seavers
OLIVER SPRINGS, TENNESSEE
Served over hot cooked noodles, this saucy chicken dinner is a lip-smacking supper. It's one dish I turn to often...whenever I'm racing against the clock or not.

Southern Sunday Chicken

PREP/TOTAL TIME: 30 min.

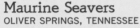

1/2 cup all-purpose flour	1/4 cup chopped onion
1 teaspoon salt, optional	1/4 cup chopped celery
1 teaspoon paprika	3 fresh mushrooms, sliced
1/4 to 1/2 teaspoon dried thyme	1 can (14-1/2 ounces) chicken broth
1/4 teaspoon celery seed	3 tablespoons all-purpose flour
1/4 teaspoon pepper	1 cup evaporated milk
1/8 teaspoon garlic powder	Hot cooked noodles
4 boneless skinless chicken breast halves (1 pound)	
2 teaspoons butter	

If using frozen chicken breasts to make a quick supper, defrosting them in cold water is fast and easy. Keep the chicken in a leakproof bag, such as a resealable plastic bag. Submerge in cold tap water and change every 30 minutes until the chicken is thawed. For every pound of chicken, allow 30 minutes of thawing time.

June Formanek
BELLE PLAINE, IOWA

As everyone who raises a garden knows, zucchini grows overnight! I never let anything go to waste, so I try adding this hearty squash to every recipe I can. Out of all the recipes I've tried, this is my family's favorite.

Turkey Vegetable Skillet

Turkey Vegetable Skillet*

PREP/TOTAL TIME: 20 min.

1 pound ground turkey breast	1/4 pound zucchini, diced
1 small onion, chopped	1/4 cup chopped dill pickle
1 garlic clove, minced	1 teaspoon dried basil
1 teaspoon vegetable oil	1/2 teaspoon pepper
1 pound fresh tomatoes, chopped	

■ In a large skillet, cook the turkey, onion and garlic over medium heat in oil until turkey is no longer pink; drain if necessary.

■ Add the remaining ingredients to the skillet. Reduce heat; simmer, uncovered, for 5-10 minutes or until heated through.

Yield: 6 servings.

✱ Nutrition Facts: 1 serving equals 135 calories, 3 g fat (0 saturated fat), 47 mg cholesterol, 104 mg sodium, 5 g carbohydrate, 0 fiber, 21 g protein. **Diabetic Exchanges:** 3 lean meat, 1 vegetable.

Twisty Pasta Primavera With Chicken

Elaine Anderson
NEW GALILEE, PENNSYLVANIA

I frequently turn to this tasty meal-in-one dish to feed my family when time is short. For a fun variation, try multicolored spirals.

PREP/TOTAL TIME: 25 min.

2	quarts water
2-1/2	cups uncooked spiral pasta
2	cups chopped broccoli
3/4	cup sliced carrots
1	cup (4 ounces) shredded part-skim mozzarella cheese
2	cups cubed cooked chicken breast
1	can (10-3/4 ounces) reduced-fat reduced-sodium condensed cream of broccoli soup, undiluted
1	cup fat-free milk
1/4	cup grated Parmesan cheese
1/8	teaspoon garlic powder
1/8	teaspoon pepper

■ In a large saucepan, bring the water to a boil. Add pasta; cook for 4 minutes. Add broccoli and carrots; cook 4-5 minutes longer or until pasta is tender. Drain and place in a bowl. Add mozzarella cheese and chicken.

■ In another saucepan, combine remaining ingredients. Bring to a boil; cook and stir until blended. Pour over pasta mixture and toss gently. Serve immediately.

Yield: 6 servings.

Pork & Ham

144

152

154

Recipes sizzling with the bold flavor of pork and ham are hands down some of the tastiest around. Whether you're having dinner guests or putting together a quick family meal, these dishes, with delicious center-stage ingredients such as pork chops, kielbasa or prosciutto, are sure to please.

Oktoberfest Roast Pork

- Sort beans and rinse with cold water. Place beans in a Dutch oven; add water to cover by 2 in. Bring to a boil; boil for 2 minutes. Remove from the heat; cover and let stand for 1 to 4 hours or until beans are softened. Meanwhile, combine the sage, salt if desired, pepper, allspice and cayenne; rub over roast.

- In a Dutch oven, brown roast in oil on all sides; drain. Drain and rinse beans, discarding liquid; stir parsley into beans. Place beans around roast. Stir in broth.

- Cover and simmer for 2 hours or until a meat thermometer reads 150°.

- Place apples and onions on top of beans; cover and simmer for 30 minutes longer or until a meat thermometer reads 160°. Let stand 10-15 minutes before slicing.

Yield: 12 servings.

Carol Stevens
BASYE, VIRGINIA

Slices of this sage-rubbed pork roast cooked and served with beans and apple slices are a popular choice at many venues. It's a sensational recipe that I try to prepare every autumn.

*Nutrition Facts: 1/4 recipe (prepared with reduced-sodium chicken broth; calculated w/o added salt) equals 378 calories, 16 g fat (0 saturated fat), 67 mg cholesterol, 59 mg sodium, 27 g carbohydrate, 10 fiber, 32 g protein. **Diabetic Exchanges:** 3-1/2 lean meat, 1-1/2 starch, 1 fat, 1/2 fruit.

Oktoberfest Roast Pork*

PREP: 10 min. + standing **COOK:** 2-1/2 hours + standing

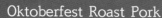

- 1 pound dried navy beans
- 1 teaspoon rubbed sage
- 1 teaspoon salt, optional
- 1/2 teaspoon pepper
- 1/8 teaspoon ground allspice

Dash cayenne pepper

- 1 boneless pork sirloin roast (3 pounds)
- 2 tablespoons canola oil
- 2 tablespoons chopped fresh parsley
- 1/2 cup chicken broth
- 2 medium tart apples, cut into wedges
- 1 large red onion, cut into wedges

Kathleen Romaniuk
CHOMEDEY, QUEBEC
Orange juice and grated orange peel lend a touch of citrus to my colorful pork-and-vegetable medley.

Orange Pork Stir-Fry

Orange Pork Stir-Fry

PREP/TOTAL TIME: 30 min.

- 2 teaspoons cornstarch
- 1/3 cup orange juice
- 1/3 cup teriyaki sauce
- 1 tablespoon Dijon mustard
- 2 teaspoons minced fresh gingerroot
- 1 teaspoon minced garlic
- 1/2 to 1 teaspoon grated orange peel

- 1 pound pork tenderloin, cut into 2-inch strips
- 1 tablespoon vegetable oil
- 1 package (16 ounces) frozen Japanese-style stir-fry vegetables

Hot cooked rice

■ Combine cornstarch and orange juice until smooth. Stir in the teriyaki sauce, Dijon mustard, ginger, garlic and orange peel; set aside.

■ In a large skillet or wok, stir-fry pork in oil until no longer pink; remove and keep warm. Add vegetables to the pan; cook and stir for 2-3 minutes or until tender. Stir orange juice mixture; add to pan. Bring to a boil; cook and stir for 1-2 minutes or until thickened. Stir in pork. Serve with rice.

Yield: 4 servings.

A great way to remove the papery peel from gingerroot is to scrape it off using the tip of a metal teaspoon. Just apply pressure and scrape the length of the root.

One-Pot Ham Dinner

Jody Cohen
MACKEYVILLE, PENNSYLVANIA
Looking for a speedy skillet supper? I add potatoes and green beans to ham steak before topping it all off with a comforting mushroom sauce.

PREP: 15 min.
COOK: 45 min.

- 1 fully cooked ham slice (1 to 1-1/2 pounds)
- 4 medium potatoes, peeled and sliced
- 1/4 to 1/2 teaspoon salt
- 1/4 teaspoon pepper
- 2 cups frozen cut green beans
- 1 medium onion, thinly sliced
- 1 can (10-3/4 ounces) condensed cream of mushroom soup, undiluted
- 1/2 cup water

■ In a large skillet over medium heat, brown the ham slice. Arrange potatoes over ham; sprinkle with salt and pepper. Top with beans and onion. Combine soup and water; pour over all. Cook for 2 minutes. Reduce heat; cover and simmer for 45-50 minutes or until potatoes are tender.

Yield: 4 servings.

Bavarian Bratwurst Supper

- In a skillet over medium heat, cook bacon until crisp. Remove with a slotted spoon to paper towels. In the drippings, cook and stir bratwurst for 10-12 minutes. Remove with a slotted spoon. Drain, reserving 2 tablespoons of drippings. Saute apple and onion in drippings until lightly browned.

- Add vinegar, brown sugar, mustard, salt, pepper and bratwurst. Cover and cook for 12 minutes or until bratwurst are no longer pink and a meat thermometer reads 160°, stirring frequently.

- Add potatoes and sauerkraut; cook and stir 12 minutes longer or until heated through. Sprinkle with bacon.

Yield: 4 servings.

Jill Cook
PERRY, IOWA

My family enjoys the flavors of hot German potato salad and bratwurst, especially during the cooler months. This original skillet recipe is truly a one-dish meal.

Bavarian Bratwurst Supper

PREP: 10 min. COOK: 50 min.

4 bacon strips, diced	1 tablespoon spicy brown mustard
4 fresh bratwurst, cut into 2-inch pieces	1/2 teaspoon salt
1 medium tart apple, chopped	1/8 teaspoon pepper
1 medium onion, chopped	4 cups frozen cubed hash brown potatoes, thawed
1/2 cup cider vinegar	1 can (14 ounces) Bavarian-style sauerkraut, drained
3 tablespoons brown sugar	

To prevent the meat from coming out of the casing as you slice the bratwurst, freeze them for about 5 minutes. They'll be much easier to cut.

Greta Igl
MENOMONEE FALLS, WISCONSIN

This meal-in-one dish is a different and delicious way to use pierogies. Best of all, I can set it on the table in less than half an hour. Now, that's fast! The apples have a sweet and sour flavor from sugar and vinegar, which is the perfect accompaniment to juicy pork chops.

Pork Chops and Pierogies

PREP/TOTAL TIME: 25 min.

8 frozen potato and onion pierogies
2 bone-in pork loin chops (3/4 inch thick)
1/2 teaspoon salt, *divided*
1/2 teaspoon pepper, *divided*
4 tablespoons butter, *divided*
1 medium sweet onion, sliced and separated into rings
1 medium Golden Delicious apple, cut into 1/4-inch slices
1/4 cup sugar
1/4 cup cider vinegar

■ Cook pierogies according to package directions. Meanwhile, sprinkle pork chops with 1/4 teaspoon salt and 1/4 teaspoon pepper. In a large skillet, cook chops in 2 tablespoons butter over medium heat until juices run clear; remove and keep warm.

■ In the same skillet, saute onion in remaining butter for 3 minutes. Add apple; saute until almost tender. Stir in the sugar, vinegar, and remaining salt and pepper. Bring to a boil. Reduce heat; simmer, uncovered, for 5 minutes. Drain pierogies. Add pork chops and pierogies to skillet; stir to coat.

Yield: 2 servings.

Zucchini and Kielbasa

Norma Fick
DECATUR, ILLINOIS

For a skillet supper that's hearty enough to satisfy even the biggest appetites in your house, consider my one-pan specialty. I like to serve it with warm corn bread muffins.

PREP/TOTAL TIME: 25 min.

2 small zucchini, cut into 1/8-inch slices
1 small onion, chopped
1/2 cup chopped green pepper
2 tablespoons olive oil
1 pound smoked kielbasa *or* Polish sausage, halved lengthwise and cut into 1/2-inch slices
1 can (15-1/4 ounces) whole kernel corn, drained
1 can (8 ounces) tomato sauce
2 teaspoons Italian seasoning
1/8 teaspoon crushed red pepper flakes

■ In a large skillet, saute the zucchini, onion and green pepper in oil until crisp-tender. Stir in the remaining ingredients; cook until heated through.

Yield: 6 servings.

Sausage Pepper Skillet

Margaret Kruse
VIRGINIA BEACH, VIRGINIA

I try to cook regularly, but it's difficult with our busy schedules. To save time, I freeze chopped onions and peppers to use in stovetop entrees like this one.

PREP/TOTAL TIME: 20 min.

1 large green pepper, julienned
1 large sweet red pepper, julienned
1 cup sliced red onion
1 garlic clove, minced
1/2 cup fat-free Italian salad dressing, *divided*
1 pound kielbasa, sliced
1 tablespoon reduced-sodium soy sauce

■ In a nonstick skillet or wok, stir-fry the peppers, onion and garlic in 1/4 cup salad dressing for 5 minutes. Add sausage and remaining dressing; stir-fry for 8-10 minutes or until sausage is heated through and vegetables are crisp-tender. Sprinkle with soy sauce.

Yield: 4 servings.

Potato Pork Skillet

- In a large skillet, brown pork in butter on both sides over medium heat. Remove and keep warm. Set aside 1/4 cup of broth. In the same skillet, add the potatoes, mustard, Worcestershire sauce, salt, pepper and remaining broth. Bring to a boil. Reduce heat; cover and simmer for 15-17 minutes or until the potatoes are tender.

- Stir in the mushrooms, onions and pork. Cover and simmer for 5 minutes longer or until meat is no longer pink.

- In a small bowl, combine the flour and reserved broth until smooth. Gradually stir into pork mixture. Bring to a boil; cook and stir for 2 minutes or until thickened.

Yield: 4 servings.

*Nutrition Facts: 1 serving (1-1/4 cups) equals 266 calories, 12 g fat (5 g saturated fat), 91 mg cholesterol, 828 mg sodium, 12 g carbohydrate, 4 g fiber, 28 g protein. **Diabetic Exchanges:** 3 lean meat, 1 starch, 1/2 fat.

Barbara Carlson
BROOKLYN PARK, MINNESOTA
I always receive wonderful comments from everyone who tries this easy meal. The red potatoes and fresh mushrooms balance out the pork nicely.

Potato Pork Skillet*

PREP: 10 min. **COOK:** 30 min.

- 1 pound pork tenderloin, cut into 1/4-inch slices
- 2 tablespoons butter
- 1 can (14-1/2 ounces) chicken broth, *divided*
- 8 small red potatoes, quartered
- 1 tablespoon Dijon mustard

- 2 teaspoons Worcestershire sauce
- 1/4 teaspoon salt
- 1/8 teaspoon pepper
- 1 cup sliced fresh mushrooms
- 1/2 cup sliced green onions
- 2 tablespoons all-purpose flour

Red potatoes make a perfect choice in this skillet specialty because they tend to hold their shape better than many other varieties.

Christine Ward
AUSTIN, TEXAS

I'm always looking for dinners that I can put together quickly. I re-created a favorite pasta dish from an Italian restaurant by using grocery store convenience products. Add crusty bread or a salad and supper is ready!

Creamy Prosciutto Pasta

Creamy Prosciutto Pasta

PREP/TOTAL TIME: 10 min.

1 package (9 ounces) refrigerated fettuccine *or* refrigerated linguine	1 package (10 ounces) fresh baby spinach
1/2 pound sliced fresh mushrooms	1 jar (17 ounces) Alfredo sauce
1 small onion, chopped	1/3 pound thinly sliced prosciutto, chopped
1 tablespoon butter	

■ Cook pasta according to package directions. Meanwhile, in a large saucepan, saute the mushrooms and onion in butter until tender. Add spinach. Bring to a boil. Reduce heat; cook just until spinach is wilted.

■ Stir in Alfredo sauce and prosciutto; cook for 1-2 minutes or until heated through. Drain pasta; add to sauce and toss to coat.

Yield: 4 servings.

Leftover ham sitting in the refrigerator? Tired of ham sandwiches? Use it up in this pasta dish. Cooked ham is a simple replacement for the prosciotto that the recipe calls for.

Garlic Potatoes And Ham

Melody Williamson
BLAINE, WASHINGTON

Not even my finicky little eaters can resist the veggies in this main dish when they're seasoned with soup mix. I sometimes replace the ham with cooked kielbasa or smoked sausage.

PREP: 10 min.
COOK: 35 min.

8 small red potatoes, cut into wedges

1 tablespoon vegetable oil

1 package (16 ounces) frozen cut broccoli, partially thawed

1 cup cubed fully cooked ham

1 envelope herb with garlic soup mix

■ In a large skillet, cook potatoes in oil over medium-high heat for 10 minutes or until lightly browned. Stir in broccoli, ham and dry soup mix. Reduce heat; cover and cook for 25 minutes or until potatoes are tender.

Yield: 4 servings.

Editor's Note: This recipe was tested with Lipton Recipe Secrets Savory Herb with Garlic soup mix.

Jean Lawson
DOVER, DELAWARE

Here's a stovetop dish that pairs tender chops with hearty carrots and potatoes. The satisfying supper, smothered in a golden sauce seasoned with thyme, is truly spirit-warming.

Country Pork Chop Dinner

Country Pork Chop Dinner*

PREP: 15 min. **COOK:** 25 min.

4 pork loin chops (1/2 inch thick)
1 small onion, chopped
1 tablespoon canola oil
4 medium red potatoes, cubed
1 cup thinly sliced carrots
1 jar (4-1/2 ounces) sliced mushrooms *or* 1 cup sliced fresh mushrooms
1 can (10-3/4 ounces) condensed cream of celery soup, undiluted
1/2 cup water
1 teaspoon salt, optional
1/2 to 1 teaspoon dried thyme

■ In a large skillet, cook pork and onion in oil until meat is browned; drain. Top with potatoes, carrots and mushrooms. Combine the soup, water, salt if desired and thyme; pour over vegetables. Bring to a boil; reduce heat. Cover; simmer for 25-30 minutes or until vegetables are tender.

Yield: 4 servings.

*✱**Nutrition Facts:** 1 serving (prepared with reduced-fat soup and fresh mushrooms and without salt) equals 282 calories, 10 g fat (5 g saturated fat), 55 mg cholesterol, 362 mg sodium, 25 g carbohydrate, 5 g fiber, 23 g protein. **Diabetic Exchanges:** 3 lean meat, 1-1/2 starch, 1 vegetable.*

When buying cabbage, look for those with crisp-looking leaves that are firmly packed. The head should feel heavy for its size.

Boiled Ham Dinner*

PREP: 10 min. **COOK:** 25 min.

1 chunk unsliced deli ham (1 pound)
6 medium carrots, halved lengthwise and cut into thirds
4 medium red potatoes, quartered
2 medium onions, cut into wedges
1 bay leaf
1 teaspoon dried thyme
1 teaspoon peppercorns
1 garlic clove, halved
1/2 teaspoon whole allspice
1/2 medium head cabbage, cut into wedges

■ Place the ham, carrots, potatoes and onions in a Dutch oven. Place the bay leaf, thyme, peppercorns, garlic and allspice on a double thickness of cheesecloth; bring up corners of cloth and tie with kitchen string. Add to pot.

■ Add water just to cover the ham and vegetables; bring to a boil. Reduce heat; cover and simmer for 10 minutes. Add cabbage; cover and simmer 15-20 minutes longer or until the vegetables are tender. Discard spice bag and cooking liquid.

Yield: 4 servings.

*✱**Nutrition Facts:** 1 serving equals 312 calories, 4 g fat (1 g saturated fat), 58 mg cholesterol, 1,300 mg sodium, 46 g carbohydrate, 8 g fiber, 26 g protein. **Diabetic Exchanges:** 4 vegetable, 3 lean meat, 1 starch.*

Janet Singleton
BELLEVUE, OHIO

I made this all-in-one dish often for my children when they were growing up. Now, I fix it when baby-sitting my grandchildren...they love it, too. It's easy to cook in one pot on the stovetop. Everyone enjoys the savory flavor.

Rebecca Baird
SALT LAKE CITY, UTAH

Here's a pasta dish that's quick to fix for everyday but is also perfect as a meal to share with someone special. I like to use different kinds of cheese, such as Parmesan or Romano, to sprinkle on top.

Asparagus Ham Fettuccine

Asparagus Ham Fettuccine

PREP/TOTAL TIME: 20 min.

4 ounces uncooked fettuccine	2 tablespoons minced fresh sage *or* 2 teaspoons rubbed sage
1/2 pound fresh asparagus, trimmed and cut into 1/2-inch pieces	1/4 teaspoon pepper
1/2 pound fully cooked ham, julienned	2 tablespoons olive oil
1/4 cup chopped walnuts	1 cup (4 ounces) shredded cheddar cheese
1 green onion, chopped	

■ Cook the fettuccine according to package directions. Meanwhile, in a large saucepan, bring 4 cups water to a boil; add asparagus. Cover and cook for 3 minutes. Drain and immediately place in ice water; drain and set aside.

■ In a skillet, saute the ham, walnuts, onion, sage and pepper in oil until onion is tender. Add asparagus; cook and stir for 1 minute. Drain fettuccine; toss with ham mixture. Sprinkle with cheese.

Yield: 2 servings.

Country Skillet

Terri Adrian
LAKE CITY, FLORIDA

When I need a fast meal-in-one, I rely on a filling combination of kielbasa, rice and veggies. It's a hearty, stick-to-your-ribs supper that's perfect on chilly nights.

PREP/TOTAL TIME: 30 min.

1 pound fully cooked kielbasa *or* Polish sausage, cut into 1/2-inch slices

1/2 cup chopped onion

1 tablespoon vegetable oil

1-1/2 cups water

1 can (10-3/4 ounces) condensed cream of celery soup, undiluted

1/2 teaspoon dried basil

1/4 teaspoon dried thyme

1/4 teaspoon pepper

1 package (10 ounces) frozen cut broccoli, thawed

1 jar (4-1/2 ounces) sliced mushrooms, drained

1 cup uncooked instant rice

1/4 cup grated Parmesan cheese

■ In a large skillet, cook sausage and onion in oil until onion is tender; drain. Combine the water, soup, basil, thyme and pepper; add to skillet.

■ Stir in broccoli and mushrooms. Bring to a boil. Stir in rice. Cover and remove from the heat. Let stand for 5-7 minutes or until rice is tender. Sprinkle with Parmesan cheese.

Yield: 4-6 servings.

Mexican Pork Stew

- In a Dutch oven or large soup kettle over medium-high heat, brown meat on all sides in 1 teaspoon oil; drain. Remove meat and keep warm.

- In the same pan, saute the onion, celery, jalapeno and garlic in remaining oil until tender. Stir in the water, chili powder, brown sugar, cumin, salt and pepper. Return meat to pan. Bring to a boil. Reduce the heat; cover and simmer for 30 minutes.

- Stir in the tomato paste, beans and tomatoes. Return to a boil. Reduce heat; cover and simmer 20 minutes longer or until meat is tender and beans are heated through. Sprinkle with cilantro.

Yield: 5 servings.

Editor's Note: When cutting hot peppers, disposable gloves are recommended. Avoid touching your face.

✱Nutrition Facts: 1-1/2 cups equals 377 calories, 9 g fat (2 g saturated fat), 50 mg cholesterol, 991 mg sodium, 43 g carbohydrate, 13 g fiber, 32 g protein. **Diabetic Exchanges:** 4 lean meat, 2 starch, 1 vegetable.

Mickey Terry
DEL VALLE, TEXAS

I heat up cold nights by serving this thick and zesty stew with corn bread. I also like to spoon leftovers into corn tortillas with a little salsa and sour cream for a satisfying snack.

Mexican Pork Stew*

PREP: 10 min. **COOK:** 55 min.

1 pound boneless pork loin roast, cut into 3/4-inch cubes	1 teaspoon ground cumin
3 teaspoons olive oil, *divided*	1/2 teaspoon salt
1 large onion, chopped	1/4 teaspoon pepper
2 celery ribs, chopped	1 can (6 ounces) tomato paste
1 jalapeno pepper, seeded and chopped	1 can (16 ounces) kidney beans, rinsed and drained
1 garlic clove, minced	1 can (15 ounces) pinto beans, rinsed and drained
1-1/2 cups water	1 can (14-1/2 ounces) diced tomatoes, undrained
1 tablespoon chili powder	2 teaspoons minced fresh cilantro
2 teaspoons brown sugar	

Add some flour tortillas to the menu when serving this Southwestern stew. Not only do they add a unique flair to weekday dinners, but they help cool taste buds when food gets too spicy.

Kathy Stephan
WEST SENECA, NEW YORK

I enjoy experimenting with herbs and spices to cut down on salt and sugar. Parsley, basil and oregano season this tasty pasta dinner perfectly without increasing the sodium. It's just as tasty with cooked and cubed chicken or turkey.

Pretty Penne Ham Skillet

PREP/TOTAL TIME: 30 min.

- 1 package (16 ounces) penne pasta
- 3 cups cubed fully cooked ham
- 1 large sweet red pepper, diced
- 1 medium onion, chopped
- 1/4 cup minced fresh parsley
- 2 garlic cloves, minced
- 1-1/2 teaspoons minced fresh basil *or* 1/2 teaspoon dried basil
- 1-1/2 teaspoons minced fresh oregano *or* 1/2 teaspoon dried oregano
- 1/4 cup olive oil
- 3 tablespoons butter
- 1 can (14-1/2 ounces) chicken broth
- 1 tablespoon lemon juice
- 1/2 cup shredded Parmesan cheese

■ Cook pasta according to package directions. Meanwhile, in a large skillet, saute the ham, red pepper, onion, parsley, garlic, basil and oregano in oil and butter for 4-6 minutes or until ham is browned and vegetables are tender.

■ Stir in broth and lemon juice. Bring to a boil. Reduce heat; simmer, uncovered, for 10-15 minutes or until liquid is reduced by half. Drain pasta; stir into ham mixture. Sprinkle with Parmesan cheese.

Yield: *6 servings.*

Sausage Squash Skillet

Marcia Albury
SEVERNA PARK, MARYLAND

I always thought yellow squash was bland until I prepared it this way. Combined with Italian sausage and a little onion, it makes a delicious, well-rounded main dish in no time.

PREP/TOTAL TIME: 15 min.

- 1/2 pound bulk Italian sausage
- 1/4 cup chopped onion
- 1 medium yellow summer squash, halved and sliced
- 1/4 cup chicken broth
- Salt and pepper to taste
- 1/3 cup seasoned salad croutons

■ In a large skillet over medium heat, cook sausage and onion until the meat is no longer pink; drain. Add the squash; cook for 3-4 minutes or until tender. Stir in the broth, salt and pepper. Cook 2 minutes longer or until heated through. Sprinkle with croutons.

Yield: *2 servings.*

Apple Ham Steak

Mildred Sherrer
FORT WORTH, TEXAS

My easy ham steak dinner with apples is always a winner.

PREP/TOTAL TIME: 30 min.

- 1-1/2 cups instant rice
- 1 medium onion, chopped
- 2 celery ribs, chopped
- 6 tablespoons butter, *divided*
- 2-1/2 cups apple juice, *divided*
- 1 teaspoon salt
- 1 pound boneless fully cooked ham steak, cut into fourths
- 2 medium tart apples, peeled and sliced
- 2 tablespoons brown sugar
- 1/4 teaspoon ground cinnamon
- 2 tablespoons raisins
- 1 tablespoon cornstarch

■ In a saucepan, saute rice, onion and celery in 2 tablespoons butter until tender. Add 1-1/2 cups apple juice and salt. Bring to a boil. Cover and remove from the heat; let stand for 5 minutes.

■ In a skillet, cook ham in remaining butter until lightly browned. Remove and keep warm. Stir in the next three ingredients until apples are almost tender, about 5 minutes. Stir in raisins.

■ Combine cornstarch and remaining apple juice just until smooth; add to the skillet. Bring to a boil; cook and stir for 2 minutes or until thickened. Return ham to skillet and heat through. Serve over rice.

Yield: *4 servings.*

Fish & Seafood

159

167

165

Cooking with fish or seafood is doubly good for home cooks because it can be prepared quickly and adds a healthy flair to weekly lineups. For a fresh change from heavier meat-and-potatoes meals, lighten up with a stovetop dinner made with succulent scallops, shrimp or fish.

Sassy Shrimp Stir-Fry

Taste of Home Test Kitchen
GREENDALE, WISCONSIN

Red pepper flakes, fresh ginger and garlic lend a spicy touch to this seafood delight. Pea pods, carrot and Chinese cabbage give the dish a fresh taste that's always welcome.

Sassy Shrimp Stir-Fry*

PREP/TOTAL TIME: 30 min.

- 2 tablespoons cornstarch
- 1-1/2 cups reduced-sodium chicken broth
- 3 tablespoons reduced-sodium soy sauce
- 2 tablespoons rice vinegar
- 1 tablespoon honey
- 2 teaspoons sesame oil
- 1 teaspoon grated orange peel
- 1 teaspoon canola oil
- 1 pound uncooked medium shrimp, peeled and deveined
- 1-1/2 teaspoons minced fresh gingerroot
- 2 garlic cloves, minced
- 1/2 teaspoon crushed red pepper flakes
- 1/2 cup julienned carrot
- 2-1/2 cups chopped Chinese *or* napa cabbage
- 2 cups fresh pea pods
- 1/4 cup thinly sliced green onions

Hot cooked rice, optional

■ In a bowl, combine the cornstarch and broth until smooth. Stir in the soy sauce, vinegar, honey, sesame oil and orange peel; set aside.

■ In a large nonstick skillet or wok, heat canola oil; stir-fry shrimp for 30 seconds. Add ginger, garlic and red pepper flakes; stir-fry 1-2 minutes longer or until shrimp turn pink. Remove and keep warm.

■ In the same pan, stir-fry the carrot for 1 minute. Stir broth mixture and stir into pan. Bring to a boil; cook and stir for 1-2 minutes or until thickened. Add the cabbage, peas, onions and shrimp mixture; heat through. Serve over rice if desired.

Yield: 4 servings.

* **Nutrition Facts:** 1-1/4 cups stir-fry mixture (calculated without rice) equals 219 calories, 5 g fat (1 g saturated fat), 168 mg cholesterol, 896 mg sodium, 20 g carbohydrate, 4 g fiber, 24 g protein. **Diabetic Exchanges:** 3 very lean meat, 1 starch, 1 vegetable, 1/2 fat.

The crisp, delicate leaves of napa cabbage add a refreshing touch to stir-fries. Choose heads with green-tipped leaves and tightly packed heads that are absent of wilting or brown spots.

Tamra Duncan
CENTERTON, ARKANSAS
This is a fun and interesting recipe to serve when entertaining. It's a great introduction to crawfish and Cajun food. Our favorite seafood restaurant has this dish on their menu and it's fabulous!

Crawfish Etoufee

Crawfish Etoufee

PREP: 15 min. **COOK:** 50 min.

1/2 cup butter	1/4 cup minced fresh parsley
1/2 cup plus 2 tablespoons all-purpose flour	1 tablespoon tomato paste
1-1/4 cups chopped celery	1 bay leaf
1 cup chopped green pepper	1/2 teaspoon salt
1/2 cup chopped green onions	1/4 teaspoon pepper
1 can (14-1/2 ounces) chicken broth	1/4 teaspoon cayenne pepper
1 cup water	2 pounds frozen cooked crawfish tail meat, thawed
	Hot cooked rice

■ In a heavy skillet or Dutch oven, melt butter; stir in flour. Cook and stir over low heat for about 20 minutes until mixture is a caramel-colored paste. Add the celery, pepper and onions; stir until coated. Add the broth, water, parsley, tomato paste, bay leaf, salt, pepper and cayenne pepper. Bring to a boil.

■ Reduce heat; cover and simmer for 30 minutes, stirring occasionally. Discard bay leaf. Add crawfish and heat through. Serve over rice.

Yield: 6-8 servings.

Citrus Scallops

Cheri Hawthorne
NORTH CANTON, OHIO
My husband and I like to eat seafood at least once a week. Oranges and lemon juice give these scallops a refreshing burst of flavor. Served with rice or pasta, it's a simple meal-in-one.

PREP/TOTAL TIME: 15 min.

1 medium green *or* sweet red pepper, julienned
4 green onions, chopped
1 garlic clove, minced
2 tablespoons olive oil
1 pound sea scallops
1/2 teaspoon salt
1/4 teaspoon crushed red pepper flakes
2 tablespoons lime juice
1/2 teaspoon grated lime peel
4 medium navel oranges, peeled and sectioned
2 teaspoons minced fresh cilantro
Hot cooked rice *or* pasta

■ In a large skillet, saute the pepper, onions and garlic in oil for 1 minute. Add scallops, salt and pepper flakes; cook for 4 minutes. Add lime juice and peel; cook for 1 minute. Reduce heat. Add the orange sections and cilantro; cook 2 minutes longer or until scallops are opaque. Serve with rice or pasta.

Yield: 4 servings.

Sea scallops are about 1-1/2 inches in diameter, which is quite a bit larger than bay scallops, which are smaller at only 1/2 inch in diameter.

Combine the cornstarch, sugar, salt and pepper. Stir in the broth, wine or additional broth and soy sauce until smooth; set aside. Cook vermicelli according to package directions.

Meanwhile, in a large nonstick skillet or wok, stir-fry the peppers, snap peas, garlic and ginger in olive oil for 2-4 minutes or until vegetables are crisp-tender. Add the scallops and the shrimp; stir-fry 2 minutes longer. Stir cornstarch mixture and add to the pan. Bring mixture to a boil; cook and stir for 2 minutes or until thickened.

Drain vermicelli; add to pan. Cook until scallops are firm and opaque and shrimp turn pink. Sprinkle with sesame oil.

Yield: 8 servings.

Seafood Pasta Delight

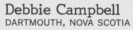

Debbie Campbell
DARTMOUTH, NOVA SCOTIA

I created this recipe after my husband gave me a pasta maker for Christmas—it's been a big hit ever since. It's a wonderful supper in the summer.

Seafood Pasta Delight

PREP/TOTAL TIME: 25 min.

2 tablespoons cornstarch
1 teaspoon sugar
3/4 teaspoon salt
Dash pepper
1/2 cup chicken broth
1/2 cup dry white wine *or* additional chicken broth
1/4 cup soy sauce
8 ounces uncooked vermicelli
1 medium sweet red pepper, julienned
1 medium sweet yellow pepper, julienned

1 cup fresh *or* frozen sugar snap peas
2 to 3 garlic cloves, minced
1 teaspoon minced fresh gingerroot
1 tablespoon olive oil
1 pound uncooked sea scallops, halved
1 pound uncooked medium shrimp, peeled and deveined
2 teaspoons sesame oil

Counting your

carbs? If so, enjoy Seafood Pasta Delight without the vermicelli. You could also decrease the amount called for by half.

Virginia Anthony
JACKSONVILLE, FLORIDA

Mediterranean flavors make my speedy seafood specialty impressive enough for company. It's loaded with orange roughy, shrimp and scallops that all simmer together in one pot. A dash of wine, fresh parsley and lemon peel give it a fresh-from-the-sea flavor.

Mediterranean Seafood Stew*

PREP/TOTAL TIME: 30 min.

1 medium onion, finely chopped	1 tablespoon tomato paste
1-1/2 teaspoons minced garlic, *divided*	1/2 teaspoon salt
1 tablespoon olive oil	1 pound orange roughy *or* red snapper fillets, cut into 1-inch cubes
1/2 pound plum tomatoes, seeded and diced	1 pound uncooked large shrimp, peeled and deveined
1 teaspoon grated lemon peel	1/2 pound sea scallops
1/4 teaspoon crushed red pepper flakes	1/3 cup minced fresh parsley
1 cup clam juice	1/3 cup reduced-fat mayonnaise
1/3 cup white wine *or* additional clam juice	

■ In a Dutch oven or large saucepan, saute onion and 1/2 teaspoon garlic in oil until tender. Add the tomatoes, lemon peel and pepper flakes; cook and stir for 2 minutes. Add the clam juice, wine or additional clam juice, tomato paste and salt. Bring to a boil. Reduce heat; cover and simmer for 10 minutes or until heated through.

■ Add the fish, shrimp, scallops and parsley. Cover and cook for 8-10 minutes or until fish flakes easily with a fork, the shrimp turn pink and scallops are opaque. Combine mayonnaise and remaining garlic; dollop onto each serving.

Yield: 6 servings.

✳ **Nutrition Facts:** 1 cup stew with 2 teaspoons mayonnaise topping equals 221 calories, 8 g fat (1 g saturated fat), 123 mg cholesterol, 607 mg sodium, 7 g carbohydrate, 1 g fiber, 28 g protein. **Diabetic Exchanges:** 4 very lean meat, 1 vegetable, 1 fat.

Fresh shrimp should have a firm texture. Avoid those with yellow meat as well as shrimp with black spots or rings on the shells (unless they are tiger shrimp).

Italian Fish Fillets*

Mindy Holliday
WESTFIELD, INDIANA

My husband and I resolved to eat healthier, so I was pleased to find this quick recipe for fish fillets. I tried it with cod and added a few twists of my own. Italian salad dressing, diced tomatoes and green pepper lend delicious flavor. We can't get enough of it!

PREP: 5 min. COOK: 20 min.

1 medium green *or* sweet yellow pepper, julienned

1 small onion, julienned

1/2 cup fat-free Italian salad dressing

1/2 teaspoon Italian seasoning

2 cans (14-1/2 ounces *each*) diced tomatoes

1-1/2 pounds fresh *or* frozen cod fillets, thawed

■ In a large nonstick skillet, cook green pepper, onion, salad dressing and Italian seasoning for 5 minutes or until vegetables are tender. Stir in tomatoes; add fillets. Bring to a boil. Reduce heat; cover and simmer for 10 minutes or until fish flakes easily with a fork. Serve with a slotted spoon.

Yield: 4 servings.

✳ **Nutrition Facts:** One serving equals 216 calories, 2 g fat (trace saturated fat), 74 mg cholesterol, 784 mg sodium, 17 g carbohydrate, 4 g fiber, 33 g protein. **Diabetic Exchanges:** 4 lean meat, 3 vegetable.

Special Seafood Skillet

- In a skillet or wok, stir-fry carrot, celery, onion, red pepper, corn and mushrooms in 1 tablespoon oil for 4-5 minutes or until crisp-tender. Remove to a bowl and keep warm.

- Add remaining oil to the skillet; stir-fry the scallops, shrimp, seafood seasoning and soy sauce for 3-4 minutes or until shrimp turn pink. Using a slotted spoon, remove seafood and add to the bowl with the vegetable mixture.

- In a small bowl, beat cream cheese, milk, cheese and nutmeg until smooth. Return seafood and vegetables to skillet; stir in cream cheese mixture and heat through. Serve over pasta or rice.

Yield: 2 servings.

Donald Boyer
NEWPORT NEWS, VIRGINIA
Packed with colorful veggies and tasty shrimp, this small-scale supper makes just the right amount for two people. I love its creamy richness.

Special Seafood Skillet

PREP/TOTAL TIME: 25 min.

- 1/4 cup *each* chopped carrot, celery, onion and sweet red pepper
- 1/4 cup whole kernel corn
- 1/4 cup sliced fresh mushrooms
- 2 tablespoons vegetable oil, *divided*
- 1/2 pound fresh *or* frozen bay scallops, thawed
- 1/4 pound uncooked medium shrimp, peeled and deveined

- 1 teaspoon seafood seasoning
- 1 teaspoon soy sauce
- 1 package (3 ounces) cream cheese, softened
- 1/2 cup milk
- 1/2 cup shredded part-skim mozzarella cheese
- 1/8 teaspoon ground nutmeg

Hot cooked pasta *or* rice

Even though

Special Seafood Skillet is ideal for two, you can easily double the ingredients for four. Pick up a package of salad greens and a bottle of dressing and swing by the bakery for an impressive, yet effortless menu.

Clara Coulston
WASHINGTON COURT
HOUSE, OHIO

I like to prepare fish and vegetables in a flavorful sauce that's easy to make with cream of mushroom soup. Made on the stovetop, it's a fast fix when you're at a loss for dinner.

Primavera Fish Fillets

Primavera Fish Fillets*

PREP/TOTAL TIME: 25 min.

2 celery ribs, sliced
1 large carrot, cut into 2-inch julienne strips
1 small onion, chopped
1/4 cup water
2 tablespoons white wine *or* chicken broth

1/2 teaspoon dried thyme
1 can (10-3/4 ounces) condensed cream of mushroom soup, undiluted
1 pound frozen cod *or* haddock fillets, thawed

■ In a large skillet, combine the first six ingredients. Bring to a boil. Reduce heat; cover and simmer for 5-7 minutes or until vegetables are crisp-tender. Stir in soup until blended; bring to a boil. Add fillets. Reduce heat; cover and simmer for 5-7 minutes or until fish flakes easily with a fork.

Yield: 4 servings.

✱ **Nutrition Facts:** 1 serving (prepared with reduced-fat and reduced sodium soup) equals 151 calories, 4 g fat (1 g saturated fat), 51 mg cholesterol, 415 mg sodium, 7 g carbohydrate, 1 g fiber, 21 g protein. **Diabetic Exchanges:** 2-1/2 lean meat, 1/2 starch.

Hurry-Up Tuna Supper

Dorothy Pritchett
WILLS POINT, TEXAS

All kinds of convenience products, including canned tuna, frozen vegetables and instant rice are used to prepare this satisfying supper.

PREP/TOTAL TIME: 15 min.

1 package (10 ounces) frozen mixed vegetables
2 cups water
2 tablespoons dried minced onion
1/2 teaspoon salt
1 can (10-3/4 ounces) condensed cream of celery soup, undiluted
1-1/3 cups uncooked instant rice
1 can (6 ounces) tuna, drained and flaked
2 teaspoons dried parsley flakes
3/4 teaspoon dried marjoram
1 teaspoon lemon juice

■ In a skillet, combine the vegetables, water, onion and salt. Bring to a boil over medium heat. Stir in the soup, rice, tuna, parsley and marjoram. Reduce heat; cover and simmer for 5-10 minutes or until the rice is tender and the liquid is absorbed. Stir in lemon juice. Serve immediately.

Yield: 4 servings.

Chunky Cod Stir-Fry*

Dorothy Colette
BOURBONNAIS, ILLINOIS

Making the most of fish is what this dinner is all about! Chunks of cod are nicely accented by a zesty sauce, vegetables and chopped peanuts.

PREP/TOTAL TIME: 30 min.

2 teaspoons cornstarch
1/3 cup chicken broth
2 tablespoons sherry or additional chicken broth
2 tablespoons reduced-sodium soy sauce
1/8 teaspoon crushed red pepper flakes
1 garlic clove, minced

1 tablespoon canola oil
1 package (16 ounces) frozen stir-fry vegetable blend, thawed
1 small sweet red pepper, julienned
1 pound cod fillets, cut into 1-inch cubes
1/4 cup chopped peanuts
4 cups hot cooked rice

■ In a bowl, combine the first five ingredients until blended; set aside. In a nonstick skillet or wok, stir-fry garlic in oil for 30 seconds. Add mixed vegetables; stir-fry for 2 minutes. Add red pepper; stir-fry for 2 minutes or until crisp-tender.

■ Remove and keep warm. Add half of the cod to skillet; gently stir-fry for 3-5 minutes or until fish flakes easily with a fork. Remove and keep warm. Repeat with remaining cod.

■ Stir reserved broth mixture and add to skillet. Bring to a boil; cook and stir for 2 minutes or until thickened. Return vegetables and fish to the pan. Add peanuts. Gently stir to coat. Cover and cook for 1 minute or until heated through. Serve over rice.

Yield: 4 servings.

✱ **Nutrition Facts:** One serving (1-1/2 cups fish mixture with 1 cup rice) equals 484 calories, 12 g fat (2 g saturated fat), 49 mg cholesterol, 1,117 mg sodium, 62 g carbohydrate, 3 g fiber, 29 g protein. **Diabetic Exchanges:** 3 starch, 3 lean meat, 1 vegetable, 1 fat.

Crab Lo Mein*

PREP/TOTAL TIME: 25 min.

4 ounces uncooked angel hair pasta *or* thin spaghetti
1 medium onion, thinly sliced
1 medium green pepper, cut into 1-inch strips
1 package (9 ounces) frozen broccoli cuts, thawed
1/4 cup sliced fresh mushrooms
2 tablespoons canola oil
1 tablespoon cornstarch
1-1/4 cups chicken broth
1/4 cup water
1/4 cup soy sauce
12 ounces imitation crabmeat, cut into 1-inch pieces

■ Cook pasta according to package directions. Meanwhile, in a large skillet or wok, stir-fry the onion, green pepper, broccoli and mushrooms in oil for 3-4 minutes or until crisp-tender.

■ In a small bowl, combine the cornstarch, broth, water and soy sauce until smooth. Gradually stir into skillet. Bring to a boil; cook and stir for 2 minutes or until thickened. Stir in crab; cook 2-3 minutes longer or until heated through. Drain pasta; toss with crab mixture.

Yield: 6 servings.

✱ **Nutrition Facts:** 1 cup (prepared with reduced-sodium chicken broth and reduced-sodium soy sauce) equals 218 calories, 5 g fat (1 g saturated fat), 28 mg cholesterol, 579 mg sodium, 29 g carbohydrate, 2 g fiber, 13 g protein. **Diabetic Exchanges:** 2 starch, 1-1/2 very lean meat.

Laura Mryyan
TOPEKA, KANSAS

I came up with this one night when I had some leftover spaghetti that I needed to finish off. When stirring up the sauce, consider replacing half of the soy sauce with oyster sauce for a richer flavor. Other than the great flavor, the best thing about this dish is that it's quick!

Jeff Brown
COLON, MICHIGAN

I've been making this stir-fry for years, often using bass since we live on a lake where bass are quite common. When I first tried the recipe, my wife declared it a surefire winner.

Potato Fish Skillet

Potato Fish Skillet

PREP/TOTAL TIME: 25 min.

4 medium red potatoes, cubed	2 cups sliced fresh mushrooms
6 tablespoons butter, cubed	1/2 cup chopped celery
2 tablespoons olive oil	1/4 cup chopped onion
1/2 cup all-purpose flour	3 garlic cloves, minced
1 pound grouper *or* other lean fish, cut into 3/4-inch pieces	4-1/2 teaspoons lemon juice
	Salt and pepper to taste

■ In a large skillet, stir-fry potatoes in butter and oil for 8-10 minutes or until lightly browned.

■ Meanwhile, place flour in a large resealable plastic bag. Add fish, a few pieces at a time, and shake to coat. Add to the skillet. Cover and cook for 4 minutes, stirring occasionally.

■ Add the mushrooms, celery, onion and garlic. Cover and cook 4-6 minutes longer or until fish flakes easily with a fork. Sprinkle with lemon juice, salt and pepper.

Yield: 4 servings.

Scallop and Potato Saute

Mildred Sherrer
FORT WORTH, TEXAS

Looking for a fast meal for one? Try this sensational idea. I brown potato slices in a bit of oil, before stirring in scallops, garlic and a hint of lemon juice.

PREP/TOTAL TIME: 30 min.

2 small red potatoes, sliced 1/4 inch thick
2 tablespoons olive oil, *divided*
1/4 pound bay scallops
1 garlic clove, minced
1 tablespoon lemon juice
1 tablespoon chopped fresh parsley
1/8 teaspoon salt
Dash pepper
Lemon slice *or* wedge, optional

■ In a small skillet over medium heat, cook potatoes in 1 tablespoon oil until golden brown and tender, about 12 minutes. Remove and keep warm. In the same skillet, heat remaining oil. Cook and stir scallops for 2 minutes. Add garlic and lemon juice; cook and stir 1-2 minutes longer or until scallops are firm and opaque.

■ Add parsley, salt and pepper. Return potatoes to pan; heat through. Serve with lemon if desired.

Yield: 1 serving.

Creamy Shrimp Noodle Skillet

- Cook noodles according to package directions; drain and set aside.

- In a large saucepan or Dutch oven, saute the onions, green pepper, celery and garlic in butter until tender. Stir in flour until blended. Gradually stir in cream. Bring to a boil; cook and stir for 2 minutes or until thickened.

- Reduce heat; add shrimp, jalapeno pepper and parsley. Simmer, uncovered, for 3 minutes. Stir in cheese; cook 3 minutes longer or until cheese is melted. Stir in the noodles; heat through.

Yield: 6-8 servings.

Editor's Note: When cutting hot peppers, disposable gloves are recommended. Avoid touching your face.

Not hot enough for you? Jazz up this seafood delight with a few dashes of hot pepper sauce or cayenne pepper. If that's not enough, use a spicy jalapeno pepper.

Cora Robin
ST. BERNARD, LOUISIANA

This is a flavorful seafood dish that draws compliments each time I serve it to family and friends. Made on the stovetop, it is easier than anyone ever suspects.

Creamy Shrimp Noodle Skillet

PREP: 15 min. **COOK:** 20 min.

1 package (16 ounces) medium egg noodles
2 medium onions, chopped
1 medium green pepper, chopped
2 celery ribs, chopped
3 garlic cloves, minced
3/4 cup butter
1 tablespoon all-purpose flour

3 cups half-and-half cream
1-1/2 pounds uncooked medium shrimp, peeled and deveined
1 jalapeno pepper, seeded and chopped
2 tablespoons minced fresh parsley
8 ounces process cheese (Velveeta), cubed

Mary Ann Palestino
BROOKLYN, NEW YORK

This recipe yields a deliciously complete and quick dinner with fish, herbed rice and plenty of veggies. Most important, it only takes a few moments to prepare so I can serve it on my busiest nights. The amazing thing is that it's healthy for you, too.

Snapper with Vegetable Medley*

PREP: 15 min. **COOK:** 55 min.

1-1/2   cups water
3/4   cup uncooked brown rice
1-1/2   teaspoons reduced-sodium beef bouillon granules
1-1/2   teaspoons dried parsley flakes
1-1/2   teaspoons dried minced onion
1/4   teaspoon garlic powder
1   medium red onion, thinly sliced
2   garlic cloves, minced
2   teaspoons canola oil
1/2   pound fresh snow peas
1-1/2   cups shredded carrots
1   tablespoon balsamic vinegar
4   red snapper fillets (5 ounces *each*)
2   teaspoons blackening seasoning

■ In a saucepan, combine the first six ingredients. Bring to a boil. Reduce heat; cover and simmer for 40-45 minutes or until rice is tender.

■ Meanwhile, in a large nonstick skillet coated with cooking spray, cook onion and garlic in oil over medium-high heat for 2 minutes. Add snow peas; cook for 2 minutes. Add carrots; cook 2 minutes longer or until vegetables are tender. Stir in vinegar. Remove and keep warm.

■ Sprinkle both sides of fillets with blackening seasoning. In the same skillet, cook fillets over medium-high heat for 4 minutes on each side or until fish flakes easily with a fork. Serve with rice and vegetables.

Yield: 4 servings.

✱ **Nutrition Facts:** 1 fish fillet with 3/4 cup vegetable mixture and 1/2 cup rice equals 353 calories, 6 g fat (1 g saturated fat), 50 mg cholesterol, 305 mg sodium, 41 g carbohydrate, 5 g fiber, 34 g protein. **Diabetic Exchanges:** 4 very lean meat, 2 starch, 2 vegetable, 1/2 fat.

You just can't beat Snapper with Vegetable Medley for a true meal-in-one sensation. Feel free to dress up the veggies with your favorite herbs, or add a handful of frozen peas to the hot rice.

Skillet Fish Dinner*

Janet Cooper Claggett
OLNEY, MARYLAND

Served over rice, this effortless meal takes very little time. We enjoy it with a spinach salad or whole wheat rolls.

PREP/TOTAL TIME: 20 min.

1   celery rib, chopped
1/2   cup chopped green pepper
1/2   cup chopped onion
1   teaspoon olive oil
2   to 3 plum tomatoes, chopped
1/4   teaspoon salt
Dash pepper
1/2   pound cod, haddock *or* orange roughy fillets
1/4   to 1/2 teaspoon seafood seasoning
Hot cooked rice
Hot pepper sauce, optional

■ In a skillet, saute the celery, green pepper and onion in oil until almost tender. Add tomatoes; cook and stir for 1-2 minutes. Sprinkle with salt and pepper. Top with fish fillets and sprinkle with seafood seasoning. Reduce heat; cover and simmer for 6 minutes. Break fish into chunks. Cook about 3 minutes longer or until fish flakes easily with a fork. Serve over rice. Serve with hot pepper sauce if desired.

Yield: 2 servings.

✱ **Nutrition Facts:** 1 serving (calculated without rice and hot pepper sauce) equals 156 calories, 3 g fat (1 g saturated fat), 49 mg cholesterol, 465 mg sodium, 10 g carbohydrate, 2 g fiber, 22 g protein. **Diabetic Exchanges:** 3 very lean meat, 1/2 starch.

page 222

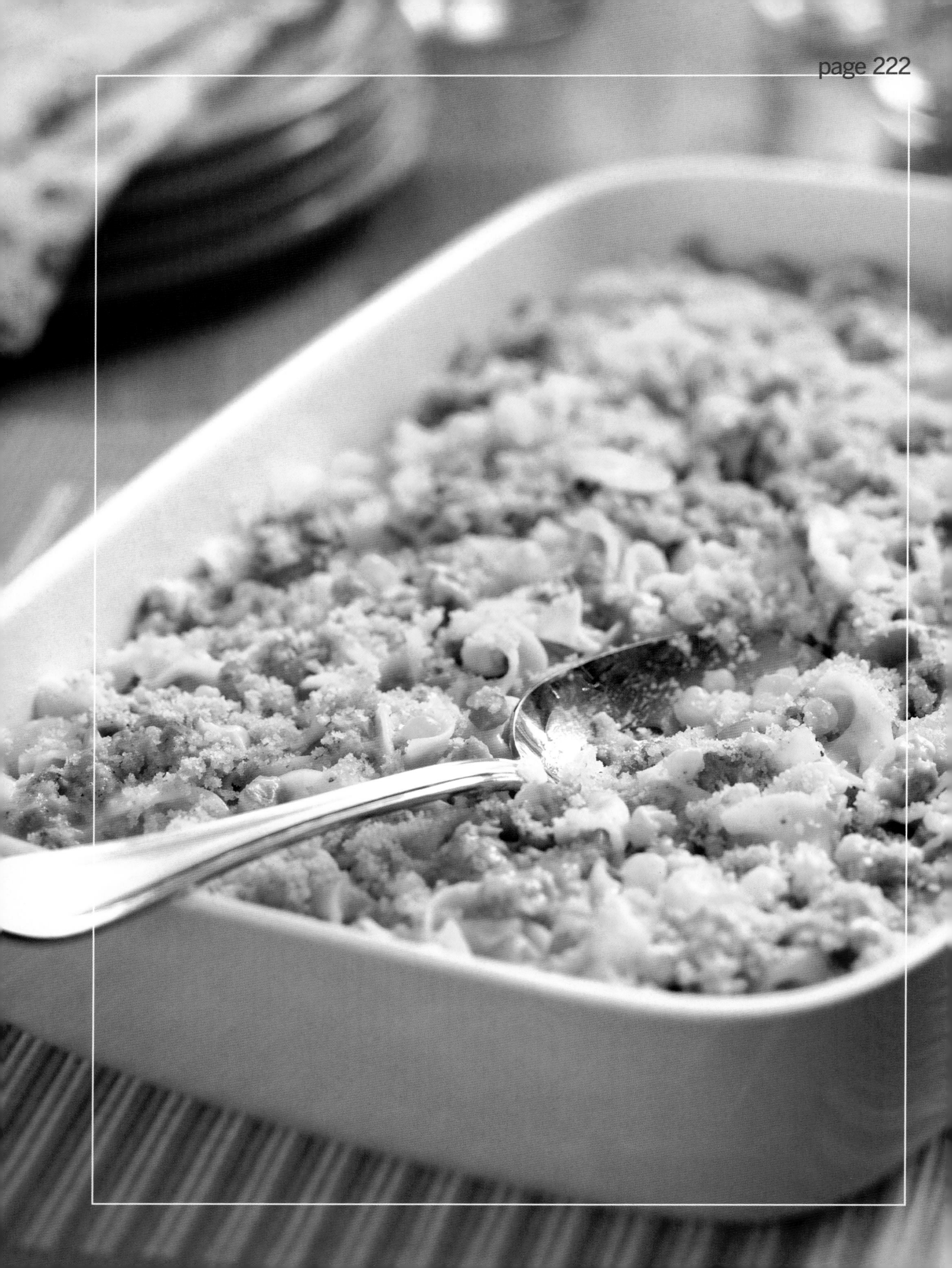

OVEN ENTREES

Beef & Ground Beef

179

184

182

Classic beef dishes are a mainstay in many cooks' repertoires because of they're popularity and reliability. These recipes have stepped it up a notch with the addition of mouth-watering new twists on favorites such as meat loaf, meatballs and pot roast.

Beef Tenderloin with Roasted Vegetables

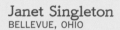

Janet Singleton
BELLEVUE, OHIO

I appreciate this recipe because the meat bakes with roasted potatoes, brussels sprouts and carrots, so I don't have to think about preparing a side dish.

Beef Tenderloin With Roasted Vegetables

PREP: 20 min. + marinating ■ BAKE: 1 hour + standing

1 beef tenderloin (3 pounds), trimmed	1-1/2 teaspoons ground mustard
3/4 cup dry white wine *or* beef broth	3 garlic cloves, peeled and sliced
3/4 cup reduced-sodium soy sauce	1 pound Yukon gold potatoes, cut into 1-inch wedges
4 teaspoons minced fresh rosemary	1 pound brussels sprouts, halved
4 teaspoons Dijon mustard	1 package (16 ounces) fresh baby carrots

■ Place tenderloin in a large re-sealable plastic bag. Combine the wine or broth, soy sauce, minced rosemary, Dijon mustard, ground mustard and garlic. Pour half of the marinade over tenderloin; seal bag and turn to coat. Refrigerate for 4-12 hours, turning several times. Cover and refrigerate the remaining marinade.

■ Place the potatoes, brussels sprouts and carrots in a greased 13-in. x 9-in. x 2-in. baking dish; add reserved marinade and toss to coat. Cover and bake at 425° for 30 minutes; stir.

■ Drain and discard marinade from tenderloin. Place tenderloin over vegetables. Bake, uncovered, for 30-45 minutes or until the meat reaches desired doneness (for medium-rare, a meat thermometer should read 145°; medium, 160°; well-done, 170°).

■ Remove the beef and let stand for 15 minutes. Check vegetables for doneness. If additional roasting is needed, cover with foil and bake for 10-15 minutes or until tender. Slice beef and serve with vegetables.

Yield: 8-10 **servings.**

Use extra beef in potpies, soups or stews. Thin slices also make wonderful sandwiches, whether they are served warm or cold.

Deby Kominski
CUPERTINO, CALIFORNIA

This colorful dish is an appealing meal for special holidays. The cranberries mixed with horseradish give the beef terrific taste. You can add any vegetables you like to fit your taste. No matter which veggies you choose, this makes a sensational dinner.

Autumn Pot Roast*

PREP: 30 min. + cooling ■ BAKE: 2-3/4 hours

1	boneless beef rump roast (about 3 pounds), tied
1/4	teaspoon salt
1/4	teaspoon pepper
2	teaspoons canola oil
3/4	cup fresh or frozen cranberries
1/2	cup water
1/4	cup sugar
1	cup reduced-sodium beef broth
1/3	cup prepared horseradish, drained
1	cinnamon stick (3 inches)
3	whole cloves
16	pearl onions
2	medium sweet potatoes (about 1-1/2 pounds), peeled and cut into 3/4-inch cubes
16	baby carrots
4	teaspoons cornstarch
2	tablespoons cold water

■ Sprinkle meat with salt and pepper. In a Dutch oven, brown meat in oil. Drain and remove from the heat. In a large saucepan, combine the cranberries, water and sugar. Cook and stir over medium heat until cranberries pop and liquid is slightly thickened, about 8 minutes. Remove from the heat.

■ Add the broth and horseradish; pour over meat. Place cinnamon stick and cloves in a double thickness of cheesecloth; bring up corners of cloth and tie with kitchen string to form a bag. Add to Dutch oven. Cover and bake at 325° for 2 hours.

■ Meanwhile, in a large saucepan, bring 6 cups water to a boil. Add pearl onions; boil for 3 minutes. Drain and rinse in cold water; peel and set aside. Add sweet potatoes to Dutch oven. Cover and cook 15 minutes longer. Add carrots and onions; cover and cook 30-40 minutes more or until vegetables and meat are tender. Remove meat and vegetables; keep warm. Discard spice bag.

■ Cool pan juices for 10 minutes; transfer to a blender. Cover and process until smooth; return to pan. Combine cornstarch and cold water until smooth. Gradually whisk into pan juices. Bring to a boil; cook and stir for 1-2 minutes or until thickened. Serve with meat and vegetables.

Yield: 6-8 servings.

* **Nutrition Facts:** 3 ounces cooked beef with 3/4 cup vegetables and 3 table-spoons gravy equals 328 calories, 9 g fat (3 g saturated fat), 83 mg cholesterol, 235 mg sodium, 31 g carbohydrate, 4 g fiber, 29 g protein. **Diabetic Exchanges:** 3 lean meat, 1-1/2 starch, 1 vegetable.

Pot roasts are done when a long-handled fork can be inserted into the thickest part of the roast easily. If the roast falls apart, the meat is overcooked.

Meal-in-One Casserole

Madge Watkins
ONTARIO, OREGON

Here's a meat-and-potatoes dish that I created. It makes a satisfying supper, and it gets me out of the kitchen in a hurry.

PREP: 15 min.
BAKE: 50 min.

1	pound ground beef
3	medium unpeeled potatoes, thinly sliced
1	medium onion, sliced and separated into rings
1	cup frozen peas
1-1/2	cups sliced mushrooms
1-1/2	teaspoons salt, optional
1/4	teaspoon pepper
1	teaspoon sesame seeds
3	tablespoons butter, melted

■ In a skillet over medium heat, cook beef until no longer pink; drain. Place potatoes in a greased 2-qt. baking dish. Top with beef and onion. Place peas in the center; arrange mushrooms around the peas. Sprinkle with salt, pepper and sesame seeds; drizzle with butter.

■ Cover and bake at 375° for 50-60 minutes or until potatoes are tender.

Yield: 4 servings.

Fries 'n' Beef Bake

Doris Pfohl
ST. JACOBS, ONTARIO

My family never turns down my meal-in-one casserole that's loaded with ground beef, fries and flavor! The day after I make it, I reheat the leftovers for a quick meal.

Fries 'n' Beef Bake

PREP: 10 min. ■ BAKE: 45 min.

1 pound ground beef	3/4 cup water
1 medium onion, chopped	2 tablespoons ketchup
1 pound frozen crinkle-cut French fries, thawed	1 teaspoon dried parsley flakes
2 cups frozen peas, thawed	1 teaspoon Worcestershire sauce
1 can (10-3/4 ounces) condensed cream of mushroom *or* cream of chicken soup, undiluted	1/2 teaspoon dried marjoram
	1/4 teaspoon ground mustard
	Salt and pepper to taste

■ In a skillet, cook beef and onion over medium heat until meat is no longer pink; drain. In a greased 13-in. x 9-in. x 2-in. baking dish, layer half of the French fries, peas and meat mixture. Repeat layers.

■ In a bowl, combine the soup, water, ketchup, parsley, Worcestershire sauce, marjoram, mustard, salt and pepper. Pour over top. Bake, uncovered, at 350° for 45-50 minutes or until heated through.

Yield: *6-8 servings.*

Mock Pot Roast

Marsha Ransom
SOUTH HAVEN, MICHIGAN

With potatoes, carrots, peas and onions, this meat loaf tastes just like a pot roast.

PREP: 25 min.
BAKE: 1-1/4 hours

1/2 cup ketchup
  2 eggs
  1 tablespoon prepared horseradish
1/2 cup quick-cooking oats
  1 teaspoon ground mustard
  1 teaspoon salt
1/4 teaspoon pepper
  2 pounds lean ground beef
  1 teaspoon steak sauce
  8 medium carrots, halved
  8 small red potatoes
16 pearl onions
  1 package (10 ounces) frozen peas, thawed

■ In a large bowl, combine the first seven ingredients. Crumble beef over mixture and mix well. Shape into a loaf in a greased 13-in. x 9-in. x 2-in. baking pan. Brush with steak sauce. Arrange carrots, potatoes and onions around loaf.

■ Cover and bake at 375° for 40 minutes. Add peas. Cover and bake 30 minutes longer. Uncover; baste with pan juices. Bake 5 minutes or until the meat is no longer pink and a meat thermometer reads 160°.

Yield: 8 servings.

Editor's Note: To peel pearl onions, immerse them in boiling water for 3 minutes; drain. Pinch at root ends and they'll slide out of their skins.

Brenda Biron
SYDNEY, NOVA SCOTIA

Here's a new twist on an old favorite. Potatoes and carrots baked alongside a ham and cheese-stuffed loaf make this a wonderful meal-in-one.

Meat Loaf Supper

Meat Loaf Supper

PREP: 20 min. ■ **BAKE:** 45 min.

1 egg	1/8 teaspoon pepper
2 tablespoons 2% milk	3/4 pound lean ground beef
3/4 cup soft bread crumbs	2 thin slices deli ham
1/2 teaspoon salt	1/2 cup shredded cheddar cheese
1/2 teaspoon dried minced onion	2 medium red potatoes, cut into chunks
1/2 teaspoon dried tarragon	2 medium carrots, halved and cut into chunks
1/2 teaspoon dried thyme	
1/4 teaspoon garlic powder	

■ In a bowl, combine the egg and milk. Stir in the bread crumbs, salt, onion, tarragon, thyme, garlic powder and pepper. Crumble beef over mixture and mix well.

■ On a piece of heavy-duty foil, pat beef mixture into a 9-1/2-in. x 6-1/2-in. x 1/2-in. rectangle. Top with ham and cheese. Roll up jelly-roll style, starting with a short side and peeling foil away while rolling. Seal seam and ends. Place in an 11-in. x 7-in. x 2-in. baking dish coated with cooking spray.

■ Arrange potatoes and carrots around loaf. Bake, uncovered, at 350° for 30 minutes. Turn potatoes and carrots. Bake 15-20 minutes longer or until a meat thermometer reads 160° and vegetables are tender.

Yield: 2 servings.

Garlic Chuck Roast

Janet Boyer
NEMACOLIN, PENNSYLVANIA

Having never made a roast before, I experimented to come up with this hearty all-in-one supper. Not only is it easy, but the tender entree gets terrific flavor from garlic, onion and bay leaves.

PREP: 15 min.
BAKE: 2-1/4 hours + standing

1	boneless beef chuck roast (3 pounds)
15	garlic cloves, peeled
1	teaspoon salt
1/4	teaspoon pepper
2	tablespoons vegetable oil
5	bay leaves
1	large onion, thinly sliced
2	tablespoons butter, melted
1-1/2	cups water
1	pound baby carrots

■ With a sharp knife, cut 15 slits in roast; insert garlic into slits. Sprinkle meat with salt and pepper. In a Dutch oven, brown meat in oil; drain. Place bay leaves on top of roast; top with onion slices. Drizzle with butter. Add water to pan. Cover and bake at 325° for 1-1/2 hours.

■ Baste roast with pan juices; add carrots. Cover and bake 45-60 minutes longer or until meat and carrots are tender. Discard bay leaves. Let roast stand for 10 minutes before slicing. Thicken pan juices if desired.

Yield: 6-8 servings.

Beef Noodle Casserole*

Karen Mathis
PENFIELD, NEW YORK

This is truly an old standby that's been in my family's recipe box for years. It can be assembled the night before and baked the next day for a quick, no-fuss meal.

PREP: 15 min. ■ **BAKE:** 25 min.

4-1/2 cups uncooked yolk-free noodles
   1 pound lean ground beef
   1 small onion, chopped
1/2 cup chopped green pepper
   1 can (10-3/4 ounces) reduced-fat reduced-sodium condensed cream of mushroom soup, undiluted

1/4 cup grated Parmesan cheese
   1 can (4 ounces) mushroom stems and pieces, drained
   1 jar (2 ounces) diced pimientos, drained
   1 tablespoon butter, melted
   1 teaspoon dried thyme
1/4 teaspoon salt

■ Cook noodles according to package directions; drain.

■ In a nonstick skillet, cook the beef, onion and green pepper over medium heat until meat is no longer pink; drain. In a large bowl, combine the soup, Parmesan cheese, mushrooms, pimientos, butter, thyme and salt; mix well. Stir in the noodles and beef mixture.

■ Transfer to a 2-qt. baking dish coated with cooking spray. Cover and bake at 350° for 25-30 minutes or until heated through.

Yield: 6 servings.

✱ **Nutrition Facts:** 1 cup equals 295 calories, 11 g fat (5 g saturated fat), 46 mg cholesterol, 527 mg sodium, 27 g carbohydrate, 3 g fiber, 21 g protein. **Diabetic Exchanges:** 2 lean meat, 1-1/2 starch, 1 vegetable, 1 fat.

Simply prepare a brownie mix and pop it into the oven when you serve the Beef Noodle Casserole, and dessert will bake on its own while you're eating. Top the brownies with vanilla ice cream for no-stress flair.

Meatballs Sausage Dinner

PREP: 25 min.
BAKE: 1 hour

   3 cups frozen chopped broccoli, thawed
   2 medium potatoes, peeled and cubed
   3 medium carrots, sliced
   1 medium onion, chopped
   1 pound smoked kielbasa *or* Polish sausage, halved and cut into 1-inch pieces
1/2 pound lean ground beef
   1 can (14-1/2 ounces) beef broth
Lemon-pepper seasoning to taste

■ In a large bowl, combine the first four ingredients. Transfer to a greased 13-in. x 9-in. x 2-in. baking pan. Evenly sprinkle the sausage over the mixture.

■ Shape beef mixture into 1-in. balls; arrange over the top. Pour broth over the casserole. Sprinkle with lemon-pepper. Bake, uncovered, at 350° for 1 hour or until meatballs are no longer pink.

Yield: 6-8 servings.

Elizabeth Martz
PLEASANT GAP, PENNSYLVANIA

One day I was having trouble deciding what to make for supper. So I combined whatever was in the refrigerator and freezer! To my surprise, everyone loved it! It has enough starch and protein to be considered a satisfying supper on its own.

Gloria Cross
CUPERTINO,
CALIFORNIA

I came across this recipe in the 1950s, and it's served me well ever since. As this meaty meal bakes, the aroma gets everyone's mouth watering!

Swiss Steak Dinner

Swiss Steak Dinner

PREP: 20 min. ■ BAKE: 1 hour and 50 min.

1/2 cup all-purpose flour
  2 teaspoons salt, *divided*
1/2 teaspoon pepper
  2 pounds boneless beef round steak, cut into 1/2-inch pieces
  2 to 3 tablespoons vegetable oil
  6 medium onions, thinly sliced
  7 to 9 small red potatoes (about 1-1/4 pounds), halved
  1 bay leaf
  1 can (10-3/4 ounces) condensed tomato soup, undiluted
  2 cups frozen cut green beans, thawed

■ In a large resealable plastic bag, combine the flour, 1-1/2 teaspoons salt and pepper. Add beef in batches and shake to coat.

■ In a large skillet over medium heat, brown beef in oil on both sides. Transfer to a greased 3-qt. baking dish. Top with onions and potatoes. Sprinkle with remaining salt; gently toss to coat. Add the bay leaf. Spoon soup over top.

■ Cover and bake at 350° for 1-1/2 hours. Place beans around edge of dish. Bake 15-20 minutes longer or until meat and vegetables are tender. Discard bay leaf.

Yield: *6 servings.*

Cheeseburger Biscuit Bake

Joy Frasure
LONGMONT, COLORADO

Popular cheeseburger ingredients create the tasty layers in my family-pleasing casserole. For the "bun," I use refrigerated biscuits to make a golden topping.

PREP: 15 min.
BAKE: 20 min.

  1 pound ground beef
1/4 cup chopped onion
  1 can (8 ounces) tomato sauce
1/4 cup ketchup
Dash pepper
  2 cups (8 ounces) shredded cheddar cheese, *separated*
  1 tube (12 ounces) refrigerated buttermilk biscuits, separated into 10 biscuits

■ In a large skillet, cook beef and onion over medium heat until meat is no longer pink; drain. Stir in tomato sauce, ketchup and pepper. Spoon half into a greased 8-in. square baking dish; sprinkle with half of the cheese. Repeat layers.

■ Place biscuits around edges of dish. Bake, uncovered, at 400° for 18-22 minutes or until the meat mixture is bubbly and biscuits are golden brown.

Yield: *5 servings.*

Beef and Potato Moussaka

Jean Puffer
CHILLIWACK, BRITISH COLUMBIA
When my son was young, he brought home this recipe for moussaka (a classic Greek entree) when he had to complete a sixth-grade assignment about Greece.

Beef and Potato Moussaka

PREP: 25 min. ■ **BAKE:** 1 hour + standing

1 pound ground beef
1 medium onion, chopped
1 garlic clove, minced
3/4 cup water
1 can (6 ounces) tomato paste
3 tablespoons minced fresh parsley
1 teaspoon salt
1/2 teaspoon dried mint, optional
1/4 teaspoon ground cinnamon
1/4 teaspoon pepper

PARMESAN SAUCE:
1/4 cup butter, cubed
1/4 cup all-purpose flour
2 cups milk
4 eggs, lightly beaten
1/2 cup grated Parmesan cheese
1/2 teaspoon salt
5 medium potatoes, peeled and thinly sliced

■ In a large skillet, cook the beef, onion and garlic over medium heat until meat is no longer pink; drain. Stir in the water, tomato paste, parsley, salt, mint if desired, cinnamon and pepper. Set aside.

■ For sauce, melt butter in a saucepan over medium heat. Stir in flour until smooth; gradually add milk. Bring to a boil; cook and stir for 2 minutes or until thickened. Remove from the heat. Stir a small amount of hot mixture into the eggs; return all to the pan, stirring constantly. Add the Parmesan cheese and salt.

■ Place half of the potato slices in a greased shallow 3-qt. baking dish. Top with half of the Parmesan sauce and all of the meat mixture. Arrange remaining potatoes over meat mixture. Top with the potatoes with remaining Parmesan sauce.

■ Bake, uncovered, at 350° for 1 hour or until potatoes are tender. Let stand for 10 minutes before serving.

Yield: 8-10 servings.

When browning

ground beef or other ground meat, consider using a pastry blender to break up large pieces shortly before the meat is completely cooked.

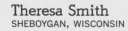

Theresa Smith
SHEBOYGAN, WISCONSIN

A combination of pasta, oregano, mushrooms and green peppers makes this beefy casserole a favorite of my husband's. It's perfect any night of the week. If you feel like getting creative, try it with different shaped pastas.

Italian Hot Dish*

PREP: 30 min. ■ BAKE: 40 min.

1-1/2 cups uncooked small pasta shells
1 pound lean ground beef
1 cup sliced fresh mushrooms, *divided*
1/2 cup chopped onion
1/2 cup chopped green pepper
1 can (15 ounces) tomato sauce
1 teaspoon dried oregano
1/2 teaspoon garlic powder
1/4 teaspoon onion powder
1/8 teaspoon pepper
1/2 cup shredded part-skim mozzarella cheese, *divided*
4 teaspoons grated Parmesan cheese, *divided*

■ Cook pasta according to package directions. Meanwhile, in a large non-stick skillet coated with cooking spray, cook the beef, 1/2 cup mushrooms, onion and green pepper until meat is no longer pink; drain. Stir in the tomato sauce, oregano, garlic powder, onion powder and pepper. Bring to a boil. Reduce heat; cover and simmer for 15 minutes.

■ Drain pasta; place in an 8-in. square baking dish coated with cooking spray. Top with meat sauce and remaining mushrooms. Sprinkle with 1/4 cup mozzarella and 2 teaspoons Parmesan.

■ Cover and bake at 350° for 35 minutes. Uncover; sprinkle with remaining cheeses. Bake 5-10 minutes longer or until heated through and cheese is melted.

Yield: 4 servings.

* Nutrition Facts: 1 serving equals 391 calories, 12 g fat (5 g saturated fat), 65 mg cholesterol, 663 mg sodium, 36 g carbohydrate, 3 g fiber, 33 g protein. **Diabetic Exchanges:** 3 lean meat, 2 starch, 2 vegetable, 1/2 fat.

Two schools of thought exist when it comes to adding olive oil to the water when cooking pasta. One belief is that adding 1 tablespoon oil to every 3 quarts water prevents the pasta from sticking together. The second school believes that the oily residue left on the pasta can cause sauces to slide off the pasta, making it difficult to eat. Our Test Kitchen home economists agree and prefer to cook pasta without adding oil to the water.

Wild Rice-Stuffed Steaks

Ardith Baker
BEAVERTON, OREGON

Thirty minutes and four ingredients are all you'll need for these scrumptious steaks. A packaged rice mixture and teriyaki sauce make them flavorful and fast.

PREP/TOTAL TIME: 30 min.

1 package (6.2 ounces) fast-cooking long grain and wild rice mix
1/4 cup chopped green onions
6 New York strip steaks (about 12 ounces *each*)
1/2 cup teriyaki sauce, *divided*

■ Cook rice according to package directions for microwave; cool. Stir in onions. Cut a pocket in each steak by slicing to within 1/2 in. of bottom. Stuff each with 1/4 cup rice mixture; secure with toothpicks. Brush steaks with 2 tablespoons teriyaki sauce.

■ Place on a broiler pan. Broil 4-6 in. from the heat for 4-6 minutes. Turn steaks; brush with 2 tablespoons of teriyaki sauce. Broil 6-8 minutes longer or until meat reaches desired doneness (for medium-rare, a meat thermometer should read 145°; medium, 160°; well-done, 170°), basting frequently with remaining sauce. Discard toothpicks.

Yield: 6 servings.

Meatball Sub Casserole

- In a small bowl, combine the onion, bread crumbs and Parmesan cheese. Add beef and mix well. Shape into 1-in. balls; place on a rack in a shallow baking pan. Bake at 400° for 8-10 minutes or until no longer pink; drain.

- Meanwhile, arrange bread in a single layer in an ungreased shallow 3-cup baking dish. Combine the cream cheese, mayonnaise, Italian seasoning and pepper; spread over bread. Sprinkle with 1/3 cup mozzarella cheese.

- In a bowl, combine the spaghetti sauce, water and garlic; add meatballs. Pour mixture over the bread. Sprinkle with remaining mozzarella. Bake, uncovered, at 350° for 25-30 minutes or until casserole is heated through.

Yield: 3 servings.

Gina Harris
SENECA, SOUTH CAROLINA

If you like meatball subs, this tangy hot bake is sure to be a favorite. It's fast, flavorful and with a green salad...becomes a no-fuss meal!

Meatball Sub Casserole

PREP: 25 min. ■ BAKE: 25 min.

2 tablespoons chopped green onion

1 tablespoon seasoned bread crumbs

1 tablespoon grated Parmesan cheese

1/3 pound lean ground beef

6 slices French bread baguette (1/2 inch thick)

2 ounces cream cheese, softened

2 tablespoons mayonnaise

1/4 teaspoon Italian seasoning

Dash pepper

2/3 cup shredded part-skim mozzarella cheese, *divided*

1 cup spaghetti sauce

1/4 cup water

1 garlic clove, minced

Round out the Meatball Sub Casserole by picking up a bag of salad greens at the grocery store. Feeding a small household? Visit supermarkets that offer a salad bar. You can select just enough fixings for your home without worrying about leftovers.

Gloria Handley
PHOENIX, ARIZONA

I originally found this recipe in our local paper. After a few additions and substitutions, it became my family's favorite. I prepare it at least two times every month.

Beefy Noodle Dinner

Cheesy Beef Casserole

Sharon Crider
LEBANON, MISSOURI

Here's satisfying hot bake for busy weeknights. A hint of Southwestern flair makes it a mainstay on my supper table.

PREP: 10 min.
BAKE: 30 min.

1-1/2 pounds ground beef
   1 envelope taco seasoning
   2 cups water
   2 cups uncooked instant rice
   1 can (10-3/4 ounces) condensed cream of chicken soup, undiluted
   1 can (10-3/4 ounces) condensed cream of mushroom soup, undiluted
   1 can (4 ounces) chopped green chilies, undrained
   2 cups (8 ounces) shredded Mexican cheese blend

◼ In a large skillet, cook beef over medium heat until no longer pink; drain. Stir in the taco seasoning, water, rice, soups and chilies. Transfer to a greased 13-in. x 9-in. x 2-in. baking dish. Cover and bake at 350° for 25 minutes. Uncover; sprinkle with cheese. Bake 5 minutes longer or until heated through and cheese is melted.

Yield: 6-8 servings.

Beefy Noodle Dinner

PREP/TOTAL TIME: 30 min.

   1 pound ground beef
1/4 cup chopped onion
3/4 teaspoon salt
1/4 teaspoon pepper
Dash garlic powder
   1 can (19 ounces) ready-to-serve chunky beef vegetable soup

   4 ounces spaghetti, cooked and drained
   1 cup (4 ounces) shredded cheddar cheese
Minced fresh parsley, optional

◼ In a skillet, cook beef and onion over medium heat until meat is no longer pink; drain. Stir in salt, pepper and garlic powder. Transfer to a greased 2-qt. baking dish. Pour soup over meat mixture. Top with spaghetti and cheese.

◼ Bake, uncovered, at 350° for 15-20 minutes or until heated through. Sprinkle with parsley if desired.

Yield: 4-6 servings.

Convenience items are key to setting a hot meal on the table in a flash. Beefy Noodle Dinner, for instance, relies on canned vegetable soup and spaghetti. Feel free to use whatever soup or pasta you have.

Karla
Wiederholt
CUBA CITY, WISCONSIN

I combined two childhood classics— sloppy joes and Tater Tots—to create this home-style delight that will keep your youngsters coming back for more. Serve it with a basket of rolls, and dinner is ready!

Tater Beef Bake

Tater Beef Bake

PREP: 25 min. ■ **BAKE:** 35 min.

1-1/2 pounds ground beef	3-1/2 cups frozen cut green beans
1-1/4 cups water	
2 envelopes sloppy joe sauce mix	1 can (4 ounces) mushroom stems and pieces, drained
1 can (6 ounces) tomato paste	6 cups frozen Tater Tots
	1 cup (4 ounces) shredded cheddar cheese

■ In a Dutch oven, cook beef over medium heat until no longer pink; drain. Stir in water and sauce mix. Bring to a boil. Reduce heat; simmer, uncovered, for 3-5 minutes or until thickened. Add tomato paste; stir until blended. Add green beans and mushrooms.

■ Transfer to a greased 13-in. x 9-in. x 2-in. baking dish. Top with Tater Tots. Bake, uncovered, at 350° for 30 minutes. Sprinkle with cheese; bake 5-10 minutes longer or until heated through and cheese is melted.

Yield: *6-8 servings.*

Spice up your dinner routine by replacing the sloppy joe sauce mix with two envelopes taco seasoning. You can also mix a can of chopped jalapeno peppers when adding the mushrooms. Top it all off with Mexican cheese blend for a south-of-the-border surprise.

Meat Loaf Dinner

Florence Dollard
GRAND ISLAND, NEW YORK

When in a hurry, I substitute canned potatoes and green beans for the fresh items called for in this recipe. I like the fact that I can pop this complete supper into the oven in the late afternoon and forget about it until dinnertime.

PREP: 15 min.
BAKE: 2 hours

1 egg
1/2 cup seasoned bread crumbs
1/4 cup chopped onion
1/2 teaspoon seasoned salt
2 pounds lean ground beef
4 medium potatoes, quartered
1/2 pound fresh *or* frozen cut green beans
1 can (14-1/2 ounces) stewed tomatoes

■ In a large bowl, combine the first four ingredients. Crumble beef over mixture and mix well. Shape into a loaf in a greased roasting pan. Arrange potatoes and green beans around loaf. Pour tomatoes over all.

■ Cover and bake at 350° for 2 hours or until the meat is no longer pink and a meat thermometer reads 160°.

Yield: 8 servings.

Herbed Shepherd's Pie

Margaret Wagner Allen
ABINGDON, VIRGINIA

This one-dish dinner pleases the meat-and-potato lovers in my family. Best of all, everyone enjoys a serving or two of veggies without any extra work on my part.

Herbed Shepherd's Pie

PREP: 45 min. ■ **BAKE:** 10 min.

1 pound ground beef
1 can (14-1/2 ounces) beef broth, *divided*
3 to 4 bay leaves
2 whole cloves
1/2 teaspoon pepper
1/8 teaspoon dried thyme
1 pound potatoes, peeled and cubed
1/4 to 1/2 cup milk
2 tablespoons butter

1 tablespoon minced chives
1 teaspoon salt, *divided*
1 cup (4 ounces) shredded part-skim mozzarella cheese
2 medium onion, sliced
2 celery ribs, diced
1 large carrot, sliced
1 cup frozen corn, thawed
2 tablespoons all-purpose flour

■ In a large skillet, cook beef over medium heat until beef is no longer pink; drain. Stir in 1 cup broth, bay leaves, cloves, pepper and thyme. Bring to a boil. Reduce heat; cover and simmer for 30 minutes.

■ Meanwhile, place potatoes in a large saucepan; cover with water. Bring to a boil. Reduce heat. Cover; cook 15-20 minutes or until tender. Drain. Mash potatoes with milk, butter, chives and 1/2 teaspoon salt. Stir in cheese; keep warm.

■ Add vegetables and remaining salt to the beef mixture. Cover and simmer for 10 minutes. In a bowl, whisk the flour and remaining broth until smooth. Gradually stir into beef mixture. Bring to a boil; cook and stir for 1-2 minutes or until thickened. Remove from heat. Discard bay leaves and cloves.

■ Transfer beef mixture to a greased 11-in. x 7-in. x 2-in. baking dish. Top with mashed potatoes. Bake, uncovered, at 375° for 10 minutes or until heated through.

Yield: 4-6 servings.

Instead of making mashed potatoes for the pie, combine canned cream of celery soup with milk and frozen hash browns. Layer the mixture over the meat.

Sloppy Joe Mac and Cheese

Dorothy Leone
MEREDITH, NEW HAMPSHIRE

Combining two mealtime classics into one turned out to be a hit with my grandchildren. It's so versatile, too. I can toss in whatever items I have in my kitchen cabinet or refrigerator.

PREP: 45 min. ■ **BAKE:** 35 min.

- 1 package (16 ounces) elbow macaroni
- 1 pound lean ground beef
- 1 can (14-1/2 ounces) diced tomatoes, undrained
- 1 can (6 ounces) tomato paste
- 1 envelope sloppy joe mix
- 1 small onion, finely chopped
- 1/4 cup butter, cubed
- 1/4 cup all-purpose flour
- 1 teaspoon salt
- 1 teaspoon ground mustard
- 1/4 teaspoon pepper
- 3 cups half-and-half cream
- 1 tablespoon Worcestershire sauce
- 4 cups (16 ounces) shredded cheddar cheese, *divided*

■ Cook macaroni according to package directions. Meanwhile, in a large skillet, cook beef over medium heat until no longer pink; drain. Add the tomatoes, tomato paste and sloppy joe mix. Bring to a boil. Reduce heat; cover and simmer for 10 minutes, stirring occasionally.

■ Drain macaroni; set aside. In a large saucepan, saute onion in butter until tender. Stir in the flour, salt, mustard and pepper until smooth. Gradually add cream and Worcestershire sauce. Bring to a boil; cook and stir for 1-2 minutes or until thickened. Remove from the heat. Stir in 3 cups cheese until melted. Add macaroni; mix well.

■ Spread two-thirds of the macaroni mixture in a greased 13-in. x 9-in. x 2-in. baking dish. Spread beef mixture to within 2 in. of edges. Spoon remaining macaroni mixture around edges. Cover and bake at 375° for 30 minutes. Sprinkle with remaining cheese. Bake, uncovered, 5-6 minutes longer or until cheese is melted.

Yield: 10 servings.

Cheese-Topped Beef Bake

PREP: 20 min.
BAKE: 25 min.

- 1 package (16 ounces) medium pasta shells
- 1 pound ground beef
- 1 jar (26 ounces) spaghetti sauce
- 1 envelope taco seasoning
- 1 carton (8 ounces) spreadable chive and onion cream cheese
- 1 cup (8 ounces) sour cream
- 1 cup (4 ounces) shredded cheddar cheese

■ Cook pasta according to package directions. Meanwhile, in a large skillet, cook beef over medium heat until no longer pink; drain. Stir in the spaghetti sauce and taco seasoning. In a bowl, combine cream cheese and sour cream; set aside.

■ Drain the pasta; stir into beef mixture. Transfer to a greased 13-in. x 9-in. x 2-in. baking dish. Spread with cream cheese mixture; sprinkle with cheddar cheese. Bake, uncovered, at 350° for 25-30 minutes or until cheese is melted.

Yield: 8-10 servings.

Debbie Pirlot
GREEN BAY, WISCONSIN

I was browsing through a Taste of Home cookbook and found two easy recipes with similar ingredients. I decided to combine them. The result is this rich and delicious recipe that my family really enjoys. Best of all, it's an effortless meal-in-one.

Poultry

194

192

204

Nothing says "home" more than a hot stew or potpie. These comforting casseroles and one-dish meals are chock-full of chicken or turkey plus other wholesome ingredients, making them excellent for family gatherings, potlucks and weeknight dinners.

- In a large skillet coated with cooking spray, cook the turkey, onions, green pepper and garlic over medium heat until meat is no longer pink and vegetables are tender; drain. Sprinkle with chili powder and salt. Stir in the beans, tomatoes, water, rice and olives.

- Transfer to a 2-1/2-qt. baking dish coated with cooking spray. Cover and bake at 375° for 50-55 minutes or until rice is tender. Uncover; sprinkle with cheese. Bake 5 minutes longer or until cheese is melted.

Yield: 6 servings.

*Nutrition Facts: 1 serving equals 348 calories, 10 g fat (3 g saturated fat), 66 mg cholesterol, 508 mg sodium, 41 g carbohydrate, 9 g fiber, 24 g protein. Diabetic Exchanges: 2-1/2 lean meat, 2 starch, 2 vegetable.

Mexicali Casserole

Gertrudis Miller
EVANSVILLE, INDIANA

Kids will love this hearty yet mild tasting Southwestern-style meal. The all-in-one dish is also popular at potluck dinners. It's sure to receive lots of attention.

Mexicali Casserole*

PREP: 15 min. ■ BAKE: 55 min.

  1 pound ground turkey breast
1-1/2 cups chopped onions
  1/2 cup chopped green pepper
  1 garlic clove, minced
  1 teaspoon chili powder
  1/2 teaspoon salt
  1 can (16 ounces) kidney beans, rinsed and drained
  1 can (14-1/2 ounces) diced tomatoes, undrained
  1 cup water
  2/3 cup uncooked long grain rice
  1/3 cup sliced ripe olives
  1/2 cup shredded reduced-fat cheddar cheese

For a little extra crunch, after the casserole comes out of the oven, top it with shredded lettuce. A topping of fresh, chopped tomato adds a bit of color.

Pat Price Cook
MISSION VIEJO, CALIFORNIA

If you're looking for a dish that's sure to satisfy your group, you can't beat this hearty dinner that features layers of chicken and homemade stuffing. A rich butter sauce adds the final touch. And because it serves a crowd, it's perfect for formal and casual get-togethers alike.

Comforting Chicken Casserole

PREP: 1-3/4 hours + cooling ■ BAKE: 1 hour

- 1 broiler/fryer chicken (3 to 4 pounds)
- 3 quarts water
- 1 large onion, chopped
- 2 celery ribs, coarsely chopped
- 1 bay leaf
- 1/2 teaspoon salt
- 1/4 teaspoon pepper

STUFFING:
- 6 cups unseasoned stuffing cubes
- 1 tablespoon dried parsley flakes
- 1/2 teaspoon rubbed sage
- 1/2 cup chopped celery
- 2 tablespoons chopped onion
- 2 tablespoons butter

SAUCE:
- 1/2 cup butter, cubed
- 3/4 cup all-purpose flour
- 1-1/4 teaspoons salt
- 1/2 teaspoon pepper
- 6 eggs, beaten

■ In a soup kettle, combine the first seven ingredients. Bring to a boil. Reduce heat; cover and simmer for 1-1/2 to 2 hours or until the chicken is tender.

■ Remove chicken from broth. When cool enough to handle, remove meat from bones; dice and set aside. Strain broth and skim fat; discard onion, celery and bay leaf. Set aside 6 cups broth for sauce.

■ In a bowl, combine stuffing cubes, parsley and sage. Saute celery and onion in butter until tender. Add to stuffing mixture and mix well; set aside.

■ In a large saucepan, melt butter. Whisk in flour, salt and pepper until smooth. Gradually add reserved broth; bring to a boil. Reduce heat; cook and stir for 2 minutes. Remove from the heat. Stir a small amount into eggs; return all to the pan, stirring constantly. Bring to a gentle boil; cook and stir 2 minutes longer.

■ In a greased 13-in. x 9-in. x 2-in. baking dish, layer half of the chicken, stuffing and sauce. Repeat layers. Cover and bake at 350° for 45 minutes. Uncover; bake 15-20 minutes longer or until a knife comes out clean.

Yield: 12 servings.

Turkey Dinner Pasta Shells

Taste of Home
Test Kitchen
GREENDALE, WISCONSIN

This special pasta meal uses a variety of Thanksgiving leftovers, like stuffing, gravy and turkey. Prepare it ahead of time, chill and bake when ready.

PREP: 20 min.
BAKE: 30 min.

- 2 cups shredded cooked turkey
- 1-1/2 cups cooked stuffing
- 1/2 cup mayonnaise
- 18 jumbo pasta shells, cooked and drained
- 2 cups turkey gravy

Paprika

■ In a bowl, combine the turkey, stuffing and mayonnaise. Spoon into pasta shells. Place in a greased 13-in. x 9-in. x 2-in. baking dish. Pour gravy over shells. Sprinkle with paprika. Cover and bake at 350° for 30-35 minutes or until heated through.

Yield: 6 servings.

It's easy to make your own bread cubes. Simply cut the bread into 1/2-inch cubes, place them in a single layer on baking sheet and then let dry overnight.

Cheryl Maczko
EGLON, WEST VIRGINIA
Canned soup and a package of scalloped potato mix hurry along my creamy and comforting casserole. You can use either leftover chicken or extra turkey.

Scalloped Chicken Supper

Scalloped Chicken Supper

PREP: 10 min. ■ **BAKE:** 45 min.

1 package (4.9 ounces) scalloped potatoes
1-3/4 cups boiling water
1 can (10-3/4 ounces) condensed cream of chicken soup, undiluted

1/8 teaspoon poultry seasoning
2 cups cubed cooked chicken
1 cup shredded carrots
1/2 cup chopped celery
1/4 cup finely chopped onion

■ Place the contents of the sauce mix in a large bowl; set the potatoes aside. Whisk in the water, soup and poultry seasoning. Stir in the chicken, carrots, celery, onion and reserved potatoes.

■ Transfer to a greased 2-qt. baking dish. Bake, uncovered, at 400° for 45-50 minutes or until vegetables are tender.

Yield: 4 servings.

Save time by shredding a few extra carrots for future meals. Freeze the carrots in 1-cup portions and store them in resealable freezer bags. The next time a recipe calls for shredded carrots, you'll be a step ahead.

Ravioli Chicken Casserole

Stacie Knackmuhs
DECATUR, ILLINOIS
I threw this together one night when I had to work late and my new in-laws stopped over for the first time. The one-dish dinner was a real hit.

PREP: 20 min.
BAKE: 30 min.

1 package (24 ounces) frozen cheese ravioli
3 cups cubed cooked chicken
6 medium fresh mushrooms, sliced
1/2 cup chopped green pepper
1/3 cup chopped onion
1 jar (28 ounces) meatless spaghetti sauce
2 cups (8 ounces) shredded part-skim mozzarella cheese

■ Cook ravioli according to package directions; drain. In a greased 13-in. x 9-in. x 2-in. baking dish, layer the ravioli and chicken. Top with mushrooms, green pepper, onion and spaghetti sauce.

■ Cover and bake at 350° for 20 minutes. Uncover; sprinkle with cheese. Bake 10-15 minutes longer or until cheese is melted.

Yield: 10-12 servings.

■ In a large bowl, combine the flour, baking powder and salt. Cut in butter until crumbly. Gradually add water, tossing with a fork until dough forms a ball. Turn onto a lightly floured surface; knead 10-12 times or until smooth.

■ Set aside a third of the dough. Roll remaining dough into a 15-in. x 11-in. rectangle. Transfer to an ungreased 11-in. x 7-in. x 2-in. baking dish.

■ In a bowl, combine the turkey, cheese, soup, sour cream, onion, chilies and green onions. Spoon into crust. Roll out reserved dough; make a lattice crust. Place over filling; trim and flute edges.

■ Bake at 400° for 45-50 minutes or until crust is golden brown and filling is bubbly.

Yield: 6 servings.

Family-Style Turkey Potpie

Karen Ann Bland
GOVE, KANSAS
Despite our last name, my family likes spicy, flavorful foods like this hearty potpie seasoned with zesty green chilies and Monterey Jack cheese.

Family-Style Turkey Potpie

PREP: 20 min. ■ **BAKE:** 45 min.

3 cups all-purpose flour
1 teaspoon baking powder
1/2 teaspoon salt
1/2 cup cold butter
3/4 to 1 cup cold water
4 cups cubed cooked turkey
2 cups (8 ounces) shredded Monterey Jack cheese

1 can (10-3/4 ounces) condensed cream of chicken soup, undiluted
1 cup (8 ounces) sour cream
1 small onion, finely chopped
1 can (4 ounces) chopped green chilies
2 green onions, sliced

Potpie is an all-time favorite with families from coast to coast. Because it's a real one-dish wonder, all you need to do is add a dessert to round out the meal. Consider scoops of ice cream or slices of pound cake with fruit for a simply delightful solution.

Polish-Style Sausage 'n' Potatoes*

Victoria Zmarzley-Hahn
NORTHAMPTON, PENNSYLVANIA

This hearty layering of sliced potatoes, cabbage, onion, Polish sausage and white sauce is always in demand at my house. After all, I love any dish with cabbage and kielbasa.

PREP: 10 min. ■ **BAKE:** 1 hour

- 1 package (14 ounces) smoked turkey kielbasa, sliced
- 1 tablespoon butter
- 3 tablespoons all-purpose flour
- 1/2 teaspoon salt
- 1/4 teaspoon pepper
- 1/4 teaspoon garlic powder
- 1/4 teaspoon paprika
- 2 cups fat-free milk
- 2 cups sliced potatoes
- 2 cups shredded cabbage
- 1 medium onion, chopped

■ In a nonstick skillet, brown sausage over medium heat; set aside. For white sauce, melt butter in a saucepan. Stir in flour and seasonings until smooth. Gradually add milk. Bring to a boil; cook and stir for 2 minutes or until thickened. Remove from heat.

■ In a 3-qt. baking dish coated with cooking spray, layer a third of the potatoes, cabbage, onion, sausage and white sauce. Repeat layers twice.

■ Cover and bake at 350° for 1 to 1-1/2 hours or until the vegetables are tender.

Yield: 4 servings.

*****Nutrition Facts:** 1 serving (1-1/4 cups) equals 298 calories, 6 g fat (3 g saturated fat), 46 mg cholesterol, 1,249 mg sodium, 41 g carbohydrate, 3 g fiber, 20 g protein. **Diabetic Exchanges:** 2 starch, 2 lean meat, 1/2 fat-free milk.

To lighten the calorie load on the Rosemary Chicken Dinner, remove the skin from the chicken quarters before serving.

Rosemary Chicken Dinner

PREP: 15 min.
BAKE: 1 hour

- 3 large potatoes, peeled
- 1 broiler/fryer chicken (3 to 4 pounds), cut into quarters
- 2 tablespoons olive oil
- 1 teaspoon salt
- 1/4 teaspoon garlic powder
- 1/4 teaspoon pepper
- 2 to 3 teaspoons minced fresh rosemary *or* 1 teaspoon dried rosemary, crushed

■ Cut each potato into four wedges. Place chicken and potatoes in a greased 13-in. x 9-in. x 2-in. baking dish or shallow roasting pan. Drizzle with oil. Combine salt, garlic powder and pepper; sprinkle over chicken and potatoes. Sprinkle the rosemary over the chicken.

■ Bake, uncovered, at 375° for 45 minutes; drain. Bake 15-20 minutes longer or until potatoes are tender and chicken juices run clear.

Yield: 4 servings.

Christine Yost
NEWARK, NEW YORK

The fragrant rosemary in this scrumptious meat-and-potatoes dish makes the whole house smell wonderful! Sometimes I round out the meal with a second vegetable or a simple green salad. It looks so elegant, your family and guests would never guess it uses only seven ingredients.

Greek Pasta Bake

- Cook pasta according to package directions; drain. In a large bowl, combine the pasta, chicken, tomato sauce, tomatoes, spinach, olives, onion, green pepper, basil and oregano.

- Transfer to a 13-in. x 9-in. x 2-in. baking dish coated with cooking spray. Sprinkle with the cheeses. Bake, uncovered, at 400° for 25-30 minutes or until heated through and cheese is melted.

Yield: 8 servings.

*Nutrition Facts: 1-1/2 cups equals 366 calories, 7 g fat (2 g saturated fat), 62 mg cholesterol, 847 mg sodium, 43 g carbohydrate, 6 g fiber, 32 g protein. **Diabetic Exchanges:** 3 very lean meat, 2-1/2 starch, 1 vegetable, 1/2 fat.

Anne Taglienti, Kennett
SQUARE, PENNSYLVANIA

I've brought this hot dish to potlucks and it received rave reviews. There's never a crumb left. Best of all, it's a complete supper made with healthy, easy-to-find ingredients.

Greek Pasta Bake*

PREP: 20 min. ■ **BAKE:** 25 min.

1 package (12 ounces) whole wheat penne pasta

4 cups cubed cooked chicken breast

1 can (29 ounces) tomato sauce

1 can (14-1/2 ounces) diced tomatoes, drained

1 package (10 ounces) frozen chopped spinach, thawed and squeezed dry

2 cans (2-1/4 ounces *each*) sliced ripe olives, drained

1/4 cup chopped red onion

2 tablespoons chopped green pepper

1 teaspoon dried basil

1 teaspoon dried oregano

1/2 cup shredded part-skim mozzarella cheese

1/2 cup crumbled feta cheese

Whole wheat pasta is fast becoming a popular choice for today's family cooks. Featuring more fiber and a slightly stronger flavor than other pasta, the healthy alternative makes a nice change-of-pace to any pasta dish.

Chicken Meal-in-One*

Jina Nickel,
LAWTON, OKLAHOMA

As the parents of a young son, my husband and I don't have much time to prepare meals. While our boy is napping, I can assemble this dinner-in-a-dish in just 10 minutes and then pop it in the oven.

PREP: 10 min. ■ **BAKE:** 1-1/4 hours

4-1/2 cups frozen shredded hash brown potatoes
 2 cups frozen cut green beans, thawed
 1 cup frozen sliced carrots, thawed
 4 bone-in chicken breasts (6 ounces *each*)

 1 can (10-3/4 ounces) condensed cream of chicken *or* mushroom soup, undiluted
 3/4 cup water
 2 tablespoons dry onion soup mix
 Salt and pepper to taste

■ In an ungreased 13-in. x 9-in. x 2-in. baking dish, combine hash browns, beans and carrots. Top with chicken. Combine remaining ingredients; pour over chicken and vegetables.

■ Cover and bake at 375° for 50 minutes. Uncover; bake 25-30 minutes longer or until chicken juices run clear.

Yield: 4 servings.

✱**Nutrition Facts:** 1 serving (prepared with skinless chicken breasts, reduced-fat reduced-sodium mushroom soup and reduced-sodium onion soup mix and without salt) equals 428 calories, 5 g fat (0 saturated fat), 73 mg cholesterol, 685 mg sodium, 62 g carbohydrate, 8 g fiber, 34 g protein. **Diabetic Exchanges:** 3-1/2 starch, 3 very lean meat, 1 vegetable, 1/2 fat.

Don't have the frozen green beans called for in Chicken Meal-in-One? Simply replace them with frozen broccoli florets, corn or whatever frozen veggie you have on hand. Consider a medley of vegetables for a burst of color and flavor.

Chicken Broccoli Supper

Heather Oblinger
GAHANNA, OHIO

Here's a complete meal for two that doesn't require you to cook the chicken or macaroni first. It's very easy to assemble.

PREP: 10 min.
BAKE: 55 min.

 1/2 pound boneless skinless chicken breast, cubed
1-1/2 cups frozen broccoli florets
 1/2 cup uncooked elbow macaroni
 1/2 cup shredded cheddar cheese
 1 can (10-3/4 ounces) condensed cream of chicken soup, undiluted
 3/4 cup chicken broth
 1/4 teaspoon garlic powder
 1/4 teaspoon pepper

■ In a large bowl, combine the chicken, broccoli, macaroni and cheese. Whisk the soup, broth, garlic powder and pepper; stir into chicken mixture.

■ Transfer to a greased 1-1/2-qt. baking dish. Bake, uncovered, at 350° for 30 minutes. Stir; bake 25-30 minutes longer or until chicken juices run clear and macaroni is tender. Let stand for 5 minutes before serving.

Yield: 2 servings.

Leslie Adams
SPRINGFIELD, MISSOURI

No one would guess that these moist chicken breasts and tender potatoes are seasoned with herb- and garlic-flavored soup mix. The meal-in-one is simple to assemble, and it all bakes in one dish so there's little cleanup.

Savory Chicken Dinner

Savory Chicken Dinner

PREP: 10 min. ■ **BAKE:** 45 min.

1 envelope savory herb with garlic soup mix
3 tablespoons water
4 boneless skinless chicken breast halves (6 to 8 ounces *each*)
2 large red potatoes, cubed
1 large onion, halved and cut into small wedges

■ In a large resealable plastic bag, combine the soup mix and water. Add the chicken, potatoes and onion; seal bag and toss to coat. Transfer to a greased 13-in. x 9-in. x 2-in. baking dish.

■ Bake, uncovered, at 350° for 40-45 minutes or until vegetables are tender and chicken juices run clear, stirring vegetables occasionally.

Yield: 4 servings.

With just 10 minutes of prep time, Savory Chicken Dinner is great when time is at a premium. The dish delivers a strong garlic flavor, so consider rounding it out with a loaf of bread.

Greek Roasted Chicken and Potatoes

PREP: 10 min.
BAKE: 2 hours

1 whole roasting chicken (about 6 pounds)
Salt and pepper to taste
2 to 3 teaspoons dried oregano, *divided*
4 to 6 baking potatoes, peeled and quartered
1/4 cup butter, melted
3 tablespoons fresh lemon juice
3/4 cup chicken broth

■ Place chicken breast side up on a rack in a roasting pan. Sprinkle with salt and pepper and half the oregano. Arrange potatoes around the chicken; sprinkle with salt and pepper and the remaining oregano. Pour butter and lemon juice over chicken and potatoes. Add chicken broth to pan.

■ Bake uncovered at 350° for 2 to 2-1/2 hours or until juices run clear and a meat thermometer inserted into thigh reads 180°, basting frequently. Cover and let stand for 10 minutes before carving. If desired, thicken pan drippings for gravy.

Yield: about 8-10 servings.

Pella Visnick
DALLAS, TEXAS

You'll find this roast to be a nice menu item for company or a special Sunday supper. Seasoned potatoes bake right alongside the meat, so you can focus on other dishes, such as a salad, vegetable or dessert. And if there is leftover chicken, I make chicken salad the next day.

- In a small bowl, combine the soup mix, garlic powder and oil. Spoon half into a large resealable plastic bag; add chicken. Seal bag and turn to coat. Spoon the remaining marinade into another large resealable plastic bag; add potatoes and carrots. Seal bag and turn to coat.

- Arrange chicken and vegetables in an ungreased 11-in. x 7-in. x 2-in. baking dish. Cover and bake at 425° for 15 minutes. Uncover; bake 15-20 minutes longer or until chicken juices run clear and vegetables are tender.

Yield: 4 servings.

One-Dish Chicken with Vegetables

Katherine McKinley
NEW ALBANY, INDIANA

It's easy to set a home-cooked meal on the table with just a handful of ingredients. The first time I made the no-fuss meal, it looked so pretty I took a picture of it!

One-Dish Chicken With Vegetables

PREP: 15 min. ■ **BAKE:** 30 min.

1 envelope onion soup mix
1/2 teaspoon garlic powder
1/4 cup olive oil
4 boneless skinless chicken breast halves (4 ounces *each*)

4 medium potatoes, cut into chunks
4 medium carrots, cut into 1/4-inch slices

Olive oils are graded according to acidity. Extra-virgin olive oil is the top grade and is extremely low in acidity (1%). Virgin olive oil has a slightly higher acidity (2%), lighter color and less fruity flavor. Both of these oils are best used in dishes where strong flavors can be appreciated. Bottles simply labeled olive oil contain oil with up to 3% acidity. It offers a light color and somewhat of a mild flavor.

Chicken and Ham Lasagna

Pamela Grady
INMAN, SOUTH CAROLINA
This creamy version of lasagna goes over great at community get-togethers. Consider it the next time you need a hearty dinner solution.

■ In a large skillet, saute the mushrooms, onion and green pepper in butter until tender. Stir in flour until blended. Gradually add milk and broth. Bring to a boil; cook and stir for 2 minutes or until thickened. Stir in the broccoli, cheese, salt, pepper and nutmeg.

■ Spread 2 cups broccoli mixture in a greased 13-in. x 9-in. x 2-in. baking dish. Top with four noodles, overlapping if needed. Layer with 2 cups broccoli mixture, 1-1/2 cups of ham, 2/3 cup Swiss cheese and four noodles. Then layer with 2 cups broccoli mixture, chicken, 2/3 cup Swiss cheese, four noodles and remaining broccoli mixture, Swiss cheese and ham.

■ Cover and bake at 350° for 35-45 minutes or until heated through. Let stand for 15 minutes before cutting.

Yield: 12 servings.

Chicken and Ham Lasagna

PREP: 25 min. ■ BAKE: 35 min. + standing

3/4 pound fresh mushrooms, sliced	2/3 cup grated Parmesan cheese
1 large onion, chopped	1/2 teaspoon salt
1 large green pepper, chopped	1/4 to 1/2 teaspoon white pepper
1/4 cup butter	1/8 teaspoon ground nutmeg
1/2 cup all-purpose flour	12 lasagna noodles, cooked and drained
1-2/3 cups milk	2 cups cubed fully cooked ham
1 can (14-1/2 ounces) chicken broth	2 cups (8 ounces) shredded Swiss cheese
1 package (16 ounces) frozen chopped broccoli, thawed and drained	2 cups cubed cooked chicken

When making her lasagna, Pamela Grady often substitutes zucchini and yellow squash for the broccoli. She explains that she precooks the squash before adding it to the mushroom mixture.

Mrs. Robert Trygg
DULUTH, MINNESOTA

I'm always on the lookout for good, fast recipes. This one is easy to cook and serve and much more affordable than taking the family to dinner at a Mexican restaurant. I've found that even children like eating chicken this way.

Spanish Chicken

PREP: 25 min. ■ BAKE: 40 min.

- 4 boneless skinless chicken breast halves
- 2 tablespoons vegetable oil
- 1 medium onion, chopped
- 1/4 cup chopped green pepper
- 1 garlic clove, minced
- 1 can (14-1/2 ounces) diced tomatoes, undrained
- 1 cup water
- 3/4 cup uncooked long grain rice
- 2 teaspoons chicken bouillon granules
- 1 to 3 teaspoons chili powder
- 1/8 teaspoon ground cinnamon
- 1/8 teaspoon ground cumin
- 1/8 teaspoon pepper
- 1/2 cup picante sauce
- 1/2 cup shredded cheddar cheese
- 1 can (2-1/4 ounces) sliced ripe olives, drained

■ In a large skillet, brown chicken in oil for 2-3 minutes on each side. Remove and keep warm. In the same skillet, saute the onion, green pepper and garlic until tender. Stir in the tomatoes, water, rice, bouillon and seasonings. Bring to a boil.

■ Pour into a greased 11-in. x 7-in. x 2-in. baking dish; top with chicken. Cover and bake at 350° for 35-40 minutes or until rice is tender. Uncover; spoon picante sauce over chicken and sprinkle with cheese. Bake 5 minutes longer or until cheese is melted. Garnish with olives.

Yield: 4 servings.

Be sure to read the label on the picante sauce you purchase. If you like your food spicy, use medium or hot. Otherwise, make sure it reads "mild."

Turkey Biscuit Bake

Andy Zinkle
MT. PLEASANT, IOWA

As a college student, I appreciate stick-to-your-ribs foods like this that are also easy on the budget. I often double the recipe so I know I'll have leftovers.

PREP/TOTAL TIME: 30 min.

- 1 can (10-3/4 ounces) condensed cream of chicken soup, undiluted
- 1 cup diced cooked turkey *or* chicken
- 1 can (4 ounces) mushroom stems and pieces, drained
- 1/2 cup frozen peas
- 1/4 cup milk
- Dash *each* ground cumin, dried basil and thyme
- 1 tube (12 ounces) refrigerated biscuits

■ In a bowl, combine the soup, turkey, mushrooms, peas, milk, cumin, basil and thyme. Pour into a greased 8-in. square baking dish. Arrange biscuits over the top.

■ Bake, uncovered, at 350° for 20-25 minutes or until biscuits are golden brown.

Yield: 5 servings.

Joyce Wilson
OMAHA, NEBRASKA

This crunchy, saucy hot dish is potluck-perfect! You can make the casserole the day before and bake it the day of the get-together.

Make-Ahead Chicken Bake

Make-Ahead Chicken Bake

PREP: 25 min. + chilling ■ **BAKE:** 30 min.

5 cups cubed cooked chicken	1 teaspoon finely chopped onion
2 cups chopped celery	1 cup (4 ounces) shredded cheddar cheese
5 hard-cooked eggs, sliced	
1 can (10-3/4 ounces) condensed cream of chicken soup, undiluted	1 can (3 ounces) chow mein noodles
3/4 cup mayonnaise	1/2 cup slivered almonds, toasted
2 tablespoons lemon juice	
1 tablespoon pimientos, optional	

■ In a large bowl, combine the first eight ingredients. Transfer to a greased 3-qt. baking dish; sprinkle with cheese, chow mein noodles and almonds. Cover and refrigerate overnight.

■ Remove from the refrigerator 30 minutes before baking. Bake, uncovered, at 350° for 30-35 minutes until lightly browned and cheese is bubbly.

Yield: 12 servings.

Editor's Note: Reduced-fat or fat-free mayonnaise is not recommended for this recipe.

Ranch Chicken 'N' Rice

Erlene Crusoe
LITCHFIELD, MINNESOTA

When I clipped this recipe from a neighborhood shopper a few years ago, I couldn't wait to try it. Just as I expected, it quickly became one of the most requested recipes at my house.

PREP: 10 min.
BAKE: 35 min.

   2 cups uncooked instant rice
1-1/2 cups milk
   1 cup water
   1 envelope ranch salad dressing mix
   1 pound boneless skinless chicken breasts, cut into 1/2-inch strips
 1/4 cup butter, melted
Paprika

■ Place rice in a greased shallow 2-qt. baking dish. In a bowl, combine the milk, water and salad dressing mix; set aside 1/4 cup. Pour remaining mixture over rice. Top with chicken strips. Drizzle with butter and reserved milk mixture.

■ Cover and bake at 350° for 35-40 minutes or until rice is tender and chicken juices run clear. Sprinkle with paprika.

Yield: 4 servings.

- Cook pasta according to package directions. In a saucepan, melt butter over medium heat. Stir in the flour, salt, pepper and cayenne until smooth. Gradually add broth. Bring to a boil; cook and stir for 2 minutes or until thickened. Remove from the heat; stir in cream.

- Drain linguine; add 2 cups sauce and toss to coat. Transfer to a greased 13-in. x 9-in. x 2-in. baking dish. Make a well in center of noodles, making a space about 6 in. x 4 in.

- To the remaining sauce, add the turkey, mushrooms, pimientos, parsley and hot pepper sauce; mix well. Pour into center of dish. Sprinkle with Parmesan cheese.

- Cover and bake at 350° for 30 minutes. Uncover; bake 20-30 minutes longer or until bubbly and heated through.

Yield: 8-10 servings.

Turkey Tetrazzini

Audrey Thibodeau
GILBERT, ARIZONA

Featuring an easy, homemade white sauce, this meal-in-one casserole is comfort food at its best. Feel free to add more mushrooms or some other vegetables if you'd like.

Turkey Tetrazzini

PREP: 15 min. ■ BAKE: 50 min.

1 package (1 pound) linguine
6 tablespoons butter
6 tablespoons all-purpose flour
1/2 teaspoon salt
1/4 teaspoon pepper
1/8 teaspoon cayenne pepper
3 cups chicken broth
1 cup heavy whipping cream

4 cups cubed cooked turkey
1 cup sliced fresh mushrooms
1 jar (4 ounces) diced pimientos, drained
1/4 cup chopped fresh parsley
4 to 5 drops hot pepper sauce
1/3 cup grated Parmesan cheese

For an extra fancy touch, sprinkle the Tetrazzini with toasted slivered almonds as soon as the casserole comes out of the oven.

Pork

213

214

227

These easy-to-make meal-in-one delights are extra tasty because they are made with flavorful ingredients like sausage, spareribs, ham and kielbasa. For a more elegant flair, try one of the baked pork chop recipes, such as the Pilaf-Stuffed Pork Chops on page 224.

Pork Roast Supper

Garnett Brown Jr.
LEXINGTON, KENTUCKY
A fragrant medley of herbs and seasonings brings this pork roast to life. Loaded with potatoes, celery and carrots, it makes a well-rounded dinner when entertaining guests.

Pork Roast Supper

PREP: 20 min. ■ BAKE: 2 hours 10 min.

1 teaspoon *each* minced fresh tarragon, thyme and rosemary	2 tablespoons packed brown sugar
1 teaspoon salt	3 small onions, cut into chunks
1/2 teaspoon garlic powder	3 celery ribs, cut into chunks
1/2 teaspoon curry powder	3 medium carrots, cut into chunks
1/2 teaspoon pepper	6 medium red potatoes, cut into chunks
1 boneless pork loin roast (4 pounds), trimmed	1/3 cup vegetable oil
1 cup barbecue sauce	1/2 cup chicken broth
1-1/2 teaspoons prepared mustard	

■ In a small bowl, combine herbs, salt, garlic powder, curry powder and pepper; set aside 1 tablespoon. Rub the remaining mixture over roast; place in a greased shallow roasting pan. Combine barbecue sauce and mustard; spread over roast. Sprinkle with brown sugar.

■ In a resealable plastic bag, combine onions, celery, carrots, potatoes, oil and reserved herb mixture; toss well. Arrange vegetables around the roast. Pour broth into the pan. Bake, uncovered, at 350° for 2 hours or until a meat thermometer reads 160°. Let stand for 10 minutes before slicing.

Yield: 8 servings.

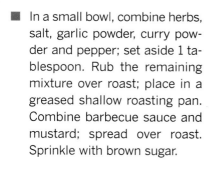

Herbed rubs give any roast a terrific taste boost. Mince the freshest herbs available to achieve the best flavor. (Mincing results in pieces no larger than 1/8 inch.) Combine the herbs and seasonings, then sprinkle the mixture over the pork roast and rub it into the surface of the meat.

Ruth Lee
TROY, ONTARIO
For a fun change of pace, consider these easy skewers. They broil nicely in the oven, so you don't even have to heat up the grill.

Smoked Sausage Kabobs

Smoked Sausage Kabobs

PREP/TOTAL TIME: 30 min.

1/3	cup honey
1/4	cup spicy brown mustard
2	tablespoons vegetable oil
1	tablespoon soy sauce
2	garlic cloves, minced
1/2	teaspoon minced fresh gingerroot
1-1/4	pounds smoked sausage, cut into 1-inch pieces
16	cherry tomatoes
8	medium fresh mushrooms
1	large green pepper, cut into 1-inch pieces
1	medium onion, cut into eight wedges
1	small zucchini, cut into 1-inch pieces

■ In a large bowl, combine the first six ingredients. Add the sausage and vegetables; toss to coat. Drain and reserve marinade.

■ On eight metal or soaked wooden skewers, alternately thread sausage and vegetables. Broil 3-4 in. from the heat for 3-4 minutes on each side or until vegetables are tender and sausage is heated through, basting occasionally with reserved marinade.

Yield: 4 servings.

Veggie Noodle Ham Casserole

PREP: 15 min.
BAKE: 50 min.

1	package (12 ounces) wide egg noodles
1	can (10-3/4 ounces) condensed cream of chicken soup, undiluted
1	can (10-3/4 ounces) condensed cream of broccoli soup, undiluted
1-1/2	cups milk
2	cups frozen corn, thawed
1-1/2	cups frozen California-blend vegetables, thawed
1-1/2	cups cubed fully cooked ham
2	tablespoons minced fresh parsley
1/2	teaspoon pepper
1/4	teaspoon salt
1	cup (4 ounces) shredded cheddar cheese, *divided*

■ Cook pasta according to package directions; drain. In a large bowl, combine soups and milk; stir in the noodles, corn, vegetables, ham, parsley, pepper, salt and 3/4 cup of cheese.

■ Transfer to a greased 13-in. x 9-in. x 2-in. baking dish. Cover and bake at 350° for 45 minutes. Uncover; sprinkle with remaining cheese. Bake 5-10 minutes longer or until bubbly and cheese is melted.

Yield: 8-10 servings.

Judy Moody
WHEATLEY, ONTARIO

This saucy main dish, packed with vegetables, egg noodles, ham and cheese is really quite versatile. Without the ham, it can be a vegetarian entree or a hearty side dish. You could also vary the type of frozen mixed veggies to suit your taste.

Pork with Apples and Sweet Potatoes

- In a small bowl, combine the salt, cinnamon, cardamom and pepper. Place sweet potatoes in a large bowl. Sprinkle with 1 teaspoon spice mixture and 3 teaspoons oil; toss to coat.

- Arrange potatoes in a single layer in a 15-in. x 10-in. x 1-in. baking pan coated with cooking spray. Bake, uncovered, at 425° for 10 minutes.

- Rub the remaining oil over pork; rub with remaining spice mixture. Place over the sweet potatoes. Bake for 15 minutes.

- Cut each apple into eight wedges. Turn pork; arrange apples around meat. Bake 15 minutes longer or until a meat thermometer reads 160°.

Yield: 6 servings.

✱**Nutrition Facts:** One serving equals 321 calories, 8 g fat (2 g saturated fat), 67 mg cholesterol, 452 mg sodium, 37 g carbohydrate, 5 g fiber, 26 g protein. **Diabetic Exchanges:** 3 lean meat, 1-1/2 starch, 1 fruit.

Linda Lacek
WINTER PARK, FLORIDA

Here's a meal-in-one that is quick, delicious and nutritious. The tenderloin is rubbed with a few seasonings, and baked apples and sweet potatoes round out the dinner perfectly.

Pork with Apples And Sweet Potatoes*

PREP: 10 min. ■ **BAKE:** 45 min.

1 teaspoon salt	4 teaspoons olive oil, *divided*
1/2 teaspoon ground cinnamon	2 pork tenderloins (3/4 pound *each*)
1/2 teaspoon ground cardamom	4 large tart apples, peeled
1/4 teaspoon pepper	
4-1/2 cups cubed peeled sweet potatoes (about 1-1/2 pounds)	

Pork tenderloin

thaws and cooks quickly, so it's great to keep in the freezer for last-minute dinners on hectic days. Thaw tenderloin using the "defrost" cycle of your microwave following the manufacturer's directions.

Evelyn Anderson Lugo
KENNER, LOUISIANA

Whenever family and friends get together, this is the dish I am asked to prepare. It's tasty, economical and oh-so easy.

Jambalaya Casserole

Jambalaya Casserole

PREP: 10 min. ■ **BAKE:** 45 min.

3 large onions, chopped	3 cups chopped fresh tomatoes
3 large green peppers, chopped	1-1/2 cups chopped green onions
3 celery ribs, chopped	1/2 cup minced fresh parsley
12 garlic cloves, minced	3 tablespoons Worcestershire sauce
1-1/2 cups butter	3 tablespoons hot pepper sauce
3 pounds smoked sausage, cut into 1/2-inch slices	3 tablespoons browning sauce, optional
9 cups chicken broth	1 tablespoon salt
6 cups uncooked long grain rice	1 tablespoon pepper

■ In a large skillet, saute the onions, green peppers, celery and garlic in butter until crisp-tender. Place in a very large bowl; stir in the remaining ingredients.

■ Transfer to three greased shallow 3-qt. baking dishes. Cover and bake at 375° for 45-50 minutes or until rice is tender, stirring twice.

Yield: 3 casseroles (8 servings each).

Pasta Ham Hot Dish

Judie Porath
BLACK DUCK, MINNESOTA

I brought this simple casserole to a potluck at work, and it was a hit. You can use a pound of cooked ground beef in place of ham.

PREP: 20 min.
BAKE: 30 min.

- 4 ounces uncooked spaghetti, broken into 2-inch pieces
- 1/4 cup chopped onion
- 1 tablespoon butter
- 2 cups cubed fully cooked ham
- 1 can (15-1/4 ounces) whole kernel corn, drained
- 1 can (14-3/4 ounces) cream-style corn
- 1 cup cubed process cheese (Velveeta)
- 1/2 teaspoon seasoned salt

■ Cook spaghetti according to package directions. Meanwhile, in a small skillet, saute onion in butter until tender. Drain the spaghetti; place in a large bowl. Add ham, corn, cheese, seasoned salt and onion mixture.

■ Transfer to a greased 2-qt. baking dish. Cover and bake at 350° for 30-35 minutes or until cheese is melted, stirring once.

Yield: 4-6 servings.

Joseph Obbie
WEBSTER, NEW YORK

I grow sweet onions and garlic, so they're always on hand when I want to make this roast. I originally fixed the supper for a church retreat, and it was a big hit. Since then, I've prepared it for large groups and family dinners over the years.

Roasted Garlic Pork Supper

PREP: 15 min. ■ **BAKE:** 3-1/2 hours + standing

2 whole garlic bulbs	6 medium red potatoes, quartered
2 teaspoons olive oil	3 cups baby carrots
1/2 teaspoon dried basil	1 large sweet onion, thinly sliced
1/2 teaspoon dried oregano	
2 tablespoons lemon juice	1-1/2 cups water
1 boneless pork loin roast (4 to 5 pounds)	1 teaspoon salt
	1/2 teaspoon pepper

■ Remove papery outer skin from garlic (do not peel or separate cloves). Cut top off garlic heads, leaving root end intact. Brush with oil; sprinkle with basil and oregano. Wrap each bulb in heavy-duty foil. Bake at 425° for 30-35 minutes or until softened. Cool for 10-15 minutes. Squeeze softened garlic into a small bowl. Add lemon juice; mix well. Rub over the roast.

■ Place roast in a shallow roasting pan. Arrange potatoes, carrots and onion around roast. Pour water into the pan. Sprinkle meat and vegetables with salt and pepper. Cover and bake at 350° for 1-1/2 hours. Uncover; bake 1-1/2 hours longer or until a meat thermometer reads 160°, basting often. Cover and let stand for 10 minutes before slicing.

Yield: 10-12 servings.

When you have leftover cooked ham from a holiday meal or family get-together, Creamy Ham 'n' Macaroni is a terrific solution. Just cube the ham and combine it with the sauce, cheese and pasta for a hearty main course. While it bakes, fix a quick broccoli side dish and serve scoops of sherbet for dessert.

Creamy Ham 'N' Macaroni

Christy Looper
COLORADO SPRINGS, COLORADO

The original comfort food, macaroni and cheese gets a makeover with the addition of cubed ham and grated Parmesan. Kids will love it!

PREP: 20 min.
BAKE: 20 min.

- 2 cups uncooked elbow macaroni
- 1/4 cup butter, cubed
- 1/4 cup all-purpose flour
- 2 cups milk
- 4 teaspoons chicken bouillon granules
- 1/4 teaspoon pepper
- 2 cups (8 ounces) shredded cheddar cheese, *divided*
- 1-1/2 cups cubed fully cooked ham
- 1/4 cup grated Parmesan cheese

■ Cook macaroni according to package directions; drain and set aside. In a large saucepan, melt butter over low heat; whisk in flour until smooth. Whisk in the milk, bouillon and pepper. Bring to a boil; cook and stir for 2 minutes or until thickened. Remove from the heat. Stir in 1 cup cheddar cheese, ham, Parmesan cheese and macaroni.

■ Transfer to a greased 2-qt. baking dish. Sprinkle with remaining cheese. Bake, uncovered, at 350° for 20-25 minutes or until bubbly. Let stand for 5 minutes before serving.

Yield: 6 servings.

Pork Chop Barley Bake

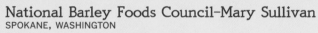

National Barley Foods Council–Mary Sullivan
SPOKANE, WASHINGTON

Orange marmalade and orange juice are the key ingredients behind this dinner's lovely glaze. Barley bakes right with the pork for a complete meal in a dish.

Pork Chop Barley Bake

PREP: 65 min. ■ **BAKE:** 1 hour

- 1   cup medium pearl barley
- 1/2 cup chopped onion
- 1/2 cup chopped celery
- 1   garlic clove, minced
- 4   tablespoons butter, *divided*
- 2   cups chicken broth
- 1   cup orange juice
- 1   teaspoon grated orange peel
- 1/2 teaspoon dried rosemary, crushed
- 1/2 cup chopped pecans, toasted

- 6   pork loin chops (1 inch thick)

Salt and pepper to taste

GLAZE:
- 1   cup orange marmalade
- 2   tablespoons orange juice
- 1   tablespoon prepared mustard
- 1/2 teaspoon ground ginger

Orange slices and fresh rosemary, optional

■ In a large saucepan, saute barley, onion, celery and garlic in 3 tablespoons butter until barley is golden brown and vegetables are tender. Add broth, orange juice, peel and rosemary; bring to a boil. Reduce heat; cover and simmer for 35 minutes or until barley is partially cooked. Add pecans.

■ Transfer to a greased 13-in. x 9-in. x 2-in. baking dish. In a skillet, brown pork chops on both sides in the remaining butter. Sprinkle with salt and pepper. Arrange over barley mixture.

■ Combine glaze ingredients; brush half over chops. Cover and bake at 350° for 45 minutes. Uncover; brush with remaining glaze. Bake 15 minutes longer or until juices run clear. Garnish with orange and rosemary if desired.

Yield: 6 servings.

Toasting nuts

before using them in a recipe intensifies their flavor. Spread the nuts on a baking sheet and bake them at 350° for 5 to 10 minutes or until they are lightly toasted. Be sure to watch the nuts carefully, so they don't burn.

Three-Cheese Kielbasa Bake

Kate Beckman
HEMET, CALIFORNIA

This hearty casserole takes advantage of garden-fresh vegetables and handy convenience items. My aunt originally made this for family gatherings. Now I fix it any night of the week.

Three-Cheese Kielbasa Bake

PREP: 55 min. ■ **BAKE:** 30 min.

12 ounces uncooked elbow macaroni	1 can (14-1/2 ounces) stewed tomatoes
2 pounds kielbasa *or* Polish sausage, halved lengthwise and sliced	1 egg, lightly beaten
1 tablespoon olive oil	1 carton (15 ounces) ricotta cheese
2 medium onions, chopped	2 cups (8 ounces) shredded cheddar cheese
2 medium zucchini, quartered and sliced	2 cups (8 ounces) part-skim shredded mozzarella cheese
2 medium carrots, grated	2 green onions, chopped
1/2 teaspoon minced garlic	
1 jar (26 ounces) spaghetti sauce	

■ Cook macaroni according to package directions. Meanwhile, in a large skillet, brown sausage in oil over medium heat; drain. Add onions, zucchini, carrots and garlic; cook and stir for 5-6 minutes or until crisp-tender.

■ Stir in spaghetti sauce and tomatoes. Bring to a boil. Reduce heat; simmer, uncovered, for 15 minutes. Drain macaroni.

■ In each of two greased 13-in. x 9-in. x 2-in. baking dishes, layer a fourth of the macaroni and meat sauce. Combine egg and ricotta cheese; spoon a fourth over sauce. Sprinkle with a fourth of the cheddar and mozzarella. Repeat layers. Top with green onions.

■ Cool one casserole; cover and freeze for up to 2 months. Cover and bake the remaining casserole at 350° for 15 minutes. Uncover; bake 15 minutes longer or until the cheese is melted.

■ **To prepare frozen casserole:** Thaw in the refrigerator for 24 hours. Remove from the refrigerator 30 minutes before baking. Cover and bake at 350° for 35-40 minutes or until heated through.

Yield: 2 casseroles (8-10 servings each).

Bavarian Casserole

Barbara LaFlair
HOUGHTON LAKE, MICHIGAN

This one-dish meal is a little different from the usual meat-and-potato casseroles. The sauerkraut and tomatoes add a nice tangy flavor to the tender chops. I've also used boneless skinless chicken breasts and turkey bacon with equally good results.

PREP: 40 min. ■ **BAKE:** 40 min.

4 medium red potatoes
6 bacon strips, diced
6 bone-in pork loin chops (3/4 inch thick)
1 large onion, chopped
1 jar (32 ounces) sauerkraut, rinsed and well drained
1 can (28 ounces) stewed tomatoes, drained
1 teaspoon caraway seeds
1/2 teaspoon salt
1/4 teaspoon pepper

■ Place potatoes in a saucepan and cover with water. Bring to a boil. Reduce heat; cover and simmer for 25-30 minutes or until almost tender. Drain; when cool enough to handle, cut into 1/4-in. slices.

■ In a large skillet, cook bacon over medium heat until crisp. Using a slotted spoon, remove to paper towels. In the drippings, brown pork chops on both sides. Remove chops; drain, reserving 1 tablespoon drippings. Saute onion in drippings until tender. Stir in sauerkraut and bacon; cook for 3-4 minutes.

■ Spoon sauerkraut mixture into a greased 13-in. x 9-in. x 2-in. baking dish. Layer with the pork chops, potato slices and tomatoes. Sprinkle with caraway seeds, salt and pepper. Cover and bake at 350° for 40-45 minutes or until a meat thermometer reads 160°.

Yield: 6 servings.

To finish a supper of Bavarian Casserole in perfect German style, just pick up a German chocolate cake from your favorite bakery. You'll have a special and satisfying dinner your family can enjoy anytime.

Scalloped Potatoes With Ham

PREP: 25 min.
BAKE: 55 min.

2 teaspoons butter
2 teaspoons all-purpose flour
1/8 teaspoon salt
1/8 teaspoon pepper
Dash Cajun seasoning
1/2 cup 2% milk
1-1/2 teaspoons sherry *or* chicken broth
1 teaspoon Worcestershire sauce
1/2 cup shredded cheddar cheese, *divided*
1 medium potato, peeled and thinly sliced
1 cup cubed fully cooked ham
1/4 cup thinly sliced onion

■ In a small saucepan, melt butter. Stir in the flour, salt, pepper and Cajun seasoning until smooth. Gradually add the milk, sherry and Worcestershire sauce. Bring to a boil; cook and stir for 1 minute or until thickened. Reduce heat; stir in 1/4 cup cheese. Remove from the heat; set aside.

■ Place half of the potato slices in a 1-qt. baking dish coated with cooking spray. Layer with ham, onion and half of the white sauce. Repeat layers.

■ Cover and bake at 350° for 50-60 minutes or until potatoes are tender. Uncover; sprinkle with remaining cheese. Bake 5-10 minutes longer or until cheese is melted.

Yield: 2 servings.

Mark Baccus
MELBOURNE BEACH, FLORIDA

When you don't want to bake a ham for a holiday dinner, this is a nice alternative. You won't want to save it just for special occasions, however. With layers of saucy, cheesy potatoes and chunks of ham, it's comfort food at its best.

Eggplant Sausage Casserole

- Cook pasta according to package directions. Meanwhile, in a large skillet, cook sausage over medium heat until no longer pink; drain. Set sausage aside.

- In the same skillet, saute the eggplant, onion and garlic in oil. Stir in the tomatoes, tomato paste, salt, basil and paprika; simmer, partially covered, for 15 minutes. Remove from the heat. Drain pasta; stir into eggplant mixture. Add sausage.

- Spread half of the sausage mixture in a greased 13-in. x 9-in. x 2-in. baking dish. Spread with ricotta cheese. Top with half of the mozzarella cheese and remaining sausage mixture.

- Cover and bake at 350° for 40 minutes. Uncover; sprinkle with remaining cheese. Bake 5 minutes longer or until cheese is melted. Let stand for 10 minutes before serving.

Yield: 12 servings.

Carol Mieske
RED BLUFF, CALIFORNIA

If you want your kids to happily eat their eggplant, serve it in this lovely layered casserole. Our whole family enjoys it. Always a popular potluck item, it's a great company dish, too.

Eggplant Sausage Casserole

PREP: 45 min. ■ **BAKE:** 45 min. + standing

- 1 package (16 ounces) penne pasta
- 2 pounds bulk Italian sausage
- 1 medium eggplant, peeled and cubed
- 1 large onion, chopped
- 2 garlic cloves, minced
- 2 tablespoons olive oil
- 1 can (28 ounces) diced tomatoes, undrained
- 1 can (6 ounces) tomato paste
- 1 teaspoon salt
- 1 teaspoon dried basil
- 1 teaspoon paprika
- 1 carton (15 ounces) ricotta cheese
- 4 cups (16 ounces) shredded part-skim mozzarella cheese, *divided*

Select a firm, heavy, round or pear-shaped eggplant with a glossy taut skin and uniformly smooth color. Choose one with intact green caps and mold-free stems, and without blemishes and rust spots. One medium eggplant (1 pound) equals 5 cups cubed.

Sparerib Casserole

Doris Voytovich
INKSTER, MICHIGAN

This is an old Southern recipe my mother passed on to me many years ago. It's especially good for a Saturday night supper since the potatoes cook in the same pan as the ribs.

PREP: 10 min. ■ **BAKE:** 55 min.

- 4 to 5 pounds pork spareribs, cut into individual ribs
- 2 teaspoons salt, *divided*
- 1/2 teaspoon pepper, *divided*
- 5 tablespoons vegetable oil, *divided*
- 6 cups cubed potatoes
- 1 medium onion, sliced
- 2 garlic cloves, minced
- 4 teaspoons all-purpose flour
- 2 tablespoons dried parsley flakes
- 1 can (12 ounces) evaporated milk
- 1/8 teaspoon paprika

■ Sprinkle ribs with 1 teaspoon salt and 1/4 teaspoon pepper. In a large skillet, brown ribs in 3 tablespoons oil in batches. Place ribs on a rack in shallow roasting pan. Bake, uncovered, at 350° for 20 minutes. Turn ribs; bake 20 minutes longer. Pat dry.

■ Place potatoes in a saucepan and cover with water; cover and bring to a boil over medium-high heat. Cook for 15-20 minutes or until tender.

■ Meanwhile, in a saucepan, saute onion and garlic in remaining oil until tender. Stir in the flour, parsley, and remaining salt and pepper until blended. Gradually stir in milk. Bring to a boil; cook and stir for 2 minutes or until thickened.

■ Drain potatoes; place in a greased 13-in. x 9-in. x 2-in. baking dish. Top with sauce and ribs. Cover and bake at 350° for 15 minutes. Uncover; sprinkle with paprika. Bake 5-10 minutes longer or until ribs are tender and potatoes are heated through.

Yield: 6 servings.

Feel free to experiment with the recipe for Pork Hash Brown Bake. Vary the types of frozen vegetables you use, or try cubed chicken in place of the pork.

Pork Hash Brown Bake

Taste of Home Test Kitchen
GREENDALE, WISCONSIN

Chock-full of colorful vegetables and tender pork, this creamy casserole is oven-ready in no time.

PREP: 15 min.
BAKE: 30 min.

- 1/4 cup all-purpose flour
- 2 teaspoons chicken bouillon granules
- 1/2 teaspoon salt
- 1 cup water
- 1/2 cup milk
- 1/4 cup sour cream
- 3 cups frozen O'Brien hash brown potatoes, thawed
- 2 cups cubed cooked pork
- 1 package (10 ounces) frozen mixed vegetables, thawed
- 1 can (4 ounces) mushroom stems and pieces, drained
- 1/2 cup crushed cornflakes
- 2 tablespoons butter, melted

■ In a saucepan, combine flour, bouillon, salt, water and milk until smooth. Bring to a boil; cook and stir for 2 minutes or until thickened. Remove from the heat; stir in sour cream.

■ In a bowl, combine the next four ingredients. Add the sour cream mixture; stir to coat well.

■ Transfer to a greased shallow 2-qt. baking dish. Toss cornflakes and butter; sprinkle over the top. Bake, uncovered, at 375° for 30-35 minutes or until heated through.

Yield: 6 servings.

Bernice Morris
MARSHFIELD, MISSOURI

Pork sausage gives this crowd-pleasing pasta casserole its savory flavor, and a can of cream-style corn adds a tasty addition without much effort. It's hard to believe that dinner can be so simple to fix yet so delicious and satisfying.

Sausage-Corn Bake

PREP: 20 min.
BAKE: 30 min.

1-1/2   pounds bulk pork sausage

1   medium green pepper, chopped

1   medium onion, chopped

4   tablespoons butter, *divided*

3   tablespoons all-purpose flour

1/2   teaspoon salt

1/2   teaspoon white pepper

1-1/2   cups milk

1   can (14-3/4 ounces) cream-style corn

3-1/2   cups (10 ounces) egg noodles, cooked and drained

1/4   cup shredded cheddar cheese

1/2   cup dry bread crumbs

■ In a large skillet, cook sausage, green pepper and onion over medium heat until the sausage is no longer pink; drain and set aside.

■ In a large saucepan, melt 3 tablespoons butter over medium heat. Stir in the flour, salt and pepper. Gradually add milk. Bring to a boil; cook and stir for 2 minutes or until thickened. Stir in corn. Add noodles and corn mixture to the sausage mixture. Fold in the cheese.

■ Transfer to a greased 13-in. x 9-in. x 2-in. baking dish. Melt remaining butter; stir in bread crumbs. Sprinkle over casserole. Bake, uncovered, at 325° for 30-40 minutes or until heated through.

Yield: *6-8 servings.*

Baked Chops and Fries

Gregg Voss
EMERSON, NEBRASKA
Convenience items like frozen vegetables and a jar of cheese sauce make it a snap to assemble this comforting pork chop supper. It's an easy meal-in-one.

Baked Chops and Fries

PREP: 20 min. ■ **BAKE:** 55 min.

6   bone-in pork loin chops (1 inch thick)

1   tablespoon olive oil

1/2   teaspoon seasoned salt

1   jar (8 ounces) process cheese sauce

1/2   cup milk

4   cups frozen cottage fries

1   can (2.8 ounces) french-fried onions, *divided*

1   package (10 ounces) frozen broccoli florets

■ In a large skillet, brown pork chops in oil; sprinkle with seasoned salt. In a bowl, combine the cheese sauce and milk until blended; spread into a greased 13-in. x 9-in. x 2-in. baking dish. Top with cottage fries and half of the onions. Arrange broccoli and pork chops over the top.

■ Cover and bake at 350° for 45 minutes. Sprinkle with remaining onions. Bake 10 minutes longer or until the meat is no longer pink and the broccoli is tender.

Yield: *6 servings.*

Pilaf-Stuffed Pork Chops

■ In a saucepan, bring water to a boil. Add rice. Remove from the heat; cover and let stand for 5 minutes. Fluff with a fork. Stir in the carrot, zucchini, onion salt and 1/8 teaspoon pepper; set aside.

■ Cut a pocket in each pork chop; sprinkle with salt and remaining pepper. In a skillet, brown chops in butter. Cool for 5 minutes. Stuff with pilaf.

■ Place in an ungreased 11-in. x 7-in. x 2-in. baking dish. Pour broth into dish. Cover and bake at 350° for 25-30 minutes or until a meat thermometer inserted into meat reads 160°.

■ Remove chops and keep warm. Pour the cooking juices into a saucepan. Combine cornstarch and cold water until smooth; stir into juices. Bring to a boil; cook and stir for 1 minute or until thickened. Stir in browning sauce if desired. Serve over pork chops.

Yield: 2 servings.

Taste of Home Test Kitchen
GREENDALE, WISCONSIN

A quick homemade gravy adds the finishing touch to these tender pork chops stuffed with rice and colorful vegetables. Try them with corn on the cob and Key lime pie.

Pilaf-Stuffed Pork Chops

PREP: 30 min. ■ **BAKE:** 25 min.

1/2 cup water	1/8 teaspoon salt
1/2 cup uncooked instant rice	1 tablespoon butter
1/4 cup shredded carrot	3/4 cup beef broth
1/4 cup shredded zucchini	1 tablespoon cornstarch
1/4 teaspoon onion salt	3 tablespoons cold water
1/4 teaspoon pepper, *divided*	1/4 teaspoon browning sauce, optional
2 bone-in pork loin chops (1-1/2 inches thick)	

To cut a pocket in a pork chop, use a sharp knife. Make a horizontal slit in the middle of the chop by slicing from the edge almost to the bone.

Jennifer Zukiwsky
GLENDON, ALBERTA
Here's a quick, tasty pizza that my family loves. It's a bit different because you use buttermilk biscuits instead of pizza dough.

Kielbasa Biscuit Pizza

Kielbasa Biscuit Pizza

PREP: 15 min. ■ **BAKE:** 35 min.

2 tubes (12 ounces *each*) refrigerated buttermilk biscuits

2-1/2 cups garden-style spaghetti sauce

1/2 pound smoked kielbasa *or* Polish sausage, cubed

1 can (8 ounces) mushroom stems and pieces, drained

1/2 cup chopped green pepper

1/2 cup chopped sweet red pepper

1 cup (4 ounces) shredded part-skim mozzarella cheese

1 cup (4 ounces) shredded cheddar cheese

■ Separate biscuits; cut each biscuit into fourths. Arrange in a greased 13-in. x 9-in. x 2-in. baking dish (do not flatten). Bake at 375° for 12-15 minutes or until biscuits begin to brown.

■ Spread spaghetti sauce over biscuit crust. Sprinkle with the sausage, mushrooms, peppers and cheeses. Bake for 20-25 minutes or until bubbly and cheese is melted. Let stand for 5 minutes before cutting.

Yield: 8 servings.

For pizza that has a taste of the tropics instead, replace the sausage with cubed cooked ham and add canned pineapple tidbits. If you like, try barbecue or pizza sauce in place of the spaghetti sauce.

Sunday Chops And Stuffing

Georgiann Franklin
CANFIELD, OHIO
This all-in-one casserole with tender chops, apples and a moist stuffing is a favorite.

PREP: 30 min.
BAKE: 30 min.

2 cups water

2 celery ribs, chopped

7 tablespoons butter, *divided*

1/4 cup dried minced onion

6 cups seasoned stuffing croutons

6 bone-in pork loin chops (3/4 inch thick)

1 tablespoon vegetable oil

1/4 teaspoon salt

1/4 teaspoon pepper

2 medium tart apples, sliced

1/4 cup packed brown sugar

1/8 teaspoon pumpkin pie spice

■ In a saucepan, combine the water, celery, 6 tablespoons butter and onion. Bring to a boil. Remove from the heat; stir in the croutons. Spoon into a greased 13-in. x 9-in. x 2-in. baking dish; set aside.

■ In a large skillet, brown pork chops on both sides in oil. Arrange chops over the stuffing. Sprinkle with salt and pepper. Combine the apples, brown sugar and pumpkin pie spice; spoon over pork chops. Dot with the remaining butter. Bake, uncovered, at 350° for 30-35 minutes or until a meat thermometer reads 160° and meat juices run clear.

Yield: 6 servings.

Rhubarb Pork Chop Bake

- In a large skillet, cook the pork chops in oil over medium heat for 2-3 minutes on each side or until chops are lightly browned; drain. Sprinkle with rosemary, salt and pepper. Remove from the heat and keep warm.

- In a large bowl, combine the rhubarb, bread cubes, brown sugar, flour, cinnamon and all-spice.

- Place half of the rhubarb mixture in a greased 11-in. x 7-in. x 2-in. baking dish. Top with chops and remaining rhubarb mixture. Cover and bake at 350° for 30-35 minutes. Uncover; bake 10 minutes longer or until a meat thermometer reaches 160°.

Yield: 4 servings.

Editor's Note: If using frozen rhubarb, measure rhubarb while still frozen, then thaw completely. Drain in a colander, but do not press liquid out.

Edie DeSpain
LOGAN, UTAH

True, it's a little unusual to combine rhubarb with meat in an entree, but my family loves this recipe! My mother created it in an effort to use abundant rhubarb from our farm garden.

Rhubarb Pork Chop Bake

PREP: 15 min. ■ **BAKE:** 40 min.

> 4 bone-in pork loin chops (1/2 inch thick and 7 ounces *each*)
>
> 2 tablespoons vegetable oil
>
> 1-1/2 teaspoons minced fresh rosemary *or* 1/2 teaspoon dried rosemary, crushed
>
> 1/4 teaspoon salt
>
> 1/8 teaspoon pepper

> 2-1/2 cups chopped fresh *or* frozen rhubarb (1/2-inch pieces)
>
> 4 slices day-old bread, crusts removed and cubed
>
> 3/4 cup packed brown sugar
>
> 2 tablespoons all-purpose flour
>
> 1/2 teaspoon ground cinnamon
>
> 1/4 teaspoon ground allspice

Store unwashed fresh rhubarb in the refrigerator for up to 1 week. Sliced rhubarb may be frozen for up to 9 months.

Great Pork Chop Bake

Sweet Potato Ham Bake

Jennette Fourne
DETROIT, MICHIGAN

Three ingredients are all I need for this colorful hot dish, sized perfectly for two. It's a good way to use up ham from the holidays.

PREP: 10 min.
BAKE: 30 min.

- 1 can (15 ounces) cut sweet potatoes, drained and quartered lengthwise
- 2 cups cubed fully cooked ham
- 1 cup (4 ounces) shredded cheddar cheese

- In a greased 1-qt. baking dish, layer half of the sweet potatoes, ham and cheese. Repeat layers. Cover and bake at 350° for 20 minutes. Uncover; bake 8-10 minutes longer or until cheese is melted.

Yield: 2-3 servings.

Rosie Glenn
LOS ALAMOS, NEW MEXICO

A friend brought this hearty meat-and-potatoes dish to our home when I returned from the hospital with our youngest child. Since then, we have enjoyed it many times.

Great Pork Chop Bake

PREP: 10 min. ■ BAKE: 55 min.

- 6 bone-in pork chops (3/4 inch thick)
- 1 tablespoon vegetable oil
- 1 can (10-3/4 ounces) condensed cream of chicken soup, undiluted
- 3 tablespoons ketchup
- 2 tablespoons Worcestershire sauce
- 1/2 teaspoon salt
- 1/4 teaspoon pepper
- 4 medium potatoes, cut into 1/2-inch wedges
- 1 medium onion, sliced into rings

- In a skillet, brown pork chops in oil. Transfer to a greased 13-in. x 9-in. x 2-in. baking dish. In a bowl, combine the soup, ketchup, Worcestershire sauce, salt and pepper. Add potatoes and onion; toss to coat. Pour over the chops.

- Cover and bake at 350° for 55-60 minutes or until meat juices run clear and potatoes are tender.

Yield: 6 servings.

To reduce tears while cutting an onion, freeze the onion for about 20 minutes before slicing or chopping. Also, use a very sharp knife and work quickly.

Fish & Seafood

232

234

231

Traditional one-dish meals, such as lasagna, quiche and rice casserole get a refreshing makeover by using fish and seafood instead of meat in this chapter. For a healthy change of scenery on your dinner table, give one a try!

- In a small bowl, combine soup and milk; set aside. Combine tuna, broccoli, 1/3 cup cheese and 3 tablespoons almonds. Stir in half of the soup mixture.

- Spoon filling down the center of each tortilla; roll up. Place seam side down in an 11-in. x 7-in. x 2-in. baking dish coated with cooking spray. Pour remaining soup mixture over top; sprinkle with tomato.

- Cover and bake at 350° for 35 minutes. Uncover; sprinkle with the remaining cheese and almonds. Bake 5 minutes longer or until cheese is melted.

Yield: 6 servings.

＊Nutrition Facts: 1 roll-up equals 321 calories, 10 g fat (3 g saturated fat), 26 mg cholesterol, 696 mg sodium, 34 g carbohydrate, 4 g fiber, 25 g protein. **Diabetic Exchanges:** 3 lean meat, 2 starch.

Broccoli Tuna Roll-Ups

Mary Wilhelm
SPARTA, WISCONSIN

In just 15 minutes, I can assemble this enchilada-like entree and set it in the oven. Featuring a creamy topping, cheese and almonds, it's a great change-of-pace for weekly menus.

Broccoli Tuna Roll-Ups*

PREP: 15 min. ■ **BAKE:** 40 min.

- 1 can (10-3/4 ounces) reduced-fat reduced-sodium condensed cream of mushroom soup, undiluted
- 1 cup fat-free milk
- 2 cans (6 ounces *each*) light water-packed tuna, drained and flaked
- 3 cups frozen chopped broccoli, thawed and drained
- 2/3 cup shredded reduced-fat cheddar cheese, *divided*
- 1/3 cup sliced almonds, *divided*
- 6 flour tortillas (7 inches)
- 1 large tomato, seeded and chopped

Tuna and tortillas can make a great pairing not only for a dinner dish such as Broccoli Tuna Roll-Ups, but also for a speedy lunch. Simply fix your favorite tuna salad recipe and spread it on tortillas. Add chopped tomato and lettuce, roll up the tortillas and serve.

Roberta Nelson
PORTLAND, OREGON

This tasty casserole is a family favorite and is my old standby for social functions. It's easy to assemble and economical, too.

Spanish Corn with Fish Sticks

Spanish Corn with Fish Sticks

PREP: 20 min. ■ **BAKE:** 40 min.

1/4 cup chopped onion	2 teaspoons sugar
1/4 cup chopped green pepper	2 cans (14-1/2 ounces *each*) stewed tomatoes
1/4 cup butter, cubed	
1/4 cup all-purpose flour	2 packages (10 ounces *each*) frozen corn, partially thawed
1-1/2 teaspoons salt	
1/4 teaspoon pepper	2 packages (12 ounces *each*) frozen fish sticks

■ In a large skillet, saute onion and green pepper in butter until tender. Stir in the flour, salt, pepper and sugar until blended. Add tomatoes; bring to a boil. Cook and stir for 2 minutes or until thickened. Reduce heat; simmer, uncovered, for 3-5 minutes or heated through, stirring occasionally. Stir in corn.

■ Transfer to two greased 11-in. x 7-in. x 2-in. baking dishes. Cover and bake at 350° for 25 minutes. Uncover; arrange fish sticks over the top. Bake 15 minutes longer or until fish sticks are heated through.

Yield: 8-10 servings.

Make dinner even easier—keep chopped onion and green pepper in the freezer so you can quickly add them to recipes such as Spanish Corn with Fish Sticks.

Shrimp 'n' Veggie Pizza*

PREP/TOTAL TIME: 30 min.

- 1/2 cup sliced onion
- 1/2 cup sliced fresh mushrooms
- 3 asparagus spears, trimmed and cut into 1-inch pieces
- 1 garlic clove, minced
- 2 teaspoons olive oil
- 4 ounces uncooked medium shrimp, peeled, deveined and halved lengthwise
- 1 prebaked thin Italian bread shell crust (10 ounces)
- 1/2 cup pizza sauce
- 1 cup (4 ounces) shredded part-skim mozzarella cheese

■ In a nonstick skillet, saute the onion, mushrooms, asparagus and garlic in oil until almost tender. Add shrimp; cook until shrimp turn pink. Remove from the heat.

■ Place the crust on a pizza pan or baking sheet. Spread with pizza sauce. Top with shrimp mixture. Sprinkle with cheese. Bake at 450° for 8-10 minutes or until cheese is melted.

Yield: 6 slices.

***Nutrition Facts:** 1 slice equals 215 calories, 7 g fat (2 g saturated fat), 38 mg cholesterol, 426 mg sodium, 24 g carbohydrate, 1 g fiber, 13 g protein. **Diabetic Exchanges:** 1-1/2 starch, 1 lean meat, 1 fat.

Terri Webber
MIAMI, FLORIDA

Just 30 minutes are all you'll need to put together my colorful, special-tasting pizza. It's a great way to use up leftover shrimp and veggies. Try it when you're in the mood for pizza that goes beyond the usual cheese-and-pepperoni variety.

Light Shrimp Rice Casserole

- In a large nonstick skillet, saute shrimp in 1 tablespoon butter for 2-3 minutes or until shrimp turn pink. Remove; set aside. In same skillet, saute mushrooms, green pepper and onion in remaining butter until tender. Stir in flour, salt and cayenne. Gradually add milk until blended. Bring to a boil; cook and stir for 2 minutes or until thickened. Add rice, 1/2 cup cheese and shrimp; stir until combined.

- Pour into a 1-1/2-qt. baking dish coated with cooking spray. Cover and bake at 325° for 30-35 minutes or until heated through. Sprinkle with remaining cheese; cover and let stand for 5 minutes or until cheese is melted.

Yield: 6 servings.

*Nutrition Facts: 1 cup equals 318 calories, 10 g fat (6 g saturated fat), 137 mg cholesterol, 621 mg sodium, 35 g carbohydrate, 4 g fiber, 24 g protein. Diabetic Exchanges: 2 starch, 2 very lean meat, 1-1/2 fat, 1 vegetable.

Marie Roberts
LAKE CHARLES, LOUISIANA
Here's a light casserole that's sure to earn you raves from everyone at the dinner table. Loaded with shrimp and veggies, it's a nice addition to weeknight lineups.

Light Shrimp Rice Casserole*

PREP: 40 min. ■ **BAKE:** 30 min.

1 pound uncooked medium shrimp, peeled and deveined
2 tablespoons butter, *divided*
12 ounces fresh mushrooms, sliced
1 large green pepper, chopped
1 medium onion, chopped

3 tablespoons all-purpose flour
3/4 teaspoon salt
1/8 teaspoon cayenne pepper
1-1/3 cups fat-free milk
3 cups cooked brown rice
1 cup (4 ounces) shredded reduced-fat cheddar cheese, *divided*

To peel and devein shrimp, begin on the underside by the head area. Pull the legs and first shell section to one side. Continue pulling the shell around the top to the other side, and pull off the shell by the tail. Cut a shallow slit along the back from the head area to the tail, then rinse the shrimp under cold water to remove the vein.

Cheddar Shrimp and Penne

- Cook pasta according to package directions. Meanwhile, in a large saucepan, cook the garlic in butter over medium heat for 1 minute. Stir in flour, salt and pepper until blended. gradually add milk. Bring to a boil; cook and stir for 2 minutes or until thickened. Reduce heat; stir in 1 cup of cheese until melted. Remove from the heat.

- Drain pasta; add pasta, shrimp and corn to cheese sauce. Transfer to a greased 2-qt. baking dish. Cover and bake at 350° for 25 minutes. Uncover; sprinkle with remaining cheese.

- Bake 10-15 minutes longer or until bubbly.

Yield: 4-6 servings.

If you don't have penne pasta on hand for Cheddar Shrimp and Penne, just substitute a different variety of pasta. For example, you could use bow ties or rotini (spiral shapes).

Brad Walker
HOLT, MICHIGAN

My wife and I take turns in the kitchen and like to experiment with new recipes. When I created this creamy seafood meal-in-one, it quickly became a favorite.

Cheddar Shrimp and Penne

PREP: 15 min. ■ **BAKE:** 35 min.

2 cups uncooked penne pasta
2 garlic cloves, minced
2 tablespoons butter
2 tablespoons all-purpose flour
1/2 teaspoon salt
1/4 teaspoon pepper

2 cups milk
1-1/2 cups (6 ounces) shredded cheddar cheese, *divided*
1 pound cooked medium shrimp, peeled and deveined
1 can (15-1/4 ounces) whole kernel corn, drained

Sheila Sjolund
DEER RIVER, MINNESOTA

This is an old recipe that I've tweaked over the years to suit my family's tastes. The comforting tuna casserole is satisfying all by itself, but you can always add to the meal by serving it with a platter of fresh veggies or a tossed green salad.

Tuna Noodle Hot Dish

PREP: 15 min.
BAKE: 30 min.

- 12 ounces uncooked egg noodles
- 2 cans (10-3/4 ounces *each*) condensed cream of chicken soup, undiluted
- 1 cup (8 ounces) sour cream
- 1/3 cup milk
- 1 can (12 ounces) tuna, drained and flaked
- 1 cup shredded process cheese (Velveeta)
- 1 medium onion, chopped
- 1 jar (2 ounces) diced pimientos, drained
- 1 can (2-1/4 ounces) sliced ripe olives, drained
- 1 cup crushed potato chips

Paprika

- Cook the noodles according to package directions; drain. In a large bowl, combine the soup, sour cream and milk. Stir in the noodles, tuna, cheese, onion, pimientos and olives.

- Pour into a greased 3-qt. baking dish. Sprinkle with potato chips and paprika. Bake, uncovered, at 375° for 30-35 minutes or until heated through.

Yield: *6-8 servings.*

Seafood Lasagna

Viola Walmer
TEQUESTA, FLORIDA

Everyone seems to enjoy this supper. I like to prepare it the day before and refrigerate it overnight. Just take it out of the fridge 30 minutes before popping it in the oven.

PREP: 15 min. ■ **BAKE:** 50 min. + standing

- 3/4 cup chopped onion
- 2 tablespoons butter
- 1 package (8 ounces) cream cheese, cubed
- 1-1/2 cups (12 ounces) 4% cottage cheese
- 1 egg, lightly beaten
- 2 teaspoons dried basil
- 1 teaspoon salt
- 1/4 teaspoon pepper
- 1 can (10-3/4 ounces) condensed cream of shrimp soup, undiluted
- 1 can (10-3/4 ounces) condensed cream of mushroom soup, undiluted
- 1/2 cup white wine *or* chicken broth
- 1/2 cup milk
- 2 packages (8 ounces *each*) imitation crabmeat, flaked
- 1 can (6 ounces) small shrimp, rinsed and drained
- 9 lasagna noodles, cooked and drained
- 1/2 cup grated Parmesan cheese
- 3/4 cup shredded Monterey Jack cheese

- In a large skillet, saute onion in butter until tender. Reduce heat. Add cream cheese; cook and stir until melted and smooth. Stir in the cottage cheese, egg, basil, salt and pepper. Remove from the heat and set aside. In a large bowl, combine the soups, wine or broth, milk, crab and shrimp.

- Arrange three noodles in a greased 13-in. x 9-in. x 2-in. baking dish. Spread with a third of cottage cheese mixture and a third of the seafood mixture. Repeat layers twice. Sprinkle with Parmesan cheese.

- Cover and bake at 350° for 40 minutes. Uncover; sprinkle with the Monterey Jack cheese. Bake 10 minutes longer or until cheese is melted and lasagna is bubbly. Let stand for 15 minutes before serving.

Yield: 12 servings.

Imitation crabmeat consists of mild-flavored, white-fleshed fish, usually pollack and/or whiting. It is available in the seafood section of most grocery stores and comes in different forms: flaked, chunked and whole "legs." A tasty addition to pasta, salads and soups, it can often be substituted for real crab, shrimp or scallops.

- Cook pasta according to package directions. Meanwhile, in a large skillet, saute the onions and mushrooms in butter until tender. Stir in the soup, milk, Worcestershire sauce, salt and pepper until blended; bring to a boil. Remove from the heat.

- Drain pasta. Add the pasta, salmon, peas, pecans and pimientos to the skillet. Transfer to a greased shallow 3-qt. baking dish.

- Cover and bake at 350° for 30-35 minutes or until heated through. Sprinkle with chips.

Yield: 12 servings.

Pecan Salmon Casserole

Edna Coburn
TUCSON, ARIZONA

Peas, pecans and pimientos complement the salmon in my potluck-friendly dish. I top it with crushed potato chips to give it an added crunch. It's great for family dinners, too!

Pecan Salmon Casserole

PREP: 55 min. ■ **BAKE:** 30 min.

1 package (16 ounces) small shell pasta	1 teaspoon salt
2 medium onions, finely chopped	1/2 teaspoon pepper
1/2 pound sliced fresh mushrooms	2 cans (14-3/4 ounces *each*) salmon, drained, bones and skin removed
1/4 cup butter, cubed	2 cups frozen peas
2 cans (10-3/4 ounces *each*) condensed cream of mushroom soup, undiluted	1 cup chopped pecans, toasted
1-1/2 cups milk	1 jar (2 ounces) diced pimientos, drained
2 teaspoons Worcestershire sauce	1/2 cup crushed potato chips

Not a salmon lover? You can still take advantage of this recipe. Simply replace the salmon with canned tuna. You could also try leftover chicken, turkey or even ham.

Salmon Rice Puff

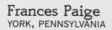

Frances Paige
YORK, PENNSYLVANIA

This simple recipe is from the 1930s, but it's just as delicious today. My mother served it with creamed vegetables, but it's a comforting meal on its own.

Salmon Rice Puff

PREP: 15 min. ■ **BAKE:** 30 min.

2 eggs	1/4 cup chopped celery
1/2 cup milk	4 tablespoons lemon juice
1 can (14-3/4 ounces) salmon, drained, bones and skin removed	1/2 teaspoon Worcestershire sauce
1 cup cooked long grain rice	1/2 cup shredded cheddar cheese
1/4 cup chopped green onion	

■ In a bowl, whisk the eggs and milk. Stir in the salmon, rice, onions, celery, lemon juice and Worcestershire sauce. Transfer to a greased shallow 1-1/2-qt. baking dish. Bake, uncovered, at 375° for 20 minutes. Sprinkle with cheese; bake 10 minutes longer or until cheese is melted.

Yield: 3-4 servings.

Crab Quiche

Maryellen Hays
WOLCOTTVILLE, INDIANA

With three types of cheese, mushrooms and flaked crabmeat, this is a wonderful meal any time of day. A packaged pastry shell makes preparation a snap.

PREP: 15 min.
BAKE: 45 min. + standing

- 1 unbaked deep-dish pastry shell (9 inches)
- 3 tablespoons all-purpose flour
- 4 eggs
- 1 cup milk
- 1/4 teaspoon salt
- 1/8 teaspoon pepper
- 1/8 teaspoon ground nutmeg
- 1 can (6 ounces) crabmeat, drained, flaked and cartilage removed
- 1 can (4 ounces) mushroom stems and pieces, drained
- 1/2 cup shredded Swiss cheese
- 1/2 cup shredded cheddar cheese
- 1/2 cup grated Parmesan cheese
- 1/2 cup french-fried onions

■ Bake unpricked pastry shell at 425° for 5 minutes. Meanwhile, in a bowl, combine the flour, eggs, milk, salt, pepper and nutmeg until smooth. Add the crab, mushrooms and cheeses. Pour into pastry shell.

■ Bake at 350° for 35 minutes. Top with onions. Bake 10 minutes longer or until a knife inserted near the center comes out clean. Let stand for 10 minutes before serving.

Yield: 8 servings.

Broccoli Tuna Squares

Janet Juncker
GENEVA, OHIO

Family and friends always ask for this recipe because it's different than traditional tuna casserole. I make it when I need something quick, which is often. We're always on the go!

PREP: 15 min. ■ **BAKE:** 35 min.

1 tube (8 ounces) refrigerated crescent rolls	2 tablespoons mayonnaise
1 cup (4 ounces) shredded Monterey Jack cheese	3/4 teaspoon onion powder
3 cups frozen chopped broccoli, cooked and drained	1/2 teaspoon dill weed
4 eggs	1 can (12 ounces) tuna, drained and flaked
1 can (10-3/4 ounces) condensed cream of broccoli soup, undiluted	1 tablespoon diced pimientos, drained

■ Unroll crescent roll dough into one long rectangle; place in an ungreased 13-in. x 9-in. x 2-in. baking dish. Seal seams and perforations; press onto bottom and 1/2 in. up the sides. Sprinkle with cheese and broccoli.

■ In a bowl, combine the eggs, soup, mayonnaise, onion powder and dill; mix well. Stir in tuna and pimientos; pour over broccoli.

■ Bake, uncovered, at 350° for 35-40 minutes or until a knife inserted near the center comes out clean. Let stand for 10 minutes before serving.

Yield: 8 servings.

If you have family members who aren't wild about eating fish, try serving types that are milder in flavor. For example, flounder, cod, haddock, sole and walleye are all pleasantly mild and have a delicate texture. Fish with more distinctive flavors and firmer textures include halibut, red snapper, orange roughy, catfish, sea bass, trout and salmon.

Flounder Zucchini Bundles*

PREP/TOTAL TIME: 30 min.

- 8 flounder fillets (3 ounces *each*)
- 1/4 teaspoon lemon-pepper seasoning
- 1 medium lemon, thinly sliced
- 1 medium zucchini, cut into 1/4-inch slices
- 12 cherry tomatoes, halved
- 1/4 teaspoon dill weed
- 1/4 teaspoon dried basil

■ For each bundle, place two fillets on a double thickness of heavy-duty foil (18 in. x 15 in.); sprinkle with lemon-pepper. Top with lemon slices, zucchini and tomatoes. Sprinkle with dill and basil.

■ Fold the foil around the fish and seal tightly. Place on a baking sheet. Bake at 425° for 15-20 minutes or until fish flakes easily with a fork.

Yield: 4 servings.

✱**Nutrition Facts:** 1 bundle equals 159 calories, 2 g fat (trace saturated fat), 80 mg cholesterol, 160 mg sodium, 5 g carbohydrate, 1 g fiber, 29 g protein. **Diabetic Exchanges:** 4 very lean meat, 1 vegetable.

Isabelle Rooney
SUMMERVILLE, SOUTH CAROLINA

A hint of lemon accents this colorful meal-in-one featuring tender fish fillets, zucchini slices and tomatoes. My husband isn't normally a fish eater, but he enjoys this recipe. An added bonus is that it's low in fat and calories.

- In a nonstick skillet, cook onion in oil over medium heat for about 2 minutes. Stir in zucchini and mushrooms; cook and stir 2 minutes longer. Sprinkle with pepper and garlic powder; stir in lemon juice. Cook and stir 30 seconds longer. Remove from heat; stir in 1 teaspoon cheese.

- Place fillets in a 13-in. x 9-in. x 2-in. baking dish coated with cooking spray. Top each fillet with about 1/4 cup onion mixture. Drizzle with butter and sprinkle with remaining cheese.

- Bake, uncovered, at 375° for 18-22 minutes or until fish flakes easily with a fork.

Yield: 4 servings.

*Nutrition Facts: One fillet equals 250 calories, 9 g fat (3 g saturated fat), 156 mg cholesterol, 166 mg sodium, 6 g carbohydrate, 2 g fiber, 35 g protein. **Diabetic Exchanges:** 4 lean meat, 1 vegetable.

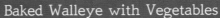
Baked Walleye with Vegetables

Sondra Ostheimer
BOSCOBEL, WISCONSIN

A medley of zucchini, mushrooms and onion make a bake-along side dish in this delightful recipe for walleye fillets. Best of all, it's low in fat and carbohydrates!

Baked Walleye with Vegetables*

PREP: 15 min. ■ **BAKE:** 20 min.

1 small onion, thinly sliced
1 tablespoon olive oil
2 small zucchini, julienned
1 cup sliced fresh mushrooms
1/4 teaspoon pepper
1/8 teaspoon garlic powder

2 tablespoons lemon juice
2 tablespoons grated Parmesan cheese, *divided*
4 walleye fillets (about 6 ounces *each*)
1 tablespoon butter, melted

Store uncooked fish in the coolest area of your refrigerator for no more than 1 or 2 days. Frozen fish should be thawed in its original packaging in the refrigerator. Do not refreeze it after thawing.

- In a small saucepan, saute the celery, peppers and onion in 1 tablespoon butter until almost tender. Stir in broth and carrot. Bring to a boil. Stir in stuffing mix. Remove from the heat; cover and let stand for 5 minutes. Stir in clams.

- Transfer to two 6-oz. ramekins or custard cups coated with cooking spray. Melt remaining butter; stir in lemon juice. Drizzle over the stuffing mix. Bake, uncovered, at 350° for 15-20 minutes or until heated through and golden brown.

Yield: 2 servings.

Need to feed more than two? Feel free to double or triple the recipe for Clam Stuffing Bake. After stirring together the clam stuffing, just put each additional serving into its own 6-ounce ramekin or custard cup.

Clam Stuffing Bake

Lillian Butler
STRATFORD, CONNECTICUT

My mother came up with this delightful main course, and because I love stuffed clams, it's a favorite of mine. The small-yield recipe is perfectly sized for two.

Clam Stuffing Bake

PREP/TOTAL TIME: 30 min.

2 tablespoons *each* chopped celery, green pepper and sweet red pepper
4-1/2 teaspoons chopped onion
2 tablespoons butter, *divided*
1/2 cup chicken broth

1/4 cup shredded carrot
1 cup seasoned stuffing mix
1 can (6-1/2 ounces) minced clams, drained
1/4 teaspoon lemon juice

Spinach Sole Roll-Ups*

Dixie Terry
MARION, ILLINOIS

This is an unusual but delicious combination of ingredients. For a great company meal, I serve it with sliced French bread that's been spread with butter and dried basil, then baked. A strawberry ice cream pie makes a delicious dessert.

PREP/TOTAL TIME: 30 min.

1	package (10 ounces) frozen leaf spinach, thawed and squeezed dry
1/2	cup sliced green onions
1/3	cup sour cream
1-1/4	pounds sole fillets

Lemon-pepper seasoning
1	tablespoon cornstarch
1	tablespoon water
1	can (14-1/2 ounces) stewed tomatoes, undrained

■ In a small bowl, combine the spinach, onions and sour cream. Spread into an ungreased 13-in. x 9-in. x 2-in. baking dish.

■ Cut sole fillets into 6-in. x 2-in. strips; carefully roll up and secure with toothpicks. Place over spinach mixture. Sprinkle with lemon-pepper. Bake, uncovered, at 350° for 15-20 minutes or until fish flakes easily with a fork.

■ In a saucepan, combine cornstarch and water until smooth. Gradually add tomatoes. Bring to a boil over medium heat; cook and stir for 2 minutes or until thickened. Discard toothpicks from roll-ups. Spoon tomato sauce over roll-ups and spinach mixture.

Yield: 4 servings.

*Nutrition Facts: 1 serving (prepared with reduced-fat sour cream) equals 213 calories, 4 g fat (2 g saturated fat), 75 mg cholesterol, 388 mg sodium, 14 g carbohydrate, 3 g fiber, 31 g protein. **Diabetic Exchanges:** 5 very lean meat, 1 vegetable, 1/2 starch.

Typically, fish is sold whole or cut into fillets or steaks. To avoid bones, purchase fillets, the boneless sides of the fish. A steak is a vertical cut and generally has some of the backbone, rib bone and skin still attached. Fortunately, these large bones and skin can be easily removed after cooking.

Veggie-Topped Fillets*

Joan Shirley
TREGO, MONTANA

These easy-to-prepare sole fillets are baked in a tomato-flavored sauce that tastes extra special.

PREP/TOTAL TIME: 30 min.

4	sole *or* walleye fillets (6 ounces *each*)
3/4	teaspoon salt, *divided*
1/8	teaspoon pepper
1-1/2	cups V8 juice
1/2	cup chopped celery
1/2	cup chopped onion
1/4	cup chopped green pepper
1	tablespoon lemon juice
1	teaspoon sugar
1	tablespoon butter

Hot cooked rice, optional

■ Place fillets in a 13-in. x 9-in. x 2-in. baking dish coated with cooking spray; sprinkle with 1/2 teaspoon salt and pepper. In a saucepan, combine the V8 juice, celery, onion, green pepper, lemon juice, sugar and remaining salt; bring to a boil. Cook over medium-low heat for 5-6 minutes or until vegetables are tender. Pour over fish; dot with butter.

■ Bake, uncovered, at 350° for 10-15 minutes or until fish flakes easily with a fork. Serve with rice if desired.

Yield: 4 servings.

*Nutrition Facts: One serving (1 fillet with 1/2 cup sauce, calculated without rice) equals 199 calories, 5 g fat (2 g saturated fat), 88 mg cholesterol, 779 mg sodium, 8 g carbohydrate, 1 g fiber, 29 g protein. **Diabetic Exchanges:** 4 very lean meat, 1 vegetable, 1/2 fat.

Vi Manning
SPRING HILL, FLORIDA

The first time I made this casserole, my son begged me to make it again. That was more than 20 years ago, and it's still a favorite among my family and friends.

Pineapple Shrimp Rice Bake

Pineapple Shrimp Rice Bake

PREP: 30 min. ■ **BAKE:** 15 min.

2 cups chicken broth	2 teaspoons soy sauce
1 cup uncooked long grain rice	1/4 teaspoon ground ginger
1 garlic clove, minced	1-1/2 pounds cooked medium shrimp, peeled and deveined
1 medium onion, chopped	
1 medium green pepper, julienned	1-1/2 cups cubed fully cooked ham
2 tablespoons vegetable oil	3/4 cup pineapple tidbits, drained

■ In a large saucepan, bring broth to a boil. Stir in rice. Reduce heat; cover and simmer for 25 minutes or until tender.

■ Meanwhile, in a large skillet, saute the garlic, onion and green pepper in oil until tender. Stir in soy sauce and ginger. Add shrimp, ham and pineapple. Stir in rice.

■ Transfer to a greased 2-qt. baking dish. Bake, uncovered, at 350° for 15-20 minutes or until heated through. Stir before serving.

Yield: 8 servings.

For minced garlic, put your fresh garlic clove through a garlic press or chop it finely with a knife. To save time, buy minced garlic in a jar from the grocery store. A half teaspoon is equal to one clove.

Salmon Supper

Debra Knippel
MEDFORD, WISCONSIN

With a husband and four children to cook for, I'm always on the look-out for quick recipes. This one-dish wonder was given to me many years ago by my mother-in-law.

PREP/TOTAL TIME: 30 min.

1/3 cup chopped green pepper

3 tablespoons chopped onion

2 tablespoons vegetable oil

1/4 cup all-purpose flour

1/2 teaspoon salt

1-1/2 cups milk

1 can (10-3/4 ounces) condensed cream of celery soup, undiluted

2 pouches (3 ounces *each*) boneless skinless pink salmon

1 cup frozen peas

2 teaspoons lemon juice

1 tube (8 ounces) refrigerated crescent rolls

■ In a large skillet, saute green pepper and onion in oil for 3-4 minutes or until crisp-tender.

■ In a small bowl, combine the flour, salt, milk and soup until blended. Add to the skillet. Bring to a boil. Reduce heat; cook and stir for 2 minutes or until smooth. Stir in salmon, peas and lemon juice.

■ Pour into an ungreased 11-in. x 7-in. x 2-in. baking dish. Do not unroll crescent dough; cut into eight equal slices. Arrange over salmon mixture. Bake, uncovered, at 375° for 10-12 minutes or until golden brown.

Yield: 4 servings.

General Recipe Index

Alphabetical Recipe Index

Substitutions & Equivalents

Equivalent Measures

3 teaspoons	=	1 tablespoon		16 tablespoons	=	1 cup
4 tablespoons	=	1/4 cup		2 cups	=	1 pint
5-1/3 tablespoons	=	1/3 cup		4 cups	=	1 quart
8 tablespoons	=	1/2 cup		4 quarts	=	1 gallon

Food Equivalents

Grains

Macaroni	1 cup (3-1/2 ounces) uncooked	=	2-1/2 cups cooked
Noodles, Medium	3 cups (4 ounces) uncooked	=	4 cups cooked
Popcorn	1/3 to 1/2 cup unpopped	=	8 cups popped
Rice, Long Grain	1 cup uncooked	=	3 cups cooked
Rice, Quick-Cooking	1 cup uncooked	=	2 cups cooked
Spaghetti	8 ounces uncooked	=	4 cups cooked

Crumbs

Bread	1 slice	=	3/4 cup soft crumbs, 1/4 cup fine dry crumbs
Graham Crackers	7 squares	=	1/2 cup finely crushed
Buttery Round Crackers	12 crackers	=	1/2 cup finely crushed
Saltine Crackers	14 crackers	=	1/2 cup finely crushed

Fruits

Bananas	1 medium	=	1/3 cup mashed
Lemons	1 medium	=	3 tablespoons juice, 2 teaspoons grated peel
Limes	1 medium	=	2 tablespoons juice, 1-1/2 teaspoons grated peel
Oranges	1 medium	=	1/4 to 1/3 cup juice, 4 teaspoons grated peel

Vegetables

Cabbage	1 head	=	5 cups shredded	Green Pepper	1 large	=	1 cup chopped
Carrots	1 pound	=	3 cups shredded	Mushrooms	1/2 pound	=	3 cups sliced
Celery	1 rib	=	1/2 cup chopped	Onions	1 medium	=	1/2 cup chopped
Corn	1 ear fresh	=	2/3 cup kernels	Potatoes	3 medium	=	2 cups cubed

Nuts

Almonds	1 pound	=	3 cups chopped	Pecan Halves	1 pound	=	4-1/2 cups chopped
Ground Nuts	3-3/4 ounces	=	1 cup	Walnuts	1 pound	=	3-3/4 cups chopped

Easy Substitutions

When you need...		Use...
Baking Powder	1 teaspoon	1/2 teaspoon cream of tartar + 1/4 teaspoon baking soda
Buttermilk	1 cup	1 tablespoon lemon juice or vinegar + enough milk to measure 1 cup (let stand 5 minutes before using)
Cornstarch	1 tablespoon	2 tablespoons all-purpose flour
Honey	1 cup	1-1/4 cups sugar + 1/4 cup water
Half-and-Half Cream	1 cup	1 tablespoon melted butter + enough whole milk to measure 1 cup
Onion	1 small, chopped (1/3 cup)	1 teaspoon onion powder or 1 tablespoon dried minced onion
Tomato Juice	1 cup	1/2 cup tomato sauce + 1/2 cup water
Tomato Sauce	2 cups	3/4 cup tomato paste + 1 cup water
Unsweetened Chocolate	1 square (1 ounce)	3 tablespoons baking cocoa + 1 tablespoon shortening or oil
Whole Milk	1 cup	1/2 cup evaporated milk + 1/2 cup water

Cooking Terms

Here's a quick reference for some of the cooking terms used in *Taste of Home* recipes:

Baste—To moisten food with melted butter, pan drippings, marinades or other liquid to add more flavor and juiciness.

Beat—A rapid movement to combine ingredients using a fork, spoon, wire whisk or electric mixer.

Blend—To combine ingredients until just mixed.

Boil—To heat liquids until bubbles form that cannot be "stirred down." In the case of water, the temperature will reach 212°.

Bone—To remove all meat from the bone before cooking.

Cream—To beat ingredients together to a smooth consistency, usually in the case of butter and sugar for baking.

Dash—A small amount of seasoning, less than 1/8 teaspoon. If using a shaker, a dash would comprise a quick flip of the container.

Dredge—To coat foods with flour or other dry ingredients. Most often done with pot roasts and stew meat before browning.

Fold—To incorporate several ingredients by careful and gentle turning with a spatula. Used generally with beaten egg whites or whipped cream when mixing into the rest of the ingredients to keep the batter light.

Julienne—To cut foods into long thin strips much like matchsticks. Used most often for salads and stir-fry dishes.

Mince—To cut into very fine pieces. Used often for garlic or fresh herbs.

Parboil—To cook partially, usually used in the case of chicken, sausages and vegetables.

Partially Set—Describes the consistency of gelatin after it has been chilled for a small amount of time. Mixture should resemble the consistency of egg whites.

Puree—To process foods to a smooth mixture. Can be prepared in an electric blender, food processor, food mill or sieve.

Saute—To fry quickly in a small amount of fat, stirring almost constantly. Most often done with onions, mushrooms and other chopped vegetables.

Score—To cut slits partway through the outer surface of foods. Often used with ham or flank steak.

Stir-Fry—To cook meats and/or vegetables with a constant stirring motion in a small amount of oil in a wok or skillet over high heat.